Springer Series on ADULTHOOD and AGING

Series Editor: Bernard D. Starr, Ph.D.

Advisory Board: Paul D. Baltes, Ph.D., Jack Botwinick, Ph.D., Carl Eisdorfer, M.D., Ph.D., Donald E. Gelfand, Ph.D., Lissy Jarvik, M.D., Ph.D., Robert Kastenbaum, Ph.D., Neil G. McCluskey, Ph.D., K. Warner Schaie, Ph.D., Nathan W. Shock, Ph.D., and Asher Woldow, M.D.

Volume 1   **Adult Day Care:** Community Work with the Elderly
Philip G. Weiler and Eloise Rathbone-McCuan, with contributors

Volume 2   **Counseling Elders and Their Families:**
Practical Techniques for Applied Gerontology
John J. Herr and John H. Weakland

Volume 3   **Becoming Old:** An Introduction to Social Gerontology
John C. Morgan

Volume 4   **The Projective Assessment of Aging Method (PAAM)**
Bernard D. Starr, Marcella Bakur Weiner, and Marilyn Rabetz

Volume 5   **Ethnicity and Aging**
Donald E. Gelfand and Alfred J. Kutzik, with 25 contributors

Volume 6   **Gerontology Instruction in Higher Education**
David A. Peterson and Christopher R. Bolton

Volume 7   **Nontraditional Therapy and Counseling
with the Aging**
S. Stansfeld Sargent, with 18 contributors

Volume 8   **The Aging Network:** Programs and Services, 2nd ed.
Donald E. Gelfand

Volume 9   **Old Age on the New Scene**
Robert Kastenbaum, with 29 contributors

Volume 10   **Controversial Issues in Gerontology**
Harold J. Wershow, with 36 contributors

Volume 11   **Open Care for the Aging:**
Comparative International Approaches
Virginia C. Little

Volume 12   **The Older Person as a Mental Health Worker**
Rosemary McCaslin, with 11 contributors

Volume 13   **The Elderly in Rural Society:**
Every Fourth Elder
Raymond T. Coward and Gary R. Lee, with 16 contributors

Volume 14   **Social Support Networks and the
Care of the Elderly:**
Theory, Research, and Practice
William J. Sauer and Raymond T. Coward, with 17 contributors

William J. Sauer, Ph.D., is Associate Professor of Business Administration in the Graduate School of Business at the University of Pittsburgh. He received his doctorate in sociology from the University of Minnesota in 1975 where he studied under a fellowship from the Midwest Council for Research on Aging. Dr. Sauer has published in the *Journal of Gerontology*, *The Gerontologist*, and other journals on a variety of issues regarding the elderly. His current research focuses on consumer problems of the elderly and social support networks.

Raymond T. Coward, Ph.D., is Research Professor for the Center of Rural Studies and Professor of Social Work at the University of Vermont. He received his doctorate in 1974 from Purdue University. Professor Coward has published in *The Gerontologist*, the *Journal of Gerontological Social Work*, and various other journals on topics related to the aged. He is also coeditor with William M. Smith of *The Family in Rural Society* and *Family Services: Issues and Opportunities in Contemporary Rural America*, and with Gary R. Lee of *The Elderly in Rural Society*. His current research interests are in rural health care and services for the elderly. Currently, Professor Coward is the editor of the *Journal of Rural Health*.

SOCIAL SUPPORT NETWORKS
AND THE **CARE**
OF THE **ELDERLY**

Theory, Research, and Practice

William J. Sauer, Ph.D.
Raymond T. Coward, Ph.D.

Editors

Springer Publishing Company
New York

Springer Publishing Company, Inc.
536 Broadway
New York, New York 10012

85 86 87 88 89 / 10 9 8 7 6 5 4 3 2 1

Library of Congress Cataloging in Publication Data

Main entry under title:
Social support networks and the care of the elderly.
  (Springer series on adulthood and aging ; v. 14)
  Includes bibliographies and index.
  1. Aged—United States—Social conditions—Addresses, essays, lectures. 2. Aged—
United States—Economic conditions—Addresses, essays, lectures. 3. Aged—United
States—Care and hygiene—Addresses, essays, lectures. I. Sauer, William J.
II. Coward, Raymond T. III. Series.
HV1461.S56 1985   305.2′6′0973   85-8162
ISBN 0-8261-4270-2

Printed in the United States of America

For
Fary F. and Meta C. Sauer
and in memory of
E. Walter and Carrie E. Coward,
our parents,
who have inspired us to take the path we have
and who are always in our thoughts.

Contents

Preface   ix
Introduction   xi
Contributors   xv

Part I   State of the Art   1

   1 The Role of Social Support Networks in the   3
      Care of the Elderly
      William J. Sauer and Raymond T. Coward

   2 Theoretical Perspectives on Social   21
      Networks
      Gary R. Lee

Part II   Family Relations   39

   3 Children and Their Elderly Parents   41
      Sandra M. Hanson and William J. Sauer

   4 Husband and Wife Networks   67
      Beth B. Hess and Beth J. Soldo

   5 The Role of Siblings as Family Caregivers   93
      Victor G. Cicirelli

   6 Extended Kin as Helping Networks   108
      Barbara Shore

Part III Community Relations   121

   7 The Role of Friends and Neighbors in   123
      Providing Social Support
      George R. Peters and Marvin A. Kaiser

8 Social Support for Elders Through   159
   Community Ties: The Role of Voluntary
   Associations
   Nicholas L. Danigelis

9 Relationships Between Informal and   178
   Formal Organizational Networks
   John A. Krout

**Part IV Social Networks Under Special   197
           Circumstances**

10 The Social Networks of Ethnic Minorities   199
    David Guttman

11 The Support Systems of Women   219
    Charles F. Longino, Jr., and Aaron Lipman

12 Social Support for the Frail Elderly   234
    Eloise E. Rathbone-McCuan,
    Nancy Hooyman, and Anne E. Fortune

**Part V The Applications of Theory and   249
          Research**

13 The Application of Network Theory and   251
    Research to the Field of Aging
    David E. Biegel

Index   **275**

Preface

In the spring of 1980 several of us who were interested in the area of social support systems for the elderly noticed that at the previous year's Gerontological meetings there seemed to be a small but significant increase in the number of papers presented relating to this topic. Early in 1981, a careful review of the 1980 program revealed that the number of presentations had doubled. The consensus following that effort was that future research and training would be enhanced by the availability of a systematic review of the current state of knowledge about the social support networks of the elderly and an identification of the most glaring gaps in our understanding.

Shortly thereafter, we undertook the leadership of a project that was designed to produce state-of-the-art reviews focused on the different components that make up the elderly person's social support network. Several years have passed since that initial decision was made. In the interim, however, our commitment has not changed. From the onset we felt the need for a volume that would summarize current research regarding the support networks available to the older person. Thus we assembled this volume, devoted to issues surrounding the development and use of social support systems that help the elderly person maintain his or her independence and meet his or her needs in time of crisis. While the publication of this volume represents the culmination of efforts we started five years ago, we make no apologies. Given the changes that have transpired since we first began this project—such as federal cutbacks in social programs, the recognition of problems among special groups such as the rural elderly and ethnic minorities, and the continually increasing costs of health care— we now view the need for a thorough understanding of the older person's support system as more vital than ever before. It is our hope that this volume will help to provide that understanding.

The creation of a collection of readings is a major undertaking and requires the sustained efforts of many individuals. First and foremost are the authors. They have given freely of their time, expertise, and experience. Their commitment to increasing both the quality of service and the quality of life of the elderly is reflected in the chapters they have written for this volume. The early versions of this manuscript were critiqued by us. The contributors of this volume have worked hard to produce a body of work that reflects the current thought in their areas of expertise. To them we are sincerely grateful, for without their effort our plans would not have come to fruition. We would also like to acknowledge the support of the many professional friends who encouraged us to pursue this project. Similarly, the cooperation and resources provided by our respective institutions have contributed greatly to this effort. In this respect we are indebted to the Graduate School of Business at the University of Pittsburgh and the Center for Rural Studies at the University of Vermont.

In addition, we owe a debt of gratitude to our secretarial staff: Cecile Fennell (University of Vermont) and Loretta Riles, Andria Jones, and Lily Maskew (University of Pittsburgh). They have provided earnest, sustained, and competent assistance from the very beginning of this project. Our appreciation is extended to them for their patience with the many revisions to the manuscript.

Finally, our most heartfelt thanks is extended to our families, for most often it is they who absorb the brunt of the lost time when commitments of this type are undertaken. Both of us are fortunate to have been blessed with companions and children who have understood the nature and role of work in our lives and have always encouraged us to pursue our goals.

Introduction

This collection of readings focuses on the role of social support networks in maintaining the social, psychological, and physical well-being of elderly Americans. Its exclusive concentration on the elderly distinguishes it from other volumes that have centered on support networks. It is the desire of the authors and the editors that this volume serve as a catalyst to promote both further innovation in the delivery of services to the elderly and research in this area.

While we have not articulated a theoretical framework for the book, there is an overriding principle which we believe has guided its development. That principle, simply stated, is that community intervention that is based on primary group–based care will provide the elderly with the most effective support both in times of crisis and in carrying out the daily tasks of living necessary to maintain their independence. By primary group–based services we mean those services that (1) take into account the ramifications of elderly people's crises for their family, friends, or neighbors who make up their informal helping network, (2) are based on empirical knowledge of the dynamics of both intergenerational and primary group relations, and (3) involve family, friends, and neighbors in the intervention process when necessary.

The chapters which follow were written exclusively for this book. They are intended to be research based with the emphasis on the integration of past and current work in the field. Each chapter focuses on a specific type of support system, the current state of knowledge regarding that phenomenon, the major issues in the area, research gaps, and research priorities. By following this process the student is introduced to (1) the current role of, and need for, different types of helping networks, (2) the quality of helping networks, (3) those factors which facilitate or inhibit the development and/or functioning of helping networks, and (4) priorities for future research. The book offers the reader the opportunity to review and analyze current issues regarding the role of helping networks in the delivery of services to the elderly. For current service providers the book is a framework into which they can place their own personal experience and, hopefully, insights to new opportunities to allow them further to stretch their limited resources in providing community services to the elderly.

This volume is organized into five parts. The two chapters in Part I, "State of the Art," provide a background for the remainder of the book. In the opening chapter, William J. Sauer and Raymond T. Coward introduce the role of social support networks in the provision of care for the elderly. They discuss (1) the nature of social networks, (2) changes in networks over the life span, (3) the relationship of networks to well-being, and (4) the role of support networks.

The second chapter, by Gary R. Lee, reviews the predominant theoretical approaches in social gerontology. Lee argues that neither activity theory nor disengagement theory seriously addresses the issues of social involvement. He further suggests that exchange theory offers a more suitable framework through which to examine social relationships and then discuss the implications of the exchange process for network involvement.

Part II, "Family Relations," is on support provided by children, husbands and wives, and siblings. The initial chapter of this section, by Sandra M. Hanson and William J. Sauer, suggests that while the relationship between adult children and elderly parents is the hub of the extended kin network, many factors come into play, resulting in a great deal of variation with regard to helping patterns.

In the next chapter Beth B. Hess and Beth J. Soldo focus on support provided by husbands and wives, pointing out that typically it is better to be married than single in old age. Married couples not only have more material resources, but also provide each other with social support. When taken together, these two factors greatly enhance the elderly person's independence and quality of life.

Chapter 5, by Victor G. Cicirelli, examines helping patterns among siblings. It appears that while sibling rivalries subside in old age, support tends to be more psychological in nature along with the expectation of being on standby should primary sources such as children or spouse not be available.

In Chapter 6, Barbara Shore cites evidence that older people are not alienated from or neglected by their families. In fact, she points out, usually the first person called on for help by an older person is a family member, followed by friends or neighbors.

George R. Peters and Marvin A. Kaiser discuss in the next chapter the help provided to the elderly, especially those without nearby relatives, by neighbors. Included in this type of help are services, emotional support, and intimacy. These authors point out the need for government agencies to take neighbors and neighboring into account when planning and implementing programs aimed at helping the elderly.

In Part III, "Community Relations," the emphasis shifts to social support provided by volunteers and by formal organizations working through informal support networks. In Chapter 8, Nicholas L. Danigelis reviews the role of voluntary associations in providing social support for the elderly. John A. Krout, in the following chapter, discusses the provision of services by formal agencies and the need to provide support for informal caregivers as well.

Part IV, "Social Networks Under Special Circumstances," examines the support provided to special groups of elderly. In Chapter 10, David Guttman focuses on ethnic minorities. Unlike other elderly, Guttman points out, ethnic minorities generally live in poverty, lack the educational and linguistic skills to deal with bureaucracies, and because of cultural pride do not reap many of the benefits to which they are entitled. As a result they live in enclaves or near extended family, depending heavily on informal support systems made up of friends, neighbors, and relatives.

In the second chapter of this section, Charles F. Longino, Jr., and Aaron Lipman discuss the benefits to the elderly woman of long years of socialization to maintaining family and friendship ties. As a result, they suggest, women have a larger support network to draw upon and generally are better off than their male counterparts in their later years regardless of marital status.

Next, Eloise E. Rathbone-McCuan, Nancy Hooyman, and Anne E. Fortune discuss the state of knowledge about the frail elderly. While they advocate the importance of informal caregiving for this group of elderly, they also indicate that little is known about its impact on the caregiver and on the quality of care provided. They suggest that a balance of shared responsibility between family and state is the critical issue facing support for the frail elderly.

Finally, in Part V, "The Applications of Theory and Research," David E. Biegel examines the nature of intervention via natural helpers. He discusses the strengths and weaknesses of informal support systems, current models of intervention, and obstacles and difficulties in the development of natural helping networks.

As is often the case in volumes of this nature, more questions are raised than are answered. The contributions in this collection were

intended to reflect the complexity of natural helping networks. Nevertheless, the assembly of these different facets of informal systems
should provide a framework for better understanding the dynamics of
this type of service delivery. To the extent that it accomplishes that
goal and stimulates further research in the field, the purpose of this
volume will be served.

Contributors

David E. Biegel, Assistant Professor, School of Social Work, University of Pittsburgh, Pittsburgh, Pennsylvania.

Victor G. Cicirelli, Professor, Department of Psychological Sciences, Purdue University, West Lafayette, Indiana.

Nicholas L. Danigelis, Associate Professor, Department of Sociology, University of Vermont, Burlington, Vermont.

Anne E. Fortune, Associate Professor, School of Social Work, Virginia Commonwealth University, Richmond, Virginia.

David Guttman, Director, The Center for the Study of Pre-Retirement and Aging, The Catholic University of America, Washington, D.C.

Sandra M. Hanson, Senior Research Analyst, Decision Resources Corporation, Washington, D.C.

Beth B. Hess, Associate Professor, Department of Sociology, County College of Morris, Dover, New Jersey.

Nancy Hooyman, Associate Professor, School of Social Work, University of Washington, Seattle, Washington.

Marvin A. Kaiser, Assistant Professor, Department of Sociology, Kansas State University, Manhattan, Kansas.

John A. Krout, Assistant Professor, Department of Sociology and Anthropology, State University of New York at Fredonia, Fredonia, New York.

Gary R. Lee, Associate Professor, Departments of Sociology and Rural Sociology, Washington State University, Pullman, Washington.

Aaron Lipman, Professor, Department of Sociology, University of Miami, Coral Gables, Florida.

Charles F. Longino, Jr., Associate Professor, Department of Sociology, University of Miami, Coral Gables, Florida.

George R. Peters, Professor, Department of Sociology and Center for Aging, Kansas State University, Manhattan, Kansas.

Eloise E. Rathbone-McCuan, Associate Professor of Social Work, College of Education and Social Services, University of Vermont, Burlington, Vermont.

Barbara Shore, Professor, School of Social Work, University of Pittsburgh, Pittsburgh, Pennsylvania.

Beth J. Soldo, Senior Research Scholar, Center for Population Research, Kennedy Institute, Georgetown University, Washington, D.C.

Part I
State of the Art

1

The Role of
Social Support Networks
in the Care of the Elderly

William J. Sauer
Raymond T. Coward

This book is about helping networks. More specifically, it is about those people who help older people—not only those who provide assistance as a function of their position or role as a formal helper in a public or private social service agency, but also those informal helpers who provide aid because they are a relative, a friend, or a neighbor. Such assistance is often in response to an elder confronting a social, psychological, or physical problem. This opening chapter will serve as an introduction into the nature of these network relationships—whether they are informal, formal, or both—and the impact they have on the quality of life of elders. The remaining chapters in the book will illuminate and illustrate the nuances of these relationships and sharpen our understanding of the significance of social support in the care of the elderly.

While the concept of social support networks is not new (Barnes, 1954; Bott, 1971; Mitchell, 1969), its practical applicability to the field of gerontology is only just beginning to be recognized fully. Prior research and intervention which has focused on the day-to-day problems and crises of the elderly has been concentrated primarily on the ability of families to cope with the needs of their older loved one or with the role of the formal social agency in bringing resources to bear on problems. The nature of both of these sources of aid, however, has undergone considerable change in recent years—such as the greater geographical separation of adult children from their elderly parents and the current period of austerity in the government funding of social service programs—and, therefore, social gerontologists have been forced to examine new models for the delivery of services to the elderly and to consider alternative means for meeting the needs of the aged in our society.

In examining the aid provided to elders, this book will cast a wide net and focus comprehensively on the social context in which American elders conduct their lives. Thus, we will examine not only formal social service agencies and family members but also friends, neighbors, relatives, and volunteers—all of whom are significant parts of the larger helping network.

In this opening chapter we will first examine the nature and common characteristics of informal support networks and then move to a discussion of the role of formal helpers in maximizing the quality of life of the aged. Also included is an introduction of the issues surrounding the cooperation between the informal and formal systems. The themes and concepts that are briefly raised and discussed in this opening chapter will be expanded upon in the subsequent text.

The Nature of Informal Social Networks

The central notion behind the concept of informal social support networks is the provision of assistance during times of crisis. Such aid takes many different forms and is delivered by a variety of means. In the professional literature, authors have used a wide range of terms to refer to such relationships, including effective networks (Epstein, 1961), natural support networks (Hirsh, 1977), informal support systems (Wingspread Report, 1978), natural neighbors or natural helping networks (Froland, Pancoast, Chapman, & Kimboko, 1979), family social networks (Unger & Powell, 1980), and informal local or community helpers (D'Augelli, Vallance, Danish, & Young, 1981). Despite the variety of terms that have been used, there does seem to be a core set of concepts common across authors.

Walker, McBride, and Vachon (1977), for example, defined informal social networks as "that set of personal contacts through which the individual maintains his social identity, and receives emotional support, material aid, services and information" (p. 35). Maguire (1980) viewed these networks as "preventive forces or buffers" which assist individuals in coping with "transition, stress, physical problems, and social emotional problems without resorting to the still somewhat stigmatized formal social services" (p. 42). A definition that perhaps captures the essence of all of these variants is that offered by Gottlieb (1983). He described social support as consisting of "verbal and/or nonverbal information or advice, tangible aid, or action that is proffered by social intimates or inferred by their presence and has beneficial emotional or behavioral effects on the recipient" (pp. 28–29).

The type of aid that is provided by helping networks varies along several dimensions. Unger and Powell (1980) have speculated, for example, that social networks provide three types of aid: instrumental, emotional, and informational. Warren (1981), while in basic agreement with these dimensions, provided a more detailed description which included giving emotional support; providing specific information; filling in when a close relationship is severed by death, illness, divorce, or separation; helping identify arenas of good professional help; and serving in place of professionals when they are not trusted or not available. Finally, Gourash (1978) has further described the major role of social networks as facilitating help seeking by buffering the experience of stress; frequently precluding the necessity for professional assistance by providing both instrumental and affective support; acting as screening and referral agents to facilitate the use of professional services; and transmitting attitudes, values, and norms about help seeking.

It is important to recognize that while all of the above authors seem to describe the role of social networks as providing aid that facilitates the independence of the person in need, they also suggest three quite different types of help to achieve this goal: (1) providing direct aid or assistance with the tasks of daily living; (2) helping the person in need to expand social contacts and enter into new social roles, thus increasing his or her social network; and (3) providing information and referral about formal agencies that may provide the necessary aid required to maximize independence.

Within informal support networks, Collins and Pancoast (1977) have suggested that it is possible to identify "central figures" who "have won the confidence of their associates because of their personal characteristics, and [because] they have demonstrated their ability to cope successfully with problems similar to those that their co-workers or neighbors face" (p. 26). These central figures need not come by their position as a "helper" only because they are a relative of the person in need or because they are a professional helper. Rather, they may hold jobs that tend to bring them in contact with those in need— such helpers may be bartenders, beauticians, barbers, checkers, or druggists. Kahn (1979) has described another feature of social support networks that he calls "convoy." Antonucci elaborates on the meaning of this concept:

> . . . the individual is surrounded from early childhood by a variety of network members who are sources of social support. Beginning with the well documented phenomenon of attachment to primary caregivers, the individual develops a variety of interpersonal relationships which become the basis for the support convoy. Many of the members continue and maintain a relationship with the focal person. As the individuals involved grow and mature, the nature of their relationships develops and changes. At different points in the life course, members of the convoy may be lost either through death or less significant changes. At the same time, as the individual matures, experiences different life events and transitions, new convoy members are added. (Antonucci, in press, p. 7)

Thus, according to Kahn and Antonucci (1980), social support networks are in force over the entire life span, but either the structure or the participants (e.g., central figures) or both may be subject to change. "The term Convoy of social support," Antonucci (in press) concluded, "is designed to emphasize [the] dynamic aspect of social interactions" (p. 8).

Pilisak and Minkler (1980) have argued, moreover, that the extent to which changes in function and composition occur, and the degree to which these networks fulfill those functions critical to the needs of their members in an efficient and effective manner, may be influenced by specific characteristics of the social support network. Research to this point, however, has generally not dealt with these issues and focused primarily on the size, geographic dispersion, member homogeneity, strength of ties, reciprocity, multiplicity, and density of the networks that surround elders.

Changes in Informal Social Support Networks

While elders can suffer from various losses with regard to physical and mental capacities as age increases, some social gerontologists have suggested that the most threatening loss (and, for that matter, a partial cause of the former two) may well be the lesser prestige that our society accords the aged. Rosow (1967) has suggested that individuals are integrated into their society by "forces which place them within the system and govern their participation and patterned association with others" (p. 9). According to Rosow, this network of bonds consists of the social values, formal and informal group memberships, and social roles through which individuals gain meaning for, and perspective on, their existence. From this point of view, the greater the continuity between the lifestyles of elders before they reach retirement and their activities as senior citizens, the greater their integration into society. In contrast, Rosow (1967) has speculated that "the greater the change, the greater [the] risk of personal demoralization and alienation from society" (p. 9).

Some research has indicated that informal social networks tend to decline for many elders with advancing age and that in addition to major losses in role functions (such as employee, spouse, and active parent), there is also a reduction in both the amount and variety of interactions that occur with others. As a consequence, a small but disturbing number of elders live very isolated lives (Rathbone-McCuan & Hashimi, 1982).

More recently, Pilisak and Minkler (1980) have suggested that several social forces have contributed to significant changes in the availability and structure of informal social support resources. First, the increase in fertility rates in the early 1900s, coupled with the increase in longevity, has resulted in a proportionately larger elderly population in the United States. In 1900 approximately 4% of the population of the United States was 65 years of age or older. Today, however, that figure is approaching 12%. Furthermore, a greater proportion than ever before of these elderly are women, widowed, and very old. Consequently, those who may be in greater need of supportive services from their children have children who themselves may have already reached retirement age or who are torn between the often competing needs of their adolescent children and their aging parents (Treas, 1977).

A second set of factors that has implications for the functioning of natural networks, and one that has been amply noted throughout the literature, is the mobility of younger generations in the United States since World War II. The loss of networks (or a decline in their ability to provide daily assistance) as a function of the mobility of younger generations may be most detrimental to those elders who reside in small towns and rural communities (Lee & Cassidy, 1981).

A final factor mentioned by Pilisuk and Minkler (1980) relates to the changing role of women. In the early 1900s only one woman in five was employed outside the home. In contrast, it has been estimated that by 1985 more than 51% of the adult female population in the United States will be engaged in the work force and that three out of every five working women will be married (Boone & Kurtz, 1983). Since

women have traditionally been a critical force through which relationships and helping networks across generations have been initiated and
maintained, their entrance into the labor force in such large numbers
has serious consequences for the provision of social support to the
elderly.

These three factors, taken together, suggest that the amount of
service provided by informal and formal helpers is in a constant state
of realignment as social forces mold and shape new realities. Nevertheless, the informal social support network—in particular the family—has been in the past and still remains the preeminent force in the
care of the elderly.

In recent years, new research has been added to the already
sizable literature attesting to the pervasiveness of family caregiving in
the lives of the elders. Stoller and Earl (1983) have noted that among
their sample of elders (65 years of age or older) who reported impaired task capacity, family members provided the major portion of
the assistance that was being received (from a low of 53.0% in aid with
bathing to a high of 96.3% in food preparation). In an ethnically diverse
sample from California, Weeks and Cuellar (1981) found that family
members were named by at least half of the elders they interviewed
(60 years of age or older) as the first person to whom the respondents
would turn in eight categories of need (from a low of 51% for the item
"someone to talk to" to a high of 75% for "sickness"). Finally, from a
random survey of noninstitutionalized elders in the Northeast, Coward
and Crawford (1983) reported that 58.0% of the 1,301 nonspousal
helpers reported by their respondents ($n = 900$) were family members—indeed, sons and daughters accounted for one-third of all of the
help provided.

Thus we can conclude (and the subsequent chapters of this book
will provide vivid evidence for this deduction) that contrary to popular images of family abandonment, the majority of elders are embedded in a social support system that provides significant help and
assistance with the tasks of daily living (Bair & Hiltner, 1982; Powers &
Bultena, 1974; Shanas, 1979a, 1979b). We must ask ourselves, then,
what the positive and negative effects are of such relationships in the
lives of elders. It is to this topic that we now direct our attention.

Social Support and Well-being

The linkage between social support networks and the well-being and
good health of elders has been suggested by several researchers. In a
comprehensive review of the literature on this topic, Cassel (1976)

focused on the positive role of the social environment with regard to the resistance of individuals to disease. His view of the environment went beyond the traditional concerns with physical and microbiological factors, to include social variables. Specifically, he was interested in the effect on health of the presence or absence of other individuals. According to Cassel, social subgroups act as buffers against stress and illness by providing the information necessary to deal with adverse conditions. Similarly, Weiss (1969, 1974) has postulated that each person needs a set of relationships that over the life course will socially integrate them into a helping network that can be relied upon during times of difficulty and stress.

Killiea (1982), in an excellent review of the literature on social support systems and coping strategies, points to a number of studies that examined the relationship between social networks and well-being or ill health:

- Gottlieb (1975) investigated the mutual support systems of subgroups of adolescent males.
- Tolsdorf (1976) studied the social networks of a population of schizophrenic adult males, whereas Hammer, Makiesky-Barrow, and Gutwisth (1978) focused on social networks and schizophrenia, and Mueller (1980) on psychiatric disorders.
- Colletta (1979) explored the social support system after divorce and Gerstel and Riessman (1981) the networks of separated and divorced respondents.
- Berkman and Syme (1979) have examined the relationship between social networks, host resistance, and mortality.
- Cochran and Bassard (1979) studied the child development and personal networks of parents, whereas, Colletta and Gregg (1981) examined the networks of adolescent mothers.
- McQueen and Celentano (1981) investigated the social support networks of women problem drinkers and Goldberg (1981) the networks of older married women.

The fundamental conclusion common to all of these studies is that a breakdown in the social support system of an individual greatly increases the likelihood of stressors having serious detrimental effects on health and well-being. Stated more positively, the availability of a supportive social network seems to significantly enhance the ability of an individual to cope with both physical and psychological stressors (McCubbin, Sussman, & Patterson, 1983).

Although both the direct and "buffering" effects of social support on health and well-being are becoming better established and understood, there is still much to be learned about the causal connections between these phenomena. Gottlieb (1983), after a recent and comprehensive review of the literature, concluded that in addition "to identifying the circumstances under which different sources and forms of support mitigate stress, researchers will need to attend more closely to questions surrounding the way support accomplishes its health-protective effects" (p. 49).

There is, however, another side to social support—one less written about and less frequently discussed. Social support systems are not *always* a useful and positive force in the lives of individuals in crisis. Despite the good intentions of informal helpers and their desire to improve the situation of the person in need, their actions do not always serve to improve circumstances (Coward, 1983; Rathbone-McCuan & Coward, in press). Indeed, in certain circumstances and under certain conditions, the intrusion of informal helpers into the situation can actually make things worse. Unfortunately, our level of understanding of these complex relationships is such that we are not able to predict precisely those circumstances or factors that will result in positive or negative ramifications.

The Role of Formal Helping Networks

It is only in the past two decades that public social welfare policy has reflected a strong commitment to the elderly. Perhaps the most tangible evidence of the magnitude and strength of this commitment to improve the life circumstances of the aged is reflected in the objectives of the Older Americans Act of 1965. Those objectives included an adequate income for all elders; full restorative services; opportunities for employment; retirement in health; honor and dignity; the pursuit of meaningful activity; efficient community services; immediate benefits from proven research; and the free exercise of individual initiatives in planning and managing their own lives. In the 20 years since the landmark Older Americans Act, these themes have become more pervasive and the notion of creating an environment that allows the elderly to maintain their independence has been stressed repeatedly as an objective of our national social policies.

In response to these commitments, America has witnessed the emergence of a vast network of formal agencies and programs to accomplish these goals. The Older Americans Act and the Social Security Act have been the principal legislative vehicles which have spawned and funded these initiatives (Estes, 1979). Increasingly, however, legislators and social service providers have recognized that even the enormous resources that are now expended on formal agencies of social intervention for the aged are often inadequate to ensure that the original objectives are achieved. Furthermore, other competing national needs are forcing policymakers to reexamine the magnitude of our social responsibility to the aged.

There is, however, a potentially viable partner in this enterprise—and professionals are now becoming aware of its nature. The collaboration between informal social support networks and human service practitioners and agencies has become the latest in a long line of service delivery "bandwagons" (Froland, Pancoast, Chapman, & Kimboko, 1979; Hooyman, 1983; Whittaker & Garbarino, 1983). For many elderly, then, the ability to maintain their independent living status and to enhance the quality of their later years will increasingly depend on the ability of formal and informal helpers to work in concert to maximize aid.

The Relationship Between Informal Social Support Networks and Formal Service Providers

The formal helping network has never been, and certainly is not today, in a position to replace, or substitute in large measure for, the significant amounts of aid provided to elders by the informal helping network. Coward and Crawford (1983), from interviews with 900 randomly selected elders in the Northeast, reported that the informal network accounted for three-fourths of all the nonspousal helpers named ($n = 1,301$) in the four task areas they studied (transportation, household chores, home repair and maintenance, and health care). Moreover, only a minority of the elderly sample (32.2%) were currently receiving help from the formal network in any of the task areas. The only realistic goal for those committed to serving the needs of elders, then, is to forge a collaborative relationship between the two systems that enhances their individual strengths, minimizes their weaknesses, and maintains their separate identity and integrity (Coward, 1983; Myers-Walls & Coward, 1983).

The relevancy of developing responsible methods for enhancing collaborations between the two sources of aid has been substantiated by recent explorations of the shifting role of formal and informal networks throughout the life course of elders. Using cross-sectional data taken from telephone interviews, for example, Coward (in press)

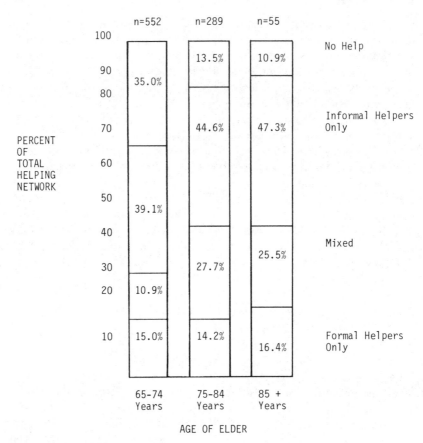

FIGURE 1.1: Helping network composition by age

has demonstrated that 17.2% of a sample of noninstitutionalized respondents over the age of 65 years ($n = 900$) were utilizing simultaneously the services of both formal and informal helpers. More importantly, there were significant shifts (chi square <.001) in the relative
proportions of different network compositions as age increased (see
Figure 1.1). There was a relatively small percentage (10.9%) of
younger elders (65 to 74 years) that were receiving services simultaneously from both formal and informal helpers; this was the least prevalent pattern in this age category. The most common patterns in this
age-group were receipt of help from informal helpers (39.1%) and no

help received (35.0%). In contrast, in the older aged categories about one-quarter of the elders (27.7% of the elders aged 75–84 years and 25.5% of the elders 85 years of age or more) reported that their helping networks consisted of individuals from both the formal and informal network. In the two oldest categories, the mixed pattern was the second most prevalent configuration observed, and there was a dramatic reduction of the number of elders reporting complete independence. Since it is these older age categories that are experiencing the fastest rate of growth in the United States, the relevancy of refining the technology and skills for intersystem collaboration is quite apparent.

The ease with which this goal of collaboration will be achieved, however, is dependent on many factors. For professionals planning and implementing health and human service programs, it will require a closer examination and consideration of the social context in which the elderly person functions. Given this socio-ecological perspective, Unger and Powell (1980) have suggested three ways of utilizing social networks: (1) forming linkages between human service agencies and social networks in order to bridge the gap between individuals in need and organizations with the resources relevant to those needs; (2) providing services that strengthen the social network of the individual in need by encouraging the development of active mutual aid groups and the acquisition of the personal skills required to sustain relationships; and (3) mobilizing networks to intervene in times of crisis. Warren (1981) has similarly articulated a range of interfaces between formal and informal helpers along the continuum of care:

> In prevention: Identifying and mapping the density, distribution, and vitality of natural helping networks can aid in program planning and evaluation by directing attention to where professional services should be increased, maintained, or can be reduced to avoid duplication, and where a local informal solution is just as successful. . . . In treatment: Most professionals see a patient who has first been in touch with many natural helpers. Patients often go as a last resort or because they trust the advice of the person who sent them to the professional; they are otherwise fearful and misinformed about formal helpers and . . . ninety percent of the cases of so-called self-referral really involve a person who has talked with at least one natural helper first—a spouse, friend, neighbor, co-worker—before he or she goes to an agency for help. . . . After care: Here the case for the natural helper is extremely strong. Many kinds of illness and social service help require the cooperation of natural helpers in the environment of the patient or client. . . . Many programs of community placement—returning the person to the community—depend for their success on the strength and role of informal helpers. (pp. 210–211)

While the potential for using informal helping networks in the delivery of human services and the promotion of health has been viewed as particularly attractive, agencies must proceed to do so in a manner that does not destroy or discourage the actions and aid of the naturally occurring social support system. Warren (1981) has warned that all too often the attempts by formal agencies to collaborate with informal helpers has resulted in the bureaucratization of the informal network. Glazer (1971) further emphasized the need for caution when forming cooperative relationships between formal agencies and the informal helping network to avoid the substitution of government interventions for more traditional, naturally occurring structures. Consequently, while the potential of a collaborative relationship exists between human service agencies and social networks, the implementation of such initiatives is not without its problems. In Chapter 13 in this volume, Biegel expands further on the difficulties, dangers, and obstacles to collaboration and cooperation.

Building Professional–Social Network Relationships

While many might anticipate a natural antagonism between human service professionals and members of informal helping networks (because of potential differences in orientation, training, style, responsibilities, and perhaps goals), this is rarely the case. Despite areas of disagreement, these two groups are generally supportive of the efforts and contributions that each is able to make on behalf of those in need.

Nevertheless, Tracy and Gussow (1976) have suggested that informal social support networks seem to flourish primarily in areas in which professionals have a lesser interest or where a large number of clients are involved. Furthermore, Kleiman, Mantell, and Alexander (1976) have indicated that conflict between formal and informal providers is most likely to emerge when professionals are unwilling to relinquish their dominance or control over a situation.

While previous research indicates that most collaborations between formal and informal networks arise spontaneously in response to shared needs (Butler et al., 1979; Gartner & Riesman, 1977; Katz, 1976), several authors have argued that the following steps meet with the greatest probability of success (Hooyman, 1980; Naperstek & Biegel, 1982; Plaut, 1982). First, the geographic area in which the partnership is to be developed should be identified. Partnerships between social networks and professionals should be locality-based. That is, they should be specific to a particular neighborhood, or rural area, and take into account the social demographic and geographic nature of that area and its differing needs and resources. Second, the "natural helpers" or "central figures" need to be identified. While Collins and Pancoast (1976) have discussed a variety of strategies for doing this, the most common has been simply to ask people which individuals in their community are good sources of advice or help. Once these individuals and their networks have been identified, the final step requires that the formal helpers establish credibility with the natural helpers. To accomplish this objective, Naperstek and Biegel (1982) have suggested that ". . . professionals . . . , human service administrators [and] community representatives, must be able to interact as peers" (p. 273).

The development of any partnership requires some form of equality. Although in the arena of helping, professionals generally hold the upper hand with regard to controlling resources (such as money and expertise), nevertheless, to the extent that they can set aside these inequalities and accept natural helpers with genuine empathy and understanding, their credibility will be enhanced (Hooyman, 1980). Once these actions have been accomplished, the basis for a reciprocal relationship between professionals and the informal helping networks will exist, and together they will be poised to deliver the support and aid needed by many elders to maintain their quality of life.

Conclusions

The current high level of interest regarding social support has generated an impressive set of new research examining the magnitude, composition, and impact of social networks in the care of the elderly. Much of this new literature will be examined in the subsequent chapters of this volume. Unfortunately, these interests in the role of social support have become entangled with the frenetic search for alternative, less expensive forms of meeting the needs of the elderly. For those who have argued that the pendulum of social intervention has swung too far (or too quickly) into the lives of Americans, and that the cost of social welfare policies has extracted too large a burden on the national budget, there is a great deal of appeal to the call for shifting some components of the responsibilities for caring for the elderly back to the informal network. Yet those researchers and practitioners most familiar with the potential, positive power of social support also understand the enormous burden that the care of an aged loved one can place on caregivers (Robinson & Thurnher, 1979; Silverstone &

Human, 1982) as well as the potential negative effects informal helpers can have in the lives of elders. The possibility of swift, unanticipated, wholesale shifts in the responsibility for care to the elderly is, therefore, alarming.

A balance in the relative role of informal and formal helpers is the ideal toward which most services to the elderly are moving. Nevertheless, "[f]inding the appropriate place for the fulcrum of this balance," Coward (1983) has argued, "will require a thorough understanding of the operation of natural support systems, the factors that sustain them, and the appropriate means for maintaining their integrity" (p. 301). As a step toward this understanding, the chapters that follow illuminate various elements of this support and offer state-of-the-art critiques of the knowledge base which must at this point serve as the foundation for theory, research, and practice.

References

Antonucci, Toni C. (in press). Personal characteristics, social support, and social behavior. In R. H. Binstock & E. Shanas (Eds.), *Handbook of aging and the social sciences* (2nd ed.). New York: Van Nostrand Reinhold.

Bair, C. W., and Hiltner, J. (1982). *The independent elderly: Medical and social service needs and use by older persons in Northwest Ohio*. Toledo: Department of Medicine, Medical College of Ohio.

Barnes, John A. (1954). Class and committees in a Norwegian island parish. *Human Relations, 7*, 43.

Berkman, L. F., & Syme, S. L. (1979). Social networks, host resistance and mortality: A nine year follow-up study of Alameda County residents. *American Journal of Epidemiology, 109*, 186-204.

Boone, L. E., & Kurtz, D. L. (1983). *Contemporary marketing*. Chicago: The Dryden Press.

Bott, Elizabeth. (1971). *Family and social networks* (2nd ed.). London, England: Tavistock Publications.

Butler, R., et al. (1979-1980). Self-care, self-help and the elderly. *International Journal of Aging and Human Development, 10*, 97-117.

Cassel, J. C. (1976). The contribution of the social environment to host resistance: The fourth Wade Hampton Frost lecture. *American Journal of Epidemiology, 104*, 107-123.

Cochran, M. M., & Bassard, J. A. (1979). Child development and personal social networks. *Child Development, 50*, 601-616.

Colletta, N. C. (1979). Support systems after divorce: Incidence and impact. *Journal of Marriage and the Family, 41*, 837-846.

Colletta, N. C., & Gregg, C. H. (1981). Adolescent mothers' vulnerability to stress. *Journal of Nervous and Mental Disease, 169*, 50-54.

Collins, A. H., & Pancoast, D. L. (1977). *Natural helping networks: A strategy for prevention.* New York: National Association of Social Workers.

Coward, R. T. (1983). Cautions about the role of natural helping networks in programs for the rural elderly. In N. Stinnett et al. (Eds.), *Family strengths 4: Positive support systems* (pp. 291–306). Lincoln, NE: The University of Nebraska Press.

Coward, R. T. (In press). Factors associated with the configuration of the helping networks of noninstitutionalized elders. *The Journal of Gerontological Social Work.*

Coward, R. T., and Crawford, C. O. (1983). *Personal health care patterns among the elderly: The influence of residence on natural helping networks.* Paper presented at the Seventh Annual Institute of the American Rural Health Association, North Lake Tahoe, NV, June.

D'Augelli, A. R., Vallance, T. R., Danish, S. J., & Young, C. E. (1981). The community helpers project: A description of a prevention strategy for communities. *Journal of Prevention, 1,* 209–224.

Epstein, A. L. (1961). The network and urban social organization. *Rhodes-Livingstone Journal, 29,* 29–62.

Estes, Carrol L. (1979). *The aging enterprise.* San Francisco: Jossey-Bass.

Froland, C., Pancoast, D. L., Chapman, N. J., & Kimboko, P. J. (1979). *Professional partnerships with informal helpers: Emerging forms.* Paper presented at the Annual Meetings of the American Psychological Association, New York.

——— (1981). *Helping networks and human services.* Beverly Hills, CA: Sage Publications.

Gartner, A., & Riessman, F. (1977). *Self-help in human services.* San Francisco: Jossey-Bass.

Gerstel, N., & Riessman, C. K. (Nov. 1981). *Social networks in a vulnerable population: The separated and divorced.* Paper presented at the annual meetings of the American Public Health Association, Los Angeles.

Glazer, Nathan. (1971). The limits of social policy. *Commentary, 52,* 51–58.

Goldberg, E. (Nov. 1981). *Social networks as a factor in the health of older married women.* Paper presented at the annual meetings of the American Public Health Association, Los Angeles.

Gottlieb, B. H. (1983). The contribution of natural support systems of primary prevention among four subgroups of adolescent males. *Adolescence, 10,* 207–220.

Gourash, N. (1978). Help-seeking. A review of the literature. *American Journal of Community Psychology, 6,* 499–517.

Hammer, M., Makiesky-Barrow, S., & Gutwirth, L. (1978). Social networks and schizophrenia. *Schizophrenia Bulletin, 4,* 522–545.

Hirsch, B. J. (Aug. 1977). *The social network as a natural support system.* Paper presented at the Annual Meetings of the American Psychological Association, San Francisco.

Hooyman, Nancy R. (1980). *Mutual help organizations for rural older women.*

Paper presented at the Annual Meetings of the Gerontological Society, San Francisco.

Hooyman, Nancy R. (1983). "Social support networks in services to the elderly." In J. K. Whittaker and J. Garbarino (Eds.), *Social support networks: Informal helping in the human services* (pp. 133–164). New York: Aldine.

Kahn, R. L. (1979). Aging and social support. In M. W. Riley (Ed.), *Aging from birth to death: Interdisciplinary perspectives*. American Association for the Advancement of Science Symposia Series. Boulder, CO: Westview Press.

Kahn, R. L., & Antonucci, T. C. (1980). Convoys over the life course: Attachment roles and social support. In P. B. Baltes & O. G. Brim (Eds.), *Lifespan development and behavior*. New York: Academic Press.

Katz, A. H. (1976). Self-help health groups: Some clarifications. *Social Science and Medicine, 13*, 491–494.

Killilea, Marie. (1982). Interaction of crisis theory, coping strategies, and social support systems. In H. C. Schulberg & M. Killilea (Eds.), *The modern practice of community health: A volume in honor of Gerald Caplan*. San Francisco: Jossey-Bass.

Kleiman, M. A., Mantell, J. E., & Alexander, E. S. (1976). Collaboration and its discontents: The perils of partnership. *Journal of Applied Behavioral Science, 12*, 403–410.

Lee, G. R., & Cassidy, M. C. (1981). Kinship systems and extended family ties. In R. T. Coward and W. M. Smith Jr. (Eds.), *The family in rural society*. Boulder, CO: Westview Press.

Maguire, L. (1980). The interface of social workers with personal networks. *Social Work with Groups, 3*, 39–49.

McCubbin, H. I., Sussman, M. B., and Patterson, J. M. (1983). *Social stress and the family: Advances and developments in family stress theory and research*. New York: Haworth Press.

McQueen, D. V., & Celentano, D. (Nov. 1981). *The role of social support systems and problem drinking among women*. Paper presented at the annual meetings of the American Public Health Association, Los Angeles.

Mitchell, J. Clyde. (1969). The concept and use of social networks. In J. Clyde Mitchell, *Social networks in urban situations*. Manchester, England: University of Manchester Press.

Mueller, D. P. (1980). Social networks: A promising direction for research on the relationship of the social environment to psychiatric disorders. *Social Science and Medicine, 14A*, 147–161.

Myers-Walls, J. A., & Coward, R. T. (1983). Natural helping networks: Their role in community services for rural families. In R. T. Coward & W. M. Smith, Jr. (Eds.), *Family services: Issues and opportunities in contemporary rural America*. Lincoln, NE: University of Nebraska Press.

Naparstek, A. J., & Biegel, D. E. (1982). A policy framework for community support systems. In D. E. Biegel & A. J. Naparstek (Eds.), *Community support systems and mental health: Practice, policy, research.* New York: Springer.

Pilisak, Marc, & Minkler, Meredith. (1980). Supportive networks: Life ties for the elderly. *Journal of Social Issues, 36,* 95–116.

Plaut, T. (1982). Primary prevention in the 80's: The interface with community support systems. In D. E. Biegel & A. J. Naparstek (Eds.), *Community support systems and mental health: Practice, policy and research.* New York: Springer.

Powers, E. A., & Bultena, G. L. (1974). Sex differences in intimate friendships of old age. *Journal of Marriage and the Family, 38,* 739–747.

Rathbone-McCuan, E., and Coward, R. T. (In press). "Respite and adult day care services." In A. Monk (Ed.), *Handbook of gerontological services.* New York: Brunner/Mazel.

Rathbone-McCuan, E., and Hashimi, J. (1982). *Isolated elders: Health and social intervention.* Rockville, MD: Aspen Systems Corporation.

Robinson, B., and Thurhner, M. (1979). Taking care of aged parents: A family cycle transition. *The Gerontologist, 19,* 586–594.

Rosow, I. (1967). *Social integration of the aged.* New York: Free Press.

Shanas, E. (1979a). The family as a social support system in old age. *The Gerontologist, 19,* 169–174.

Shanas, E. (1979b). Social myth as hypothesis: The case of the family relations of old people. *The Gerontologist, 19,* 3–9.

Silverstone, B., & Hyman, H. K. (1982). *You and your aging parent* (rev. ed.). New York: Pantheon Books.

Stoller, E. P., and Earl, L. L. (1983). Help with activities of everyday life: Source of support for the noninstitutionalized elderly. *The Gerontologist, 23*(1), 64–70.

Tracy, G. S., & Gussow, Z. (1976). Self-help groups: A grassroots response to a need for services. *Journal of Applied Behavioral Science, 12,* 381–396.

Treas, J. (1977). Family support systems for the aged: Some social and demographic considerations. *The Gerontologist, 17,* 486–491.

Tolsdorf, C. C. (1976). Social networks, support, and coping: An explanatory study. *Family Process, 15,* 407–417.

Unger, D. G., & Powell, D. R. (1980). Supporting famlies under stress: The role of social networks. *Family Relations, 29,* 566–574.

Walker, K. N., McBride, A., & Vachon, M. L. S. (1977). Social support networks and the crisis of bereavement. *Social Science and Medicine, 11,* 35–41.

Warren, D. I. (1981). *Helping networks: How people cope with problems in the urban community.* Notre Dame, IN: University of Indiana Press.

Week, J. R., & Cuellar, J. B. (1981). The role of family members in the helping network of older people. *The Gerontologist, 21,* 388–394.

Weiss, R. S. (1969). The fund of sociability. *Transactions, 6,* 36–43.

Weiss, R. S. (1974). The provisions of social relationships. In Z. Rubin (Ed.), *Doing unto others.* Englewood Cliffs, NJ: Prentice-Hall.

Whittaker, J. K., and Garbarino, J. (Eds.) (1983). *Social support networks: Informal helping in the human services.* New York: Aldine.

Wingspread Report. (1978). *Strengthening families through informal support systems.* Racine, WI: The Johnson Foundation.

2

Theoretical Perspectives on Social Networks

Gary R. Lee

The idea of "theory" is probably the most misunderstood concept in all of science, and particularly in the social and behavioral sciences. Since this chapter is about theory, it behooves us to agree on what we are going to be talking about. I begin by stipulating what theory is not, then proceed to discuss what it is.

First, a theory is not speculative fact. In other words, a theory is not simply a guess, educated or otherwise, about some state of affairs which has yet to be confirmed. Theories do not become facts upon confirmation. A detective in a murder mystery may have a "theory," and when at the end of the novel or movie, we discover that the butler really did it, the detective's theory becomes a fact and is no longer "just a theory." That is all well and good for detectives and murder mysteries but is of no use to science, for reasons that will become apparent shortly.

Second, a theory is not a collection of interrelated concepts which serve to organize experience. While conceptual frameworks have frequently been employed to great advantage in the early stages of theory development in subdisciplines such as family sociology (see Holman & Burr, 1980), they are not theories in themselves. For many reasons, the increasingly popular analytical tool known as "social network theory" (see, for example, Mitchell, 1969; Sarason et al., 1977; Snow & Gordon, 1980; Tolsdorf, 1976) may be more appropriately described as a conceptual scheme or "paradigm" than as a theory, at least in its current form. Conceptual frameworks are important in the early stages of theory development as organizational tools, but do not by themselves constitute theory.

A theory is, thus, neither a speculative fact nor a conceptual calculus, although a well-developed theory will, in one form or another, include both of these components. According to Carl Hempel,

> Empirical science has two major objectives: to describe particular phenomena in the world of our experience and to establish general principles by means of which they can be explained and predicted. The explanatory and predictive principles of a scientific discipline are stated in its hypothetical generalizations and its theories; they characterize general patterns or regularities to which the individual phenomena conform and by virtue of which their occurrence can be systematically anticipated. (Hempel, 1952, p. 1)

Consistent with Hempel's usage, we may take the term "theory" to be loosely synonymous with the term "explanation." A theory is a systematic explanation of some class of events or phenomena, that allows us to understand their patterns of occurrence and to predict their occurrence in future or unknown situations. Theoretical statements are the general principles that give rise to hypotheses, or speculative facts. To the extent that hypotheses derived from a theory are supported by empirical evidence, the theory becomes more credible. If hypotheses derived from a theory are not supported by data, then there is something wrong with the data, the method by which the hypotheses were derived from the theoretical statements, and/or the theoretical statements themselves. Theories give rise to questions (hypotheses) which hopefully provoke answers (empirical generalizations). The answers are then employed to modify or otherwise improve the theoretical statements, giving birth to new hypotheses, and the process continues (Wallace, 1969).

This is how scientific theories are supposed to work. Unfortunately this is rarely the case, at least in the social and behavioral sciences. In social gerontology we have no rigorous theory that is capable of explaining or predicting any significant component of the aging process. This is due in large part to the intransigence of the subject matter, and the enormous variability of human behavior in general and the aging process in particular. There are, however, two widely employed perspectives in social gerontology that have served to guide research, organize the results of research, and give rise to hypotheses. Since both of these perspectives deal with the involvement of the elderly in social networks, each perspective will be examined briefly, paying particular attention to implications it has for social network involvement. We will then turn to another theoretical strategy which, while not at all gerontological in origin, is gaining increasing prominence in the discipline.

Major Theoretical Approaches in Social Gerontology

The guiding principles underlying most research in social gerontology for several decades are now collectively described as "activity theory." The basic premise of activity theory is that, for the elderly, social activity such as role incumbency, social interaction, and general involvement with others positively affects aging individuals' abilities to cope with aging, their self-concepts, and their emotional adjustment. The theory has been most explicitly stated and formalized by Lemon, Bengston, and Peterson (1972), who define activity as "any regularized or patterned action or pursuit that is regarded as beyond routine physical or personal maintenance" (p. 513). For our purposes, however, we will restrict the discussion of activity to social activity, involving interaction with at least one role partner.

Lemon et al. succinctly summarize the logic behind activity theory as follows:

> Activity provides various role supports necessary for reaffirming one's self-concept. The more intimate and the more frequent the activity, the more reinforcing and the more specific will be the role supports. Role supports are necessary for the maintenance of a positive self-concept, which in turn is associated with high life satisfaction. (p. 515)

Activity theory clearly hinges on the hypothesis that social involvement and emotional adjustment are positively related among the elderly. Most research has supported this hypothesis, in a variety of forms (see George, 1980; Larson, 1978; and Palmore, 1981, for recent reviews). According to activity theory, then, elderly persons who are highly involved in social roles and social networks benefit from this involvement, are better adjusted in a variety of ways than their less involved counterparts, and are, in fact, no different than younger persons in these respects.

Perhaps the greatest problem with activity theory resides in its inherent simplicity. In spite of its formalization by Lemon et al., its concepts and hypotheses are not sufficiently differentiated to account for the complexities in the relationships between the social interaction and adjustment variables. In their own data, for example, Lemon et al. found that only informal activity with friends was significantly related to a measure of life satisfaction. Interaction with relatives, interaction with neighbors, and participation in voluntary associations were all unrelated to life satisfaction. Many studies and reviews have since documented the surprising fact that interaction with relatives (including children, grandchildren, siblings, and other kin) is unrelated to emotional adjustment among the elderly (Lee, 1979; Lee & Ellithorpe, 1982; Lee & Ihinger-Tallman, 1980; Lowenthal & Robinson, 1976; Wood & Robertson, 1978). Activity theory by itself, however, does not suggest why different kinds of interaction, such as friendship versus kinship, should have differential consequences for the emotional well-being of older persons.

Furthermore, activity theory clearly implies that the loss of major social roles which frequently accompany old age should have adverse effects on the adjustment of persons experiencing these losses. Yet, in spite of widespread beliefs to the contrary (Wolozin, 1981), most research shows that retirement does not result in significant decreases in measures of adjustment (Atchley, 1976; George & Maddox, 1977; Palmore, 1981; Streib & Schneider, 1971). Even widowhood, independent of associated decreases in financial status, does not substantially decrease morale or life satisfaction (Balkwell, 1981; Chatfield, 1977; Morgan, 1976).

On the other hand, Lowenthal and Haven (1968) have shown that the existence of even one very intimate friend or confidant may allow older people to maintain positive self-images and high levels of emotional well-being regardless of the occurrence of potentially traumatic events such as retirement or widowhood. Tolsdorf (1976), in a study comparing the social networks of psychiatric and surgical hospital patients, found not only that the networks of the psychiatric patients were smaller, but also that psychiatric patients were less likely to reciprocate services received from network members and had less intimate relations with these members. These findings and many others suggest that the sheer volume or amount of social activity may be less important than the nature of relationships among network members. While this is not inconsistent with activity theory, these complexities are not clearly derivable from its premises.

The major alternative to activity theory for the past two decades has been disengagement theory (Cumming & Henry, 1961). While this theory currently has few real proponents, it has generated many influential ideas and a great deal of research in recent years. This theory capitalizes on the observation (that is not, incidentally, disputed by the premises of activity theory) that social involvement tends to decrease in later life. This decrease in social involvement, or withdrawal from social roles and relationships, is a major part of the process of disengagement. The unique aspect of disengagement theory is not the assertion that the disengagement process exists among older people, but rather that it is (1) a normal part of the aging process; (2) largely voluntary, and thus partially independent of other age-related phenomena such as failing health, declining resources, enforced retirement, and widowhood, and (3) mutually beneficial for society and for aging individuals (Dowd, 1975; Rose, 1964).

While disengagement theory is quite complex, it cannot be considered a well-developed scientific theory because it is inherently unfalsifiable (Hochschild, 1975). Most scholars interpret the theory to say that disengagement, rather than involvement, is associated with emotional adjustment in old age (Dowd, 1975; Hochschild, 1975; Palmore, 1981). Most available data do not support this hypothesis (see Larson, 1978, for a review), although as we have noted it is by no means the case that all instances of role loss decrease adjustment or that adjustment is increased by high levels or frequencies of any type of interaction.

The issue of involvement in social networks among the elderly is critical to both activity theory and disengagement theory, at least in terms of the consequences of such involvement. From an activity theory perspective, such involvement should have positive consequences for the elderly (as, indeed, it should for members of any other age category). The empirical support for this simple hypothesis, however, shows the necessity of so many qualifications that the overall level of its support must be classified as marginal at best. Activity theory is not sufficiently differentiated to allow prediction of circumstances under which social interaction or involvement is or is not rewarding to older individuals. Relevant data, by their very equivocality, make it clear that there are some circumstances under which social involvement is not rewarding.

Disengagement theory is not really much help in this regard because, in spite of its greater complexity, it predicts only that disengagement is inevitable and ultimately gratifying to aging individuals. It stipulates that the disengagement process is gradual and uneven, may proceed at different rates and in different ways for different individuals, and may result in a temporary decrease in emotional adjustment (Cumming, 1963, 1975; Hochschild, 1975). These stipulations *allow* for individual variability but do not allow for the *prediction* or *explanation* of such variability. Thus the consequences of network involvement for older people, particularly in terms of emotional adjustment, cannot be predicted from either activity or disengagement theory with sufficient accuracy or complexity to address the realities of social life in concrete situations or for specific individuals.

Furthermore, neither theory is designed to predict or explain network involvement itself, with one small exception. This exception involves the fact that disengagement theory capitalizes on the known propensity of aging individuals to reduce their levels of social involvement and explains this process as both voluntary and involuntary. It is a small exception, however, because disengagement theory does not produce verifiable explanations of individual variability in disengagement. The best the theory can do is to predict a negative correlation between age and social involvement (engagement), but even this correlation is not expected to be particularly strong since recognition of individual variation in disengagement is built into the theory.

As we noted above, activity theory does not, in general, dispute the point that social involvement declines with age. The difference between activity theory and disengagement theory in this regard is that the former takes declining social involvement as a given, a fact either not subject to explanation or attributable entirely to age-related changes in health, energy, employment status, and marital status. Activity theory pertains to the consequences of social involvement among the elderly and lets the antecedents take care of themselves. Disengagement theory, on the other hand, posits that age itself is a cause of disengagement, with the weak theoretical justification that disengagement occurs because both individuals and societies will be better off if it does.

This issue is summarized succinctly by Dowd:

> The specific difference between the two theories concerns whether the observed negative association between aging and social interaction is voluntary and preceded by psychological disengagement on the part of the individual or imposed unilaterally on the individual by the structural requirements of the society. . . . Neither theory, however, while focusing for the most part on descriptive accounts of the peculiar relationships between social interaction and life satisfactions attempts to offer anything but the most perfunctory of explanations for the decreased social interaction itself. Rather, this phenomenon is given the status of a sociological "given"; that it is treated as something requiring no additional explanation. (Dowd, 1975, p. 585)

Most studies agree that, in general, social activity does decline with age (Gordon & Gaitz, 1976), although longitudinal studies show considerable variation in this pattern across individuals and different types of social activities (Palmore, 1981). Dowd (1975) argues that this decline merits more systematic theoretical attention than it has received, or than either activity theory or disengagement theory is capable of providing. To assess the implications of age-related decreases in social activity for the social networks of the elderly, we need to shift into more general sociological and social psychological theories of social interaction and social relationships.

Social Networks and Social Exchange

Dowd (1975) argues that neither activity theory nor disengagement theory seriously addresses the issue of declining social involvement of aging persons as an object of explanation. Activity theory assumes that this decline is a natural consequence of the concomitants of aging: declining health, diminished financial resources, widowhood, and so forth. Disengagement theorists see decreased social involvement as an intrinsic part of the aging process itself and assert that disengagement occurs in spite of, or independently of, physical and financial capacities. Neither perspective delves intensively into the reasons individuals may voluntarily decrease their social involvements, although disengagement theory asserts that they do.

Dowd (1975, 1978, 1980, 1981), however, contends that decreases in social participation that accompany age may be explained in terms of social exchange theory. Like disengagement theory, Dowd addresses declines in social involvement which are independent of age-related changes in health, finances, marital status, and so on, and attempts to explain these declines in terms of changes in the structure of social relations rather than as innate properties characteristic of the aging process. According to exchange theory,

> All social interaction may be viewed as an exchange between two actors
> . . . of rewarding behaviors. . . . Human behavior tends to be oriented
> towards the expectations of other people; it is also motivated by a desire
> to maximize one's rewards and to minimize one's costs. People tend to
> avoid the undesirable and to seek that which is perceived as pleasant or
> rewarding. (Dowd, 1980, p. 596)

Rewards which are sought through social interaction are counterbalanced to some varying degree by costs entailed in the interaction. Costs may involve only the rewards that would be derived from alternative behaviors or relationships, or they may involve undesired consequences of a relationship itself. Actors evaluate the desirability of relationships in which they are engaged in terms of subjectively calculated "profit"—rewards minus costs (Emerson, 1976; Homans, 1961; Stolte & Emerson, 1977). Actors enter into social relationships because of expectations of profit, and continue to participate in these relationships if their expectations are realized. "In other words, actors engaged in an exchange of behavior will continue their exchange only so long as the exchange is perceived as being more rewarding than it is costly" (Dowd, 1975, p. 587).

In order for two (or more) social actors to establish and maintain a mutually satisfactory exchange relationship, the value of the resources possessed by each must be relatively equal. If Actor A possesses more numerous or more valuable resources than Actor B, the relationship is "unbalanced." Furthermore, if Actor B requires the resources possessed by Actor A and has no alternative source of these resources, Actor B is "dependent" upon Actor A.

The dependence of actors with few resources upon actors with many resources is, in exchange theory terms, the source of social power. Those who control valued resources may demand compliance from others in exchange for access to those resources. Thus, our Actor B, if he or she is dependent upon Actor A to provide valued resources, may need to comply with the wishes of Actor A in order to gain or maintain access to the resources Actor A controls. The consequence of an unbalanced exchange relationship is that the party in the relationship whose resources are most highly valued possesses power over the dependent party in that relationship. Dependence is likely to be costly to the dependent actor, psychologically and in other ways.

The logic of exchange theory has frequently been employed in analyses of power relations between the sexes. Over a generation ago, Waller (1937, pp. 275–277) elucidated the "principle of least interest" and applied it to the courtship process: "That person is able to dictate the conditions of association whose interest in the continuation of the affair is least" (1937, p. 275). In a sense, the person who is the more emotionally involved in the relationship is dependent upon the other party for gratification. Waller argues that this dependence leads to exploitation of the dependent party, making the relationship more costly to him or her.

Exchange theory also provides the logical basis for the "resource theory" of marital power (Blood & Wolfe, 1960; Lee & Petersen, 1983; Scanzoni, 1979). Resource theory suggests that the ability to make decisions in a marital relationship derives from control of valued resources; a spouse who possesses few resources must comply with the wishes of the other spouse because of his or her dependence on that spouse's resources.

Dowd (1975, 1980) argues that exchange theory is also applicable to the analysis of relationships between members of different age categories. He contends that, in contemporary society, the resources possessed by the elderly are both diminished and devalued. They are diminished because, in an industrial economy, wealth is a consequence of labor rather than property. Given the general surplus of labor typical of industrial societies and the rapid rate of social and technological change, the skills and training of older people rapidly become obsolete (Cowgill & Holmes, 1972; Palmore & Manton, 1974). The practice of retirement becomes institutionalized, removing the elderly from the labor force and from the resources associated with this involvement. Thus, "the bargaining position of the aged social actor upon retirement quickly deteriorates as his supply of power resources becomes depleted" (Dowd, 1975, p. 588).

The power of the elderly is also reduced in modern society because the resources they do possess tend to be devalued due to the operation of "status generalization." Old age in the United States and similar societies is a negative status characteristic. Because low status is attached to old age, and because human beings tend to generalize from visible status characteristics to characteristics which are less obvious such as abilities (Berger et al., 1977; Webster & Driskell, 1978), older people are often believed to possess few resources that would be of value in an exchange relationship. This believe becomes a self-fulfilling prophecy: older people are treated as if they have few resources, regardless of the level of resources they actually possess.

> As a result of these processes, many aged are doubly disadvantaged in their social exchange relationships. On the one hand, their access to several categories of exchange resources tends to decline with age thus placing the old person in a position of negotiating from weakness, rather than strength. . . . On the other hand, the resources that the older person *does* possess are perceived as less valuable because of the "burden of proof" principle. That is, the *value* of an exchange resource—when possessed by an older actor—is not self-evident. (Dowd, 1980, p. 598)

In addition to its other disadvantages, being the dependent party in an exchange relationship is psychologically uncomfortable. According to exchange theory (Emerson, 1976), an actor in such a position may engage in a variety of strategies to rectify the power imbalance. Strategies relevant to the situation of the elderly (Dowd, 1975) include (1) extension of the power network—that is, developing other sources of valued rewards; (2) emergence of status—increasing the value of rewards controlled by the less powerful party to the more powerful party; and (3) withdrawal from the relationship.

The first two options, however, are relatively unavailable to older persons. The first balancing strategy mentioned above, extension of the power network, may, however, account for many research findings cited in support of activity theory (Dowd, 1975, p. 589). Older persons who maintain frequent interaction with a variety of partners tend to be happier and better adjusted than their less socially active counterparts (Larson, 1978). Furthermore, this logic may provide a clue as to why older people show a marked proclivity to form and maintain friendship relations with age-peers (Lowenthal & Robinson, 1976; Rosow, 1967). Homogeneity is a basic principle of friendship formation: individuals tend to form friendships with others who are similar to themselves in terms of social characteristics, and age is a critical characteristic in this regard (Hess, 1972). It may be critical because, particularly among the elderly, power resources are more evenly distributed within than between age categories. The likelihood of balanced exchange relations is therefore greater in age-homogeneous than age-heterogeneous relationships.

Increasing the value of resources possessed or controlled by the elderly is difficult in industrial societies where older people ultimately relinquish their positions in the labor force, but it may occur in certain situations. For example, Salamon and Keim (1979) report that widows in a farming community who possessed substantial land holdings employed these holdings as a power resource in their relations with younger kin, distributing both current use of the land and the possibility of inheritance to these kin in such a way as to ensure continuing relationships. However, since the elderly control relatively few resources in modern industrial societies (Balkwell & Balswick, 1981; Cowgill & Holmes, 1972; Palmore & Manton, 1974), these kinds of possibilities are severely limited and examples in the empirical literature are scarce indeed.

The final option open to older persons who find themselves at a power disadvantage in an exchange relationship is the option of withdrawal from that relationship. The older person, in effect, reduces motivational investment in the rewards which may be obtained through interaction with more powerful others because those rewards are too costly to pursue, and withdraws from such relationships. In the most critical component of his argument, Dowd (1975) contends that this may account for the process of disengagement. In other words, the elderly may withdraw or disengage from social relationships because their limited resources, or the perception of their resources as limited, place them in an uncomfortable position of dependence and power deficit in relation to others.

Suggestions that disengagement and desire to avoid dependence may be connected have been made before in the gerontological literature. Clark and Anderson (1967), in their study of elderly San Franciscans, found that those living in the community ranked dependence as the most important source of low morale, well ahead of worries about health, boredom or inactivity, and fear of dying (1967, p. 222). They also indicate a direct connection between social withdrawal and fear of dependence:

> In much of the social isolation and avoidance of others which we see among the elderly, there is also the suggestion of the need to be self-reliant, of not engaging too much in public or social activities lest others foist help upon them while they still want to try "going it alone." (Clark & Anderson, 1967, p. 64)

This logic may also explain one of the more interesting empirical findings in gerontological research which is, thus far, insufficiently understood. While it does appear that frequency of interaction with friends is positively related to morale, life satisfaction, and happiness among older people (Larson, 1978; Lemon, Bengston, & Peterson, 1972), frequency of interaction with kin (children, grandchildren, and siblings) is not (Lee, 1979; Lee & Ellithorpe, 1982; Lee & Ihinger-Tallman, 1980; Lowenthal & Robinson, 1976; Wood & Robertson, 1978). This may be attributable to the fact that, given the cultural norms which surround kinship in general and the parent–child relationship in particular, withdrawal from these relations is not a realistic possibility. As the power resources of older persons decline, they may perceive themselves as having progressively less to offer their kin, and as being potentially more dependent on them. Although many psychological and material rewards may be derived from interaction with kin, they may also be costly because of decrements in the power resources of older persons. If friendship relations become costly in this manner, they may be terminated. Kinship relations, based on sentiments of obligation and "positive concern" (Adams, 1968), must be continued.

The perspective on social relations of the elderly offered by exchange theory differs in certain key respects from those provided by disengagement theory and activity theory. Unlike disengagement theory, exchange theory does not posit that older persons must withdraw from social life in order to adjust successfully to the realities of aging; it does, however, contribute to our understanding of why they frequently *do* withdraw. And unlike most versions of activity theory, exchange theory does not imply that social activity per se is a uniformly "good thing" for older people. Instead it focuses analytic attention on the properties of specific relationships and kinds of relationships, variation in these properties, and variation in potential outcomes of social interaction for older persons. The complexities of social life highlighted by exchange theory need to be carefully considered in any analysis of the ramifications of social network involvement for the elderly.

Exchange Processes: Implications for Network Involvement Among the Elderly

The aversion of older people in the United States to reliance on community or other public agencies for the provision of needed services has frequently been noted, and just as frequently attributed to their desires for independence (Atchley, 1980; Kreps, 1977). Services provded by public agencies are paid for by others and cannot be reciprocated. The problem this causes for elderly persons in need of services is articulated clearly by Clark and Anderson:

> Since the older one gets, the more likely one will need help of some kind, old people are often obliged to admit this need and seek this help. Unfortunately for some . . . these very real and very serious circumstances often run counter to an individual's additional need for anchoring his self-esteem upon autonomy—the ability to keep on managing for oneself, to go it alone, to reaffirm that one is still a self-governing adult. (Clark & Anderson, 1967, p. 380)

It is frequently suggested that many of the needs of older persons may be met by informal, rather than formal, support networks (Horwitz, 1978; Stoller, 1979). This suggestion is worthy of careful attention from a policy point of view, but the ramifications of its implementation must be considered in light of our theoretical and empirical knowledge. This knowledge suggests that there are at least three problems which must be dealt with before the resources of informal networks may be successfully mobilized in the fulfillment of the needs of older persons.

First, although we know that real social isolation among the elderly is quite rare (see, for example, Shanas, 1979), it is nonetheless the case that the existence of social networks with respect to individual older persons is variable. Some, and perhaps many of those most in need of services, have no access to such networks. Second, those networks which do exist are not invariably or necessarily supportive (Wellman, 1981). Lopata (1978), for example, has shown that extended kin contribute only very infrequently to the support systems of widows. The terms "informal networks" and "informal support networks" are not at all synonymous.

The third problem, and the one which is most critical from the theoretical perspective developed here, is exactly the same problem which appears to deter older people from taking advantage of formal support services. This is the problem of reciprocity, of balance in exchange relationships. Older people require services to the extent that their own resources are insufficient to provide for their needs. If friends, neighbors, relatives, or others do have the resources to satisfy some of the needs of older persons, how are the older persons to reciprocate? What resources do they possess which will allow them, in exchanges with "informal" service providers, to maintain balance and thus maintain feelings of autonomy, self-esteem, and ultimately contentment? These are not trivial questions. If the only reward older people can offer to the providers of services is "the humble capacity to comply" (Dowd, 1975, p. 587), and if this resource deficit is in fact responsible for social withdrawal, diminished self-esteem, and low morale as we have suggested, then strategies designed to satisfy the needs of older people through informal networks may have more adverse than beneficial consequences.

This may be particularly problematical in the case of friendship relations. We have established that interaction with friends positively affects the emotional well-being of older people. This effect appears to be due, in large part at least, to the fact that friendship is based on consensus, equality, and reciprocity. To the extent that these relationships change from balanced to unbalanced, from equality to power-dependence, perhaps the most critical quality of such relations will be lost. We cannot, of course, predict the consequences of this loss with absolute certainty. However, we might remember Tolsdorf's (1976) finding that a primary distinguishing feature of the social networks of psychiatric patients was the absence of reciprocity: psychiatric patients were dependent on network members and offered these members little in return. We do not know the causal processes involved here, and it would be foolish to assert categorically that dependence causes mental illness. On the other hand, it would be equally foolish to ignore the connections between dependence and negative emotional states which the gerontological literature has so amply documented. Again, Clark and Anderson state the problem clearly and forcefully:

> For our sample as a whole, there are two basic goals—survival and self-esteem. . . . For most of this generation of older Americans, self-esteem is indelibly linked with the personal and cultural value of independence—autonomy and self-reliance. Yet, old age in reality is often a time when one must have help and support in order to survive. This is the fundamental dilemma. In our sample, the tragic contradiction that American culture generates for the elderly between these two basic goals is the major problem in adaptation to aging. (Clark & Anderson, 1967, p. 390)

The problem of reciprocity between older people and those who provide the services they may require for survival is serious, but may not be insurmountable. However, existing theory at this point tells us only that it is a problem; strategies for its resolution are not immediately apparent. The most useful conclusion we can currently offer is the suggestion that our attentions focus on the issue of reciprocity if we are to make full use of the potentials for support inherent in informal networks without inadvertently decreasing the quality of life in later years.

References

Adams, B. N. (1968). *Kinship in an urban setting.* Chicago: Markam Publishing Co.

Atchley, R. C. (1976). *The sociology of retirement.* Cambridge, MA: Schenkman.

Atchley, R. C. (1980). *The social forces in later life* (3rd ed.). Belmont, CA: Wadsworth.

Balkwell, C. (1981). Transition to widowhood: A review of the literature. *Family Relations, 30,* 117–127.

Balkwell, C., & Balswick, J. (1981). Subsistence economy, family structure, and the status of the elderly. *Journal of Marriage and the Family, 43,* 423–429.

Berger, J., Fisek, M. H., Norman, Z., & Zelditch, M., Jr. (1977). *Status characteristics and social interaction: An expectation-states approach.* New York: Elsevier.

Blood, R. O., Jr., & Wolfe, D. M. (1960). *Husbands and wives: The dynamics of married living.* New York: The Free Press.

Chatfield, W. (1977). Economic and sociological factors influencing the life satisfaction of the aged. *Journal of Gerontology, 32,* 593–599.

Clark, M., & Anderson, B. G. (1967). *Culture and aging: An anthropological study of older Americans.* Springfield, IL: Charles C. Thomas.

Cowgill, D. O., & Holmes, L. D. (1972). *Aging and modernization.* New York: Appleton-Century-Crofts.

Cumming, E. (1963). Further thoughts on the theory of disengagement. *International Social Science Journal, 15,* 377–393.

Cumming, E. (1975). Engagement with an old theory. *International Journal of Aging and Human Development, 6,* 187–191.

Cumming, E., & Henry, W. E. (1961). *Growing old: The process of disengagement.* New York: Basic Books.

Dowd, J. J. (1975). Aging as exchange: A preface to theory. *Journal of Gerontology, 30,* 584–594.

Dowd, J. J. (1978). Aging as exchange: A test of the distributive justice proposition. *Pacific Sociological Review, 21,* 351–375.

Dowd, J. J. (1980). Exchange rates and old people. *Journal of Gerontology, 35,* 596–602.

Dowd, J. J. (1981). Age and inequality: A critique of the age stratification model. *Human Development, 24,* 157–171.

Emerson, R. M. (1976). Social exchange theory. In A. Inkeles, J. Colman, & N. Smelser (Eds.), *Annual review of sociology* (Vol. 2). Palo Alto, CA: Annual Reviews.

George, L. K. (1980). *Role transitions in later life.* Belmont, CA: Wadsworth.

George, L. K., & Maddox, G. L. (1977). Subjective adaptation to the loss of the work role: A longitudinal study. *Journal of Gerontology, 32,* 456–462.

Gordon, C., & Gaitz, C. M. (1976). Leisure and lives: Personal expressivity across the life span. In R. H. Binstock & E. Shanas (Eds.), *Handbook of aging and the social sciences.* New York: Van Nostrand Reinhold.

Hempel, C. G. (1952). *Fundamentals of concept formation in empirical science.* Chicago: University of Chicago Press.

Hess, B. B. (1972). Friendship. In M. W. Riley, M. E. Johnson, & A. Foner (Eds.), *Aging and society, Vol. 3: A theory of age stratification.* New York: Russell Sage.

Hochschild, A. R. (1975). Disengagement theory: A critique and proposal. *American Sociological Review, 40,* 553–569.

Holman, T. B., & Burr, W. R. (1980). Beyond the beyond: The growth of family theories in the 1970's. *Journal of Marriage and the Family, 42,* 729–741.

Homans, G. C. (1961). *Social behavior: Its elementary forms.* New York: Harcourt, Brace and World.

Horwitz, A. (1978). Family, kin and friend networks in psychiatric help-seeking. *Social Science and Medicine, 12,* 297–304.

Kreps, J. (1977). Interorganizational transfer and the bureaucracy. In E. Shanas & M. B. Sussman (Eds.), *Family bureaucracy and the elderly.* Durham, NC: Duke University Press.

Larson, R. (1978). Thirty years of research on the subjective well-being of older Americans. *Journal of Gerontology, 33,* 109–125.

Lee, G. R. (1979). Children and the elderly: Interaction and moral. *Research on Aging, 1*, 335–360.

Lee, G. R., & Ellithorpe, E. (1982). Intergenerational exchange and subjective well-being among the elderly. *Journal of Marriage and the Family, 44*, 217–224.

Lee, G. R., & Ihinger-Tallman, M. (1980). Sibling interaction and morale: The effects of family relations on older people. *Research on Aging, 2*, 367–391.

Lee, G. R., & Petersen, L. R. (1983). Conjugal power and spousal resources in patriarchal cultures. *Journal of Comparative Family Studies, 14*, 23–38.

Lemon, B. W., Bengston, V. L., & Peterson, J. A. (1972). An exploration of the activity of aging: Activity type and life satisfaction among in-movers to a retirement community. *Journal of Gerontology, 27*, 511–523.

Lopata, H. Z. (1978). Contributions of extended families to the support systems of metropolitan widows: Limitations of the modified kin network. *Journal of Marriage and the Family, 40*, 355–364.

Lowenthal, M. F., & Haven, C. (1968). Interaction and adaptation: Intimacy as a critical variable. *American Sociological Review, 33*, 20–30.

Lowenthal, M. F., & Robinson, B. (1976). Social networks and isolation. In R. H. Binstock & E. Shanas (Eds.), *Handbook of aging and the social sciences*. New York: Van Nostrand Reinhold.

Mitchell, J. C. (1969). The concept and the use of social networks. In J. C. Mitchell (Ed.), *Social networks in urban situations*. Manchester University Press.

Morgan, L. A. (1976). A re-examination of widowhood and morale. *Journal of Gerontology, 31*, 687–695.

Palmore, E. (1981). *Social patterns in normal aging: Findings from the Duke longitudinal studies*. Durham, NC: Duke University Press.

Palmore, E., & Manton, K. (1974). Modernization and the status of the aged: International correlations. *Journal of Gerontology, 29*, 205–210.

Rose, A. M. (1964). A current theoretical issue in social gerontology. *The Gerontologist, 4*, 46–50.

Rosow, I. (1967). Social integration of the aged. New York: The Free Press.

Salamon, S., & Keim, A. M. (1979). Land ownership and women's power in a mid-western farming community. *Journal of Marriage and the Family, 41*, 109–119.

Sarason, S. B., Carroll, C., Maton, K., Cohen, S., & Lorentz, E. (1977). *Human services and resource networks*. San Francisco: Jossey-Bass.

Scanzoni, J. (1979). Social processes and power in families. In W. R. Burr, R. Hill, F. I. Nye, & I. L. Reiss (Eds.), *Contemporary theories about the family, Vol. 7: Research-based theories*. New York: The Free Press.

Shanas, E. (1979). Social myth as hypothesis: The case of the family relations of old people. *The Gerontologist, 19*, 3–9.

Snow, D. L., & Gordon, J. B. (1980). Social network analysis and intervention with the elderly. *The Gerontologist, 20*, 463–467.

Stoller, E. P. (1979). *Growing old in the country: The role of informal support networks.* Paper presented at the annual meetings of the Rural Sociological Society, Burlington, VT.

Stolte, J. F., & Emerson, R. M. (1977). Structural inequality: Position and power in network structures. In R. L. Hamblin & J. H. Kunkel (Eds.), *Behavioral theory in sociology.* New Brunswick, NJ: Transaction.

Streib, G. F., & Schneider, C. J. (1971). *Retirement in American society.* Ithaca, NY: Cornell University Press.

Tolsdorf, C. C. (1976). Social networks, support, and coping: An exploratory study. *Family Process, 15,* 407–417.

Wallace, W. L. (1969). *Sociological theory.* Chicago: Aldine.

Waller, W. (1937). *The family: A dynamic interpretation.* New York: Dryden.

Webster, J., Jr., & Driskell, J. E., Jr. (1978). Status generalization. *American Sociological Review, 43,* 220–236.

Wellman, B. (1981). Applying network analysis to the study of support. In B. Gottlieb (Ed.), *Social networks and social support.* Beverly Hills, CA: Sage.

Wolozin, H. (1981). Earlier retirement and the older worker. *Journal of Economic Issues, 15,* 477–487.

Wood, V., & Robertson, J. F. (1978). Friendship and kinship interaction: Differential effect on the morale of the elderly. *Journal of Marriage and the Family, 40,* 367–373.

Part II
Family Relations

3

Children and
Their Elderly Parents

Sandra M. Hanson
William J. Sauer

In this chapter, that portion of the kinship network involving children and their elderly parents will be examined. Previous research indicates that for most families, this relationship between parents and children is the "hub" or "critical core" of the extended kinship network. In our discussion of the relationships between elderly parents and their children, we attempt to avoid the commonly accepted stereotype of the "typical American family" and show how these kinship ties vary considerably across groups.

Proximity of the Elderly to Their Children

Proximity involves not only geographic distances between the separate households of elderly and their children, but also the extent to which households are shared by individuals in these two groups. In their study of the aged in three industrialized countries, Shanas et al. (1968) found that between 7 and 14% of the aged were married couples living with one or more children, and between 9 and 14% were widowed, divorced, or separated and living with one or more children. Some cultural variations with regard to shared residences have emerged in Great Britain, the United States, and Denmark, where Stehouwer (1965) has noted that 41.9, 27.6, and 20.1%, respectively, of the elderly share households with their children. Troll (1971) further notes that in the early 1970s, about one-third of the American elderly who had children lived with them.

In recent decades, however, the number of older parents sharing a home with adult offspring has steadily declined (Shanas, 1979). At the same time, the number living in one-person households has risen (Kobrin, 1976; Siegel, 1976), as has the number of older people living within 10 minutes distance of one or more of their children. Although shifts in shared residence have taken place, the proportion of elderly who either live with or near a child has remained somewhat constant. In 1976, three-fourths of all elderly persons with children lived either in the same household or within a half hour distance from a child (Shanas, 1979).

Research is consistent in showing that older parents generally prefer not to live with children. It is the ill, the unmarried, the poor, and the very old who are the most likely candidates for residence sharing (Hess & Waring, 1980; Kivett, 1976; Treas, 1975; Troll, 1971). Both generations value the privacy and independence which separate households allow; "intimacy at a distance" is the preferred arrangement (Cosneck, 1970; Rosenmayr & Kockeis, 1963). Older individuals may express a desire for children to live closer than they do, but not many prefer to live in the same neighborhood (Reiss, 1962).

The second proximity issue has to do with the geographic distribution of the separate households in which elderly parents and their children reside. A considerable amount of research on the residential proximity of extended kin began appearing in the 1950s and 1960s (e.g., Adams, 1968; Axelrod, 1956; Bell & Boat, 1957; Dotson, 1951; Litwak, 1960; Shanas, 1961). These studies were primarily motivated by the work of Parsons and others concerning the isolated nuclear family in America. The major conclusion of this research is that nuclear families are not physically isolated from their extended kin— most individuals have at least some kin living within a relatively short distance (Streib & Beck, 1980; Sussman, 1965; Troll, 1971).

Studies of proximity in which children are the respondents indicate that approximately 60% have a parent(s) living in the same community (Komarovsky, 1964) or within one hundred miles (Adams, 1968). Further studies focusing on older parents suggest that approximately 90% live less than one hour from at least one of their children (Stehouwer, 1965; see also Johnson, 1971; Kerckhoff, 1966a; Reiss, 1962; Rosenberg, 1970). While most research addressing the question of geographic proximity between older parents and their children has shown that a majority of the elderly live close to at least one child, some variation has been found to occur by residence, social class, life cycle stage, birth order and gender of child, marital status, and health of parent(s). The major findings may be stated as follows:

1. Because of population shifts, rural residents have fewer relatives near them than urban residents (Troll, 1971).
2. Both social class and income tend to be positively correlated with the distance between parents' and children's households (Harris, 1975; Kerckhoff, 1966; Lacy & Hendricks, 1980).
3. Findings on the relationship between family life cycle and proximity are inconclusive. While some researchers have suggested a decline in the percent of kin living in the same area over the family life cycle (Reiss, 1962), others have suggested an increase (Gibson, 1972; Shanas et al., 1968). Some of this incongruity in findings could be resolved if the pool of kin available over the life cycle were taken into account and more similar conceptual and operational definitions of proximity and kin were used (Gibson, 1972). Research focusing exclusively on parents and children, for example, has suggested that the period of time when parents are middle-aged and children are in their early family stages is likely to be the time when the two generations are most geographically distant (Litwak, 1960; Troll, 1971; Willmott & Young, 1960). Komarovsky (1964) found a differential proximity of children to their parents which favored the daughter's parents, while Adams (1968) and Wilkening, Gurrero, and Ginsberg (1972) presented findings which did not lend support to that conclusion.
4. Younger children are more likely than older children to live near their parent(s) (Townsend, 1963). Older women are more likely than older men to live with or near their children (Berardo, 1980; Chevan & Korson, 1972; Shanas et al., 1968).
5. The cross-cultural residence data of Shanas et al. suggest that the widowed, divorced, or separated elderly are more likely to live with their children than are married elderly (Streib, 1977). A similar relationship has been found between marital status of the aged person and proximity to kin (Gibson, 1972).
6. Parents in poorer health tend to live closer to their children than do those in good health (Rosow, 1967).

The Quantity and Quality of Contact Among Elderly Parents and Their Children

Contact between kin is another aspect of family networks which has received a great deal of attention in the past few decades. Most of this effort has focused on dispelling the myth of the isolated nuclear family (see, e.g., Adams, 1970; Axelrod, 1956; Johnson, 1971). It should be noted that in this chapter we have separated the discussions on contact and assistance. In this section we focus on the amount and quality of social interaction that takes place, while in later sections we discuss the functional aspects of interaction such as services, aid, and support exchanged between children and their parents. Several flaws in the kinship interaction research limit somewhat our ability to make valid conclusions about the quantity and quality of contact between elderly parents and their children. For example, the focus of many studies has been primarily on quantity rather than quality of interaction. While it has been demonstrated that most kin networks involve considerable contact, very little research has examined quality of visiting patterns: Are visits brief or lengthy? Friendly or hostile? Based on affection or obligation? and so on (Shanas, 1979; Troll, 1971). In addition, Gibson (1972) has pointed out several other flaws in the empirical analysis of kinship interaction. First, there has been no real attempt to delineate the minimal amount of interaction needed to categorize families as isolated. And second, sampling is often unrepresentative and tends to rely on operational and conceptual definitions of interaction that are poor and/or inconsistent. Several researchers, for example, consider only face-to-face interaction (e.g., Reiss, 1962), while others (e.g., Berardo, 1967; Johnson, 1971) take into account phone calls and letter writing as well.

Studies that have focused on the kin network in its entirety have discovered extremely high levels of interaction (Gibson, 1972; Litwak, 1960; Reiss, 1962; Rosenberg, 1970). A large number of available kin are seen at least monthly (Gibson, 1972; Reiss, 1962), and for many interaction is weekly (Litwak, 1960; Rosenberg, 1970). The greatest amount of interaction within the kinship system has been shown to take place between parents and their children (Adams, 1968; Reiss, 1962; Shanas, 1973). As would be expected, these parent–child contacts are usually rated as the most important type of kin contacts (Brown, 1974) and are typified by considerable regularity both within families (Adams, 1970; Townsend, 1963) and across decades (Shanas, 1979). Most studies focusing on the level of interaction between elderly parents and their children are consistent in showing that approximately 70% of the elderly have weekly visits with at least one child (Harris, 1975; Shanas, 1979; Shanas et al., 1968; Townsend, 1976; Watson & Kivett, 1976). As was the case with proximity, all older parents and their children do not have similarly high levels of interaction. Variation occurs across different groups and among group members depending on their particular needs and characteristics. The major sources of this variation include geographic proximity, gender, social mobility, social class, retirement, life cycle stage, marital status, residence, and ethnicity. They may be summarized as follows:

1. Geographic proximity is a variable which is frequently included in studies of kin interaction. Previous research unanimously shows that it is one of the major factors in the amount of face-to-face interaction between kin in general and parents and children in particular (Berardo, 1967; Lee, 1980; Sussman & Burchinal, 1972). Although distance does cut down on face-to-face interaction, it does not limit other forms of contact such as phone calls and letter writing (Wilkening et al., 1972). Further, any disruptive effects of geographic migration have been shown to be temporary (Berardo, 1967; Litwak, 1960; Troll, 1971).

2. With regard to gender, present research suggests that the women in both the parent and child generations keep in touch with kin more frequently than do the men (Adams, 1970; Lee, 1980; Townsend, 1963), and that they are also more involved in kin obligations and activities (Berardo, 1967; Farber, 1964; Komarovsky, 1964). However, other researchers have found sex differences in interaction to be minimal or absent (Petrowsky, 1976; Reiss, 1962). Finally, there is some indication that middle-aged children interact with maternal kin more frequently than with paternal kin (Reiss, 1962).

3. Previous research focusing on social mobility provides inconclusive results. While some studies argue that there is no relationship between social mobility and parent–child interaction (Aldous, 1967; Klatzky, 1972), others have observed significant but small effects regarding the relationship (Booth, 1972; Bruce, 1970; Hutter, 1970; Kessing, 1971).

4. The small inverse relationship which has been inconsistently observed between social class and kin interaction may be attributable to the greater geographic distance between middle-class households (Lee, 1980), and also to the fact that the working class does less visiting and what visiting is done tends to be with relatives (Troll, 1971). In fact, when size of kin network and propinquity are controlled for, it has been found that a positive relationship exists between income and interaction with kin (Rosenberg, 1967).

5. Retirement appears to increase contact with children (Atchley, 1980; Harris, 1965b; Stehouwer, 1965).

6. Previous studies regarding kin interaction remain inconclusive. Some suggest that there is no variation over the life span (Brown, 1974; Gibson, 1972; Reiss, 1962), while others suggest that there is (Mitchell, 1963; Rosenberg & Anspach, 1973; Shanas et al., 1968; Troll, Miller, & Atchley, 1979). It may be fair to conclude that total but not proportionate interaction with all kin declines over the life cycle due to declining numbers of kin (Gibson, 1972; Lee, 1980). Interaction between parents and children, however, remains fairly constant with the chance of a small dip during the years when the children are raising families. It has been suggested, however, that this dip may disappear when geographic proximity is controlled for (Litwak, 1960; Willmott & Young, 1960).

7. Although several researchers have suggested that those who are single have fewer kin ties than those who are not (Shulman, 1975), it appears that the percentage of available kin seen monthly is higher for the single than the married (Gibson, 1972). While the widowed as a group may be no more isolated from kin than married individuals (Petrowsky, 1976), considerable evidence indicates that widowers interact less with kin than do widows and married couples (Berardo, 1967, 1980; Langford, 1962).

8. In Lee's (1980) survey of the research on kin interaction and residence, he concludes that there may be a slightly greater frequency of kin interaction among rural groups (e.g., Hendrix, 1975; Key, 1961), but that these differences appear to be largely due to migration and geographic distance.

9. Finally, greater frequencies of interaction have been found to occur among the aged belonging to minority groups (e.g., black, Mexican-American) than among the white elderly (Dowd & Bengston, 1978). Although most blacks, like whites, do not live in extended families (Martin & Martin, 1978; Scanzoni, 1971), black elderly may be more likely to live with relatives (Bourg, 1975) and to visit and exchange aid with relatives (Hays & Mindel, 1973; Hill, 1971; Soldo & Lauriat, 1976).

Turning now to the quality of elderly parent–child contacts, we will begin by examining the type of contacts that typify parent–child relationships. Kin interaction is dominated by visiting, family get-togethers, and shared leisure activities (Adams, 1968; Streib, 1965; Sussman, 1965). Other common interactions include taking care of kin when they become ill (Streib, 1965); the provision of personal and protective services (Blenkner, 1965); writing (Adams, 1970; Streib, 1965); phone calls (Adams, 1970); providing financial assistance when necessary (Streib, 1965); giving social and psychological support (Shanas, 1973); and providing business advice (Streib, 1965). Adams (1968) found that when kin live nearby, visitation often involves no more than brief conversation, while at other times it might involve shopping, recreation, or attending religious services. In Lopata's (1973) study of Chicago widows, it was demonstrated that while sons tend to provide financial aid and advice, daughters tend to provide household assistance and emotional support.

The importance of family ties can be most fully appreciated when family interactions are compared to other types of interactions. Visiting with kin has been shown to be a primary activity for many elderly—occurring at a higher frequency than visiting with friends, neighbors, and co-workers (Axelrod, 1956; Sussman, 1965). Research regarding the elderly has shown that interaction and roles involving family (usually children) take priority over those of friends (Hochshild, 1973; Johnson, 1971) and that the importance and nature of kin ties in old age are such that they are not interchangeable with other ties (Hochshild, 1973). In Lopata's (1973) sample of Chicago widows, 45% claimed that being a mother was their most important role. Although a number of extended family contacts may be maintained in old age, those ties with sons and daughters are considered to be the most significant (Brown, 1974). As individuals age, they retain fewer formal and group relationships and more personal relationships. Often, the ties to children are the "last stronghold to which the elderly cling" (Brown, 1974). Regularity, loyalty, constancy, and fidelity tend to characterize the relations between parents and children (Townsend, 1963). Even potentially disruptive events, such as the institutionalization of a parent, do not necessarily take away from good parent–child ties (Smith & Bengston, 1979).

There is some disagreement, however, over whether the cement which binds parents and children together so strongly is based on feelings of affection or obligation. Some suggest that it is the emotional, affectionate bond that is important in explaining strong parent–child ties (e.g., Krepps, 1977; Rosenfeld, 1978; Rosow, 1977; Shanas, 1979), while others suggest that obligation may be the important element in creating strong kin ties (Arling, 1976; Reiss, 1962; Troll & Smith, 1976). On the basis of present research, one must conclude that both affection and obligation are important in making the ties between parents and children as viable and durable as they are.

Types of Assistance Children
Provide Their Elderly Parents

In the following two sections, the flow of aid that goes from parents to children and from children to parents will be discussed. But first, it is necessary to say a few words about the total network involving reciprocal aid between these two groups. The amount of assistance exchanged between parents and children is greater than that between any other forms of kin (Adams, 1970; Croog, Lipson, & Levine, 1972). Although parents may provide more of certain types of assistance and children more of others, when all forms of assistance are taken into account, the reciprocal nature of exchanges becomes the most outstanding feature of the parent–child assistance network (Atchley, 1980; Hess & Waring, 1980; Hill, 1965; Riley & Foner, 1968; Streib, 1977). The amount and direction of assistance depends on the relative resources and needs of both the children and their parents (Hess & Waring, 1980; Riley & Foner, 1968). The assumption of mutual exchange or reciprocity in kin networks is reflected in the research findings of Townsend (1963), who found that when older persons can no longer give aid, they become less likely to accept aid.

Helping patterns take many forms, for example, services, gifts, advice, and financial assistance. While there may be some class differences in the types of aid exchanged between parents and children, viable exchange networks exist across all social classes (Hess & Waring, 1980). Sussman and Burchinall (1972) noted that although there may be some variation in the absolute amount of financial aid exchanged in families of different classes, there are not significant differences in the proportion of families who report exchanging some form of economic assistance.

While both parents and children expect that children will lend assistance to their parents if it is needed (Atchley, 1980; Riley & Foner, 1968), past research has shown that children support norms of filial responsibility to a greater extent than do their elderly parents (Hanson, Sauer, & Seelbach, 1981). The most frequent aid given by children involves companionship, emotional support, living nearby, providing care when ill, and providing household management (Hill, 1965; Streib, 1965; Sussman & Burchinal, 1972). Hess and Waring (1980) noted that with the inception of Medicaid, Social Security, and other forms of government assistance, children's opportunities for helping may have declined in the areas of basic maintenance, but not in socioemotional areas. Nevertheless, older parents prefer to remain independent as long as they possibly can, but when this is no longer possible, they expect their children to take on more responsibilities, and children almost inevitably do (Atchley, 1980; Townsend, 1963).

A further examination of current research reveals some interesting findings regarding the extent to which the elderly rely on services from kin (especially children) as opposed to formal organizations. The services which the elderly most often request from agencies involve housing, financial planning, and health needs (Glaser & Glaser, 1962). Maddox and Dellinger (1978) report that over 77% of the services received by the most severely impaired elderly are provided by family or friends. The work of Shanas (1979) indicates that in 1962, approximately 2% of the elderly in the community were bedfast at home and 8% were housebound. This proportion did not change significantly by 1975, in spite of the implementation of Medicare. These elderly, it appears, were being taken care of primarily by family members with minimal help from public health nurses, home health aides, and the like. In a survey of Chicago elderly, Lopata (1980) further found that the only support received by many older persons was from their primary relations. A large proportion were unaware of or unable to use services and programs which had been designed for their needs.

These findings suggest the need to examine the necessary links between family and bureaucracy that would maximize the level and quality of assistance provided to the elderly. Many aspects of life in old age are intermeshed with public programs, public facilities, and public policies (Streib & Beck, 1980). Streib (1973) discusses the notion of shared functions and states that families and formal organizations need to better coordinate their efforts, rather than compete with each other in attaining the best possible life situation for the aged. As several papers suggest (Shanas & Sussman, 1973), families are an important watchdog in the relationship between bureaucracies and the elderly. They can provide information, take part in decision making, effect entry, and supervise the ongoing relationship between elderly persons and various formal organizations. Two areas in which bureaucracies are particularly weak in their relations with the elderly, and in which families play a critical role, include immediate response to crisis situations and attention to the humanistic and individualized needs of older people.

In the area of health assistance, there is considerable evidence which suggests that children and other kin, not social service agencies, are relied upon during periods of illness. The majority of the frail and sick, for example, are taken care of at home by spouses or children (Shanas, 1979). Shanas (1962) found that 85% of older people with children named a child as the person, other than their spouse, to whom they would turn if they suffered a health crisis. The notion that sick older persons are dumped into institutions is erroneous; families turn to institutionalization as a last resort only after they have exhausted all other alternatives (Brody, 1977, 1978).

Finally, in areas of financial assistance, present research suggests that a large majority of the aged neither expect to receive (Harris, 1965b) nor actually do receive regular monetary aid from the children (Streib, 1977). Although regular financial aid is rare, over one-third of the old people in the United States do report having received occasional monetary gifts from their children (Stehouwer, 1965). A substantial portion of the support, it should be noted, may well be concealed in gifts, services, housing arrangements, and other indirect forms of aid (Riley & Foner, 1968).

Types of Assistance the Elderly Provide Their Children

When families consist of three generations, aid tends to flow outward in both directions from the middle-aged parent generation (Adams, 1970; Hill, 1965). Children, but not grandparents, tend to return considerable amounts of aid (Hill, 1965). In Hill's (1965) study of three-generation families, he found the greatest amount of giving in the middle-aged parent generation and the greatest amount of receiving in the child generation—the generation with the greatest needs. Other research focusing exclusively on two generations has concurred with Hill in showing that the amount of help given by parents to children exceeds the amount received (Kivett, 1976; Shanas, 1967; Streib, 1965). Although some have suggested that this relationship may change as parents grow older (Hill, 1965), others have found that even among elderly parents (65+) the proportion of aid given by them exceeds that which they receive (Kivett, 1976; Streib, 1965, 1973; Sussman & Burchinal, 1972).

In the area of financial aid, for example, Kivett (1976) found that 7% of the elderly in his sample received regular financial help from their children, while 12% extended financial aid to their children. After initial financial gifts at marriage, most giving is limited to emergency help and gifts at special occasions. According to Sussman (1965), another major form of financial aid to children takes place in the form of loans at low or no interest, and is twice as likely to come from parents as from sibs (Sussman, 1965). Parent–child financial assistance has also been shown to vary from country to country, with Denmark having a lower rate than either the United States or Great Britain (Stehouwer, 1965).

Finally, Streib and Beck (1980) suggest that intergenerational transfers of property within kin networks is an important component of the kin exchange network. In a study of inheritance, Sussman, Cates, and Smith (1970) found that assets tended to flow to particular children who had provided services to parents. Consequently, children who took care of parents when ill, provided them a home, or gave emotional support were rewarded with bequests.

Attitudes of the Elderly and Their Children Toward Filial Responsibility and Concomitant Stresses

In the previous section, it was noted that both elderly parents and their children expect children to provide assistance in times of need. However, with certain needs (especially health and financial), families increasingly are relying on formal social institutions to provide assistance previously considered their domain. Attitudes about filial responsibility reflect these shifts. Hanson, Sauer, and Seelbach (1983) measured support for five filial responsibility norms among three age cohorts. These norms involved having room in your home for parents; living close to parents; taking care of parents when they are sick; giving parents financial help; and visiting parents weekly if residences are close. Only the first two of these five norms were supported by a majority of the respondents. The fit between expectations and actual behaviors may not be exact. For example, Shanas (1979) found that a majority of the frail and sick are taken care of at home by spouses and children, yet only 13.2% of the respondents in the study by Hansen et al. (1983) agreed with the statement that "children should be willing to take care of their parents in whatever way necessary when they are sick." This response appears to be at extreme odds with Shanas' (1962) finding that 85% of older people with children named a child as the person (other than spouse) to whom they would turn in a health crisis. This difference, however, could be either a function of social change over the past 20 years or a function of how terms are operationalized. Researchers need to operationalize filial responsibility norms with an eye for the varying levels of responsibility which might be assumed given a particular parental need—for example, there is a critical distinction between making health care arrangements to ensure parents receive good health care and taking care of a sick parent in "whatever way necessary."

A final note on the fit between filial responsibility norms and actual filial assistance is needed. In a study of values held by older people, Kerckhoff (1966b) identified three norm–value clusters: extended family clusters with high expectations of interaction and assistance from children; nucleated family clusters with low expectations in these areas; and modified extended family clusters with moderate expectations in these areas. With regard to actual interaction and assistance, Kerckhoff concluded that for most older people, the amount of interaction and assistance closely coincided with that expected by modified extended types. Thus, extended types were apt to be disappointed, while nucleated types were apt to be pleasantly surprised.

As was the case with other aspects of elderly parent–adult children interactions, ties and expectations concerning filial responsibility varied across cohorts, residence, income, education, mobility, family size, and racial groups. Research is inconsistent in showing whether rural or urban respondents extend greater support for filial responsibility norms. Wake and Sporakowski (1972) found no differences, Dinkel (1944) found rural respondents to be more supportive, and Hanson et al. (1981) found urban respondents to be more supportive. In addition, there is inconclusive evidence on the relationship between race and support for norms of filial responsibility. Schorr (1960) found greater support among blacks, and Hanson et al. (1983) found greater support among whites, with the exception of the oldest age-group, where racial differences disappeared. With regard to cohort differences, most research suggests that older cohorts support filial responsibility norms to a lesser extent than do middle-aged cohorts, and middle-aged cohorts support them to a lesser extent than do the youngest cohort (Hanson et al., 1983; Wake & Sporakowski, 1972). Kerckhoff (1966b) found that for the older generation, blue-collar occupations, lower levels of education, having lived on a farm, lower amounts of geographic mobility, and large families were most likely to be associated with the extended family norm–value cluster.

Cohort difference in support of filial responsibility norms are no doubt tied to the elderly's desire for independence. Thus, previous data focusing on residence and indicating that greater numbers of elderly live independently repeat assertions that old people prefer living that way. Evidence such as that from Hanson et al. (1983) suggests that, compared to other cohorts, the elderly were the least supportive of filial responsibility norms involving residence, interaction, financial assistance, and health assistance; all support the notion that the aged prefer to maintain as much independence in as many areas of life for as long as possible.

Having examined attitudes toward assistance, let us now focus on the potential stresses faced by elderly parents when they accept assistance from their children. One of the most frequently discussed stresses involves that of role reversals. Parents who previously were heads of households, breadwinners, and authority figures for their children find that as they age, they become increasingly dependent on their children. These changes in roles and responsibilities are not accepted easily in all families. Clark and Anderson's research suggests that, in old age, relations with children depend on the "graces and autonomy" of old age: "there simply cannot be any happy role reversals between the generations, neither an increasing dependency of parent upon child nor a continuing reliance of child upon parent" (1967, pp. 275-276). Older men with traditional role orientations are especially vulnerable to stresses associated with role reversal (Atchley, 1980). Older women who have functioned in traditional sex roles involving dependency and nurturance may find these transitions less traumatic (Watson, 1982). Having a spouse and sufficient socioeconomic resources are the best security against the parent–child role reversal situation.

Related to the role reversal experience is the gradual loss of roles that often accompany old age (e.g., postparenthood; retirement; widowhood). When going through these difficult transitions, elderly parents often turn to their children for support. If children are also going through role transitions, such as the loss of a family member (e.g., a father or mother), or if the parent's transition requires concomitant transitions of the child, aid and support may not be forthcoming. Although these role transitions might be a source of strain, for those who do reach out to one another and experience Erikson's (1959) "generativity" as opposed to "self-absorption," the transitions and accompanying support might bring about a strengthening of family ties (Hess & Waring, 1980).

It was previously suggested that children give a considerable amount of aid and assistance to parents with declining facilities. Since these investments take time and energy from other investments, the child may feel resentment and a sense of self-sacrifice (Clark & Anderson, 1967; Hess & Waring, 1980). Although parents and children may attempt to maintain residential independence for as long as possible, there may come a time when the parent's health and frailty makes either shared residence or institutionalization inevitable. Children often feel ambivalent toward shared residence arrangements (Fendetti & Gelfand, 1976; Wake & Sporakowski, 1972). When multigenerational households are a "last resort" and members are not in the best of health, shared residence may be a strain; however, when these arrangements are chosen out of feelings of mutual affection, both generations have been known to benefit (Hess & Waring, 1980; Lynn, 1976).

The strains associated with assistance provided by children to their elderly parents may increase as a larger number of persons are living to older ages and a greater proportion of elderly have children who are also over age 65. The disabling illnesses experienced by the old-old and the financial squeezes that all family members over 65 are likely to experience have potential negative consequences for families that are already stretching their limited resources (Atchley, 1980).

The Antecedents of Relations Between Elderly Parents and Their Children

The best way to summarize the antecedents of parent–child relations in later life is to delineate the factors which enhance and detract from exchanges of contact and assistance between generations. Hess and Waring (1980) present an excellent discussion of these factors.

Turning first to those factors which might work to inhibit intergenerational exchanges, it is likely that with increased geographic and social mobility, the elderly will have a smaller proportion of children living near them. Although socioemotional ties and even some forms of aid may be maintained over distances, provisional basic day-to-day services and assistance often become more difficult. The disruptive effects of geographic mobility on kin ties, however, appear to be temporary at worst (Troll, 1971). Children's geographic mobility for purposes of occupational advancement may in fact increase the quality of family ties. Britton and Britton's (1967) research on elderly rural residents showed that while they missed their distant children, they reported increased morale and pride in their success. Troll and Smith (1976) conclude that family bonds are strong over great distances.

Today, Social Security, Medicare, and other government programs provide assistance to the elderly to meet their basic financial and health care requirements. These institutions, in combination with the desire for independence on the part of the elderly, act in concert to reduce opportunities for children to help their parents.

Differences stemming from three generationally related sets of variables might also work to detract from intergenerational contacts in later life (Hess & Waring, 1980). For example, cohort differences stem from unique social and historical events a group of people experience, such as the Depression and World War II. They also arise from unique family, work, and community commitments and resources associated with various stages of individual development and the family life cycle. Schulman (1975) suggests that although kin networks exist throughout the life cycle, they are the weakest when children are in their middle stages with their own offspring and considerable family and work responsibilities. Finally, differences in cohorts as populations may intervene. The older generation is more likely to be foreign born and to have been reared on a farm or in a rural area, to have less education, and to have worked in a blue-collar occupation. Differences in population composition, cohort experiences, and age and life stage contribute to attitude and value differences which may put strains on intergenerational contacts.

Another set of factors that might detract from intergenerational exchanges in families are the residuals of earlier parent–child conflicts and tensions which are commonplace during childhood, adolescence, and even early parenting years (Hess & Waring, 1980).

Two factors discussed in the previous section should also be mentioned—parental role losses and multigenerational households. Given the above sources of difference between generations, some elderly parents and children may have difficulties in responding to role transitions and shared residences. If unequipped in terms of mutual affection and shared values, these experiences may further detract from good intergenerational relations.

Institutionalization is often perceived as an event that either precedes or follows bad family relations. In a unique study, Smith and Bengston (1979) found that the majority of elderly persons receiving long-term institutional care were close to and involved with their families. For some, there was uninterrupted family closeness, while for others, family ties strengthened following institutionalization.

When one takes into account the diversity of factors that might take away from good parent–child relations in later life, it might be surprising to read the first few sections of this chapter, which suggest that a good amount of affectional and instrumental support flow back and forth between generations. We will now discuss factors which might be involved in contributing to these overwhelmingly good relations.

The notion of exchange or reciprocity is an important factor affecting enhanced intergenerational bonds (Hess & Waring, 1980). Parents make investments in children with the expectation that children will return this favor in old age. Guilt and anxiety revolving around being a dutiful son or daughter act as a form of social control (Simos, 1970). The reactions of other reference groups such as sibs, cohorts, neighbors, and friends also serve to reinforce the responsibilities of children for their aged parents.

In addition to these external forces, there are internal forces which enhance bonds and contacts between generations, namely shared values and norms obtained through socialization experiences. This transmission of values and orientations has been heavily documented (Bengston, 1970; Troll, 1971). Socialization experiences have important implications not only for the adult child–elderly parent generations, but also for middle-aged parents and their children. Middle-aged children who assume responsibilities for their elderly parents are acting as role models for their children, who will eventually be expected to take on that role (Hess & Waring, 1980).

Finally, the fact that today's elderly can get many of their basic needs met outside of the family (e.g., Social Security and Medicare) contributes to good intergenerational bonds. Although many of these obligations have diminished, they have not disappeared. Given the bureaucratic nature of institutions providing much of the elderly's basic maintenance, children must often be go-betweens for their parents. This sharing of functions between children and institutions no doubt contributes to intergenerational bonds. In a study by Eggert et al. (1977), the researchers concluded that increases in the provision of home care by public health and welfare agencies could induce higher levels of famly care. Without these supportive agencies, however, family resources may be overtaxed.

Since many elderly today do not present the financial, time, or energy burden for their children that they did in the past, both elderly parents and their children feel that assistance and interaction is based on a certain degree of choice and mutual affection rather than obligation. Although obligation is also a critical variable, the increasingly even balance of obligation and affection as sources of interaction and assistance is probably a healthier trend.

The Consequences of Relationships with Children for the Physical and Social Well-being of Elderly Parents

In old age, one of the major advantages of having children appears to be the medical care and services children provide which allow the older parent to avoid or at least delay long-term hospitalization and institutionalization. Children are especially important in these capacities when spouses are not present. In an earlier section, the number of homebound and disabled elderly getting care from children was documented. In Shanas' (1979) study of the health of older people, she reported that family members not only took care of the bedfast parent, but also prepared meals, cleaned house, and shopped. The women in the sample tended to be looked after by children while the men tended to be looked after by a spouse. In a study by Laurie (1978), it was shown that greatly impaired elderly who live with their spouses and children generally are not institutionalized, while those living alone usually are. The important role of children in health care of the aged is further supported by research that shows that interaction with kin increases as health fails (Maddox & Dellinger, 1978).

There is little conclusive evidence on the relationship between ties with children (or kin in general) and socioemotional well-being in later life. There is some evidence which suggests that there is no relationship; both quantity and frequency of interaction with children (Conner, Powers, & Bultena, 1979; Mancini, 1979) and exchange of aid with children (Lee & Ellithorpe, 1982) have been shown to be unrelated to morale of the elderly. A relationship has been shown to exist, however, between general family satisfaction and morale of the elderly (Medly, 1976), suggesting that the quality and perception of family relations is more important than the absolute amount of interaction. Some have suggested that the lack of a relation between ties with children and morale may be due to the value differences emerging from the generation gap (Arling, 1976), while others have suggested that since kin relations are prescribed and, unlike friendships, are not based on choice, they may not contribute to subjective well-being (Lee & Ellithorpe, 1982).

The effect of presence or absence of children on socioemotional well-being is also not known. Having children appears to add to the life satisfaction of women in their middle years; however, if women are childless and have careers, they appear to do equally well (Sears & Barber, 1977). The absence of children appears to be associated somewhat with adjustment in old age in that old men without family ties have been shown to be vulnerable to suicide, accidental death, alcoholism, and other socially generated diseases (Bock & Webber, 1972; Gove, 1973). Females may be less vulnerable to these problems since they are more successful at substituting friendship for family ties (Hess & Waring, 1980).

In their review of the literature, Shanas and Sussman (1977) suggest that older persons fare better in a complex bureaucratized world when they have families interceding between bureaucracies and themselves. Access to institutions and the associated benefits and aid geared toward meeting the needs of the elderly are limited when elderly have to fend for themselves.

The relationship between ties with children and community involvement is not clearly understood. Some research suggests that those who interact frequently with kin are also more likely to interact with nonkin (Booth, 1972; Croog et al., 1972). Others have shown an inverse relationship between these two variables. In a Kansas City study, for example, people with no children nearby compensated by becoming more involved in the community (Berghorn, Schafer, & Wiseman, 1977).

Finally, it should be pointed out that exchange networks involving exchanges of gifts, advice, help in emergencies, goods, and services between elderly parents and their children have been shown to be critical to the economic well-being of many older parents (Hill, 1970; Sussman, 1976).

Current Research Priorities for This Area of Study

Given the complex set of findings just reviewed on the networks involving elderly parents and their children, a number of directions for future research are suggested.

First, researchers need to focus more on the macro forces affecting the experiences of the aged and their ties with children. Shanas and Sussman (1977) point in this direction by studying the critical link of families between the aged and complex institutions. Given the large elderly population facing America in the near future, more work along the lines initiated by Eggert et al. (1977) is needed to examine ways in which aid from certain programs and institutions can be distributed to the elderly and their families—aid which might help the elderly maintain a certain level of independence and avoid unnecessary institutionalization. An even more timely question involves the effects of cutbacks in programs geared toward the aged and to what extent informal networks can fill the resultant service gaps.

In addition, more attention needs to be placed on the historical or period variables which impinge on the aging experience. These might involve historical changes in attitudes about aging or historical changes in social structures, or the interaction between the two. Cohort analyses like those of Hareven (1983) give us important information on the unique historical experiences of different cohorts and generations, and their implications on aging experiences.

Finally, macro approaches such as the "Minority Group" approach suggested by Levine and Levine (1982) are needed in order to expand our understanding of the aged (and their families) beyond the individual level. As in the case of race studies, the traditional focus on the aging individual, and the documentation of inevitable decline which this focus involves, creates a tendency to see the problems of the aged as a result of individual decline and not as a result of ageist attitudes and behaviors built into the society, thus "blaming the victim." Social scientists need to examine more thoroughly the attitudinal and institutional sources of discrimination experienced by the aged and the role of family members in providing a buffer against this prejudice.

There are micro as well as macro issues that need our attention. An especially important area for future research involves the cohort and life course perspective suggested by Elder (1977) with regard to the family in general, and by Hareven (1983) with regard to the aging family in particular. Longitudinal studies which explore the dynamics of parent–child interaction over the life course and the intersection of these life courses with cohort and period effects will provide a rich body of knowledge and allow a more dynamic understanding of family development through the later years.

Social scientists need to gather information on several previously ignored, unique populations, for example, the old-old and children over the age of 65 who have living parents. There is reason to believe that the financial and health problems of these growing populations will present families with unique challenges.

Finally, more extensive information on the composition of networks which include elderly parents and their children is needed. For example, elderly parents' ties with *all* children should be examined, not just one or two and information on the quality and content of ties, as well on the level of interaction that typifies them, is needed. More rigorous theoretical application and precise methods are also necessary if we are to understand the complexity of parent–child networks in later life and sort out the inconsistent findings which have typified research in this area.

References

Adams, B. N. (1968). *Kinship in urban setting*. Chicago: Markham.
Adams, B. N. (1970). Isolation, function and beyond: American kinship in the 1960's. *Journal of Marriage and the Family, 32*, 375–397.

Aldous, J. (1967). Intergenerational visiting patterns: Variations in boundary maintenance as an explanation. *Family Process, 6*, 235–251.

Arling, G. (1976). The elderly widow and her family, neighbors and friends. *Journal of Marriage and the Family, 38*, 757–768.

Atchley, R. C. (1980). *The social forces in later life: An introduction to social gerontology.* Belmont, CA: Wadsworth.

Axelrod, M. (1956). Urban structure and social participation. *American Sociological Review, 21*, 13–18.

Bell, W., & Boat, M. D. (1957). Urban neighborhood and informal social behavior. *American Journal of Sociology, 62*, 391–398.

Berardo, F. (1967). Kinship interaction and communications among space-age migrants. *Journal of Marriage and the Family, 29*, 541–554.

Berardo, F. (1980). Survivorship and social interaction: The case of the aged widower. In J. S. Quandango (Ed.), *Aging, the individual and society.* New York: St. Martin's.

Berghorn, F. L., Schafer, D. E., & Wiseman, R. F. (1977). *The urban elderly: A study of life satisfaction.* Montclair, NJ: Alenheld, Osman.

Bengston, V. L. (1970). The generation gap: A review and typology of social-psychological perspectives. *Youth and Society, 2*, 7–32.

Blenkner, M. (1965). Social work and family relationships in later life with some thoughts on filial maturity. In E. Shanas & G. F. Streib (Eds.), *Social structure and the family.* Englewood Cliffs, N.J.: Prentice-Hall.

Bock, E. W., & Webber, I. L. (1972). Suicide among the elderly: Isolating widowhood and the mitigating alternatives. *Journal of Marriage and the Family, 34*, 24–31.

Booth, A. (1972). Sex, and social participation. *American Sociological Review, 37*, 183–192.

Bourg, C. J. (1975). Elderly in a southern metropolitan area. *The Gerontologist, 15*, 15–22.

Britton, J. H., & Britton, J. O. (1967). The middle-aged and older rural person and his family. In E. G. Youmans (Ed.), *Older rural Americans.* Lexington, KY: University of Kentucky Press.

Brody, E. (1977). *Long-term care for older people.* New York: Human Sciences Press.

Brody, E. (1978). The aging of the family. *The Annals of Political and Social Science, 438*, 13–27.

Brown, A. S. (1974). Satisfying relationships for the elderly and their patterns of disengagement. *The Gerontologist, 14*, 258–262.

Bruce, J. M. (1970). Intragenerational occupational mobility and visiting with kin and friends. *Social Forces, 49*, 117–127.

Chevan, A., & Korson, I. H. (1972). The widowed who live alone: An examination of social demographic factors. *Social Forces, 51*, 45–53.

Clark, M., & Anderson, B. (1967). *Culture and aging.* Springfield, IL: Charles C. Thomas.

Conner, K. A., Powers, E. A., & Bultena, G. L. (1979). Social interaction and life satisfaction: An empirical assessment of late-life patterns. *Journal of Gerontology, 34*, 116–121.

Cosneck, B. J. (1970). Family patterns of older widowed Jewish people. *The Family Coordinator, 19*, 368–373.

Croog, S. H., Lipson, A., & Levine, S. (1972). Help patterns in severe illness: The roles of kin network, non-family resources and institutions. *Journal of Marriage and the Family, 34*, 32–41.

Dinkel, R. (1944). Attitudes of children toward supporting aged parents. *American Sociological Review, 9*, 370–379.

Dotson, F. (1951). Patterns of voluntary association among urban working-class families. *American Sociological Review, 16*, 687–693.

Dowd, J. J., & Bengston, V. L. (1978). Aging in minority populations: An examination of the double jeopardy hypothesis. *Journal of Gerontology, 33*, 427–436.

Eggert, G. M., et al. (Oct. 1977). Caring for the patient with long-term disability. *Geriatrics*, 102–114.

Elder, G. H. (1977). Family history and the life course. *Journal of Family History, 2*, 279–304.

Erikson, E. (1959). Identity and the life cycle. In G. Klein (Ed.), *Psychological issues*. New York: International.

Farber, B. (1964). *Family: Organization and interaction*. San Francisco: Chandler.

Fendetti, D. V., & Gelfand, D. E. (1976). Care of the aged: Attitudes of white ethnic families. *The Gerontologist, 16*, 545–549.

Gibson, G. (1972). Kin family network: Overheralded structure in past conceptualization of family functioning. *Journal of Marriage and the Family, 34*, 13–23.

Glaser, D. H., & Glaser, L. N. (1962). Role reversal and conflict between aged parents and their children. *Marriage and Family Living, 24*, 46–51.

Gove, W. (1973). Sex, marital status and mortality. *American Journal of Sociology, 79*, 44–67.

Hanson, S. L., Sauer, W. J., & Seelbach, W. C. (1981). Urban–rural and cohort differences in filial responsibility norms. *Journal of Minority Aging, 5*, 299–305.

Hanson, S. L., Sauer, W. J., & Seelbach, W. C. (1983). Racial and cohort variations in filial responsibility norms. *The Gerontologist, 23*(6), 626–631.

Hareven, T. (April 1983). *Transition to old age: A cohort comparison in adaptation*. Presentation at The Elderly in a Bureaucratic World: New for History of Old Age conference, Case Western Reserve University.

Harris, L. (Nov. 29, 1965a). Thoughts of loneliness haunt older Americans. *The Washington Post*.

Harris, L. (Nov. 28, 1965b). Pleasant retirement expected. *The Washington Post*.

Harris, L. (1975). *The myth and reality of aging in America*. Washington, DC: National Council on Aging.

Hays, W. C., & Mindel, C. H. (1973). Extended kinship relations in black and white families. *Journal of Marriage and the Family, 35,* 51–57.

Hendrix, L. (1975). Kinship and economic-rational migration. A comparison of micro and macro level analysis. *Sociological Quarterly, 16,* 534–543.

Hess, B. B., & Waring, J. M. (1980). Changing patterns of aging and family bonds in later life. In A. Skolnick & J. H. Skolnick (Eds.), *Family in transition.* Boston: Little, Brown.

Hill, R. (1965). Decision making and the family life cycle. In E. Chanas & G. F. Streib (Eds.), *Social structure and the family.* Englewood Cliffs, NJ: Prentice-Hall.

Hill, R. (1970). *Family development in three generations.* Cambridge, MA: Schenkman.

Hill, R. (1971). *The strengths of black families.* New York: Emerson Hall.

Hochschild, A. (1973). *The unexpected community.* Englewood Cliffs, NJ: Prentice-Hall.

Hutter, M. (1970). Transformation of identity, social mobility and kinship solidarity. *Journal of Marriage and the Family, 32,* 133–137.

Johnson, S. (1971). *Idle haven.* Berkeley, CA: University of California.

Kerckhoff, A. C. (1966a). Family patterns of morale in retirement. In I. H. Simpson & J. C. McKinney (Eds.). *Social aspects of aging.* Durham, NC: Duke University Press.

Kerckhoff, A. C. (1966b). Norm-value clusters and the strain toward consistency among older married couples. In I. H. Simpson & J. C. McKinney (Eds.), *Social aspects of aging.* Durham, NC: Duke University Press.

Kessing, K. (1971). Social and psychological consequences of intergenerational occupational mobility. *American Journal of Sociology, 77,* 1–18.

Key, H. W. (1961). Rural–urban differences and the family. *The Sociological Quarterly, 2,* 49–56.

Kivett, V. R. (1976). The aged in North Carolina: Physical, social and environmental characteristics and sources of assistance. Technical Bulletin No. 237, Raleigh, NC: Agricultural Experiment Station.

Kobrin, F. E. (1976). The primary individual and the family: Changes in living arrangements in the United States since 1940. *Journal of Marriage and the Family, 38,* 233–239.

Komarovsky, M. (1964). *Blue collar marriage.* New York: Random House.

Krepps, J. M. (1977). Intergenerational transfers and the bureaucracy. In E. Shanas & M. B. Sussman (Eds.), *Family, bureaucracy and the elderly.* Durham, NC: Duke University Press.

Lacy, W. B., & Hendricks, J. (1980). Development models of adult life: Myth or reality. *International Journal of Aging and Human Development, 11,* 89–110.

Langford, M. (1962). *Community aspects of housing for the aged.* Ithaca, NY: Cornell University Center for Housing and Environmental Studies.

Laurie, W. F. (1978). *Employing the Duke OARS methodology in cost comparisons: Home services and institutionalization.* Center Reports on Advances in Research, Vol. 2. Durham, NC: Duke University Center for the Study of Aging and Human Development.

Lee, G. R. (1979). Children and the elderly: Interaction and morale. *Research on Aging, 1*, 335–360.

Lee, G. R. (1980). Kinship in the seventies: A decade review of research and theory. *Journal of Marriage and the Family, 42*, 923–934.

Lee, G. R., & Ellithorpe, E. (1982). Intergenerational exchange and subjective well-being among the elderly. *Journal of Marriage and the Family, 44*, 217–224.

Levine, J., & Levine, W. C. (1982). *Ageism: Prejudice and discrimination against the elderly.* Belmont, CA: Wadsworth.

Litwak, E. (1960). Geographic mobility and extended family cohesion. *American Sociological Review, 25*, 385–394.

Lopata, H. Z. (1973). *Widowhood in an American city.* Cambridge, MA: Shickman.

Lopta, H. Z. (1980). Support systems of elderly urbanites: Chicago of the 1970's. In J. S. Quadango (Ed.), *Aging, the individual and society.* New York: St. Martin's.

Lynn, I. (1976). Three-generation households in the middle-class. In B. B. Hess (Ed.), *Growing old in America.* New Brunswick, NJ: Transaction.

Maddox, G. L., & Dellinger, D. C. (1978). Assessment of functional status in a program evaluation and resource allocation model. *Annals of the American Academy of Political and Social Science, 438*, 59–70.

Mancini, J. A. (1977). Family relationships and morale among people 65 years of age and older. *American Journal of Orthopsychiatry, 49*, 292–300.

Martin, E. P., & Martin, J. (1978). *The black extended family.* Chicago: University of Chicago Press.

Medley, M. L. (1976). Satisfaction with life among persons sixty-five and over. *Journal of Gerontology, 31*, 448–455.

Mitchel, W. E. (1963). Theoretical problems in the concept of kindred. *American Anthropologist, 65*, 343–354.

Petrowsky, M. (1976). Marital status, sex, and the social networks of the elderly. *Journal of Marriage and the Family, 38*, 749–756.

Reiss, P. J. (1962). The extended kinship system: Correlates of and attitudes on frequency of interaction. *Journal of Marriage and the Family, 24*, 333–339.

Riley, M. W., & Foner, A. (1968). *Aging and society.* Vol. 1: *An inventory of research findings.* New York: Russell Sage.

Rosenberg, G. S. (1967). *Poverty, aging and social isolation.* Washington, DC: Bureau of Social Science Research.

Rosenberg, G. S. (1970). *The worker grows old.* San Francisco: Jossey-Bass.

Rosenberg, G. S., & Anspach, D. F. (1973). *Working class kinship.* Lexington, MA: D. C. Heath.

Rosenfeld, A. H. (1978). *New views on older lives.* Washington, DC.

Rosenmayr, L., & Kockeis, E. (1963). Propositions for a sociological theory of aging and the family. *International Social Science Journal, 15,* 410–426.

Rosow, I. (1967). *Social integration of the aged.* New York: The Free Press.

Rosow, I. (1977). The social milieu: Neighborhood interaction of the elderly. In P. Ostwald (Ed.), *Communication and social interaction.* New York: Grune and Stratton.

Scanzoni, J. H. (1971). *The black family in modern society.* Boston: Allyn and Bacon.

Schorr, A. (1960). *Filial responsibility in the modern American family* (pp. 11–18). Washington, DC: U.S. Department of Health, Education and Welfare.

Schulman, N. (1975). Life cycle variation in patterns of close relationships. *Journal of Marriage and the Family, 37,* 813–821.

Sears, P., & Barbee, A. H. (1977). Careers and life satisfaction among Terman's gifted women. In J. Stanely, W. George, & C. Solano (Eds.), *The gifted and creative: Fifty year perspective.* Baltimore, MD: Johns-Hopkins University Press.

Shanas, E. (1961). *Family relationships of older people.* Washington, DC: Health Information Foundation.

Shanas, E. (1962). *The health of older people: A social survey.* Cambridge, MA: Harvard University Press.

Shanas, E. (1967). Family help patterns and social class in three countries. *Journal of Marriage and the Family, 29,* 257–266.

Shanas, E. (1973). Family-kin networks and aging in cross-cultural perspective. *Journal of Marriage and the Family, 35,* 505–511.

Shanas, E. (1979). Social myth as hypothesis: The case of the family relations of old people. *The Gerontologist, 19,* 3–9.

Shanas, E., & Sussman, M. B. (Eds.). (1977). *Family bureaucracy and the elderly.* Durham, NC: Duke University Press.

Shanas, E., Townsend, P., Wedderbum, D., Friis, H., Milhoj, P., & Stehouwer, J. (1968). *Old people in three industrialized societies.* New York: Atherton Press.

Siegel, J. S. (1976). *Demographic aspects of aging and the older population in the United States.* Current Population Reports, Special Study Series D-23, No. 59, Washington, DC: U.S. Government Printing Office.

Simos, B. G. (1970). Relations of adults with aging parents. *The Gerontologist, 10,* 135–139.

Smith, K. F., & Bengston, V. L. (1979). Positive consequences of institutionalization: Solidarity between elderly patients and their middle-age children. *The Gerontologist, 19,* 438–447.

Soldo, B., & Lauriat, P. (1976). Living arrangements among the elderly in the United States: A log-linear approach. *Journal of Comparative Family Studies, 7,* 351–366.

Stehouwer, J. (1965). Relations between generations and the three-generation household in Denmark. In E. Shanas & G. Streib (Eds.), *Social structure and the family: Generational relations.* Englewood Cliffs, NJ: Prentice-Hall.

Streib, G. F. (1965). Intergenerational relations: Perspectives of the two generations on the older parent. *Journal of Marriage and the Family, 27,* 469–482.

Streib, G. F. (1973). Older families and their troubles: Familial and social responses. In M. E. Lasswell & T. E. Lasswell (Eds.), *Love, marriage, family: A developmental approach* (pp. 531–540). Glenview, IL: Scott, Foresman.

Streib, G. F. (1977). Older people in a family context. In A. Kalish (Ed.), *The later years: Social applications of gerontology.* Monterey, CA: Brooks, Cole.

Streib, G. F., & Beck, R. W. (1980). Older families: A decade review. *Journal of Marriage and the Family, 42,* 937–956.

Sussman, M. B. (1965). Relationships of adult children with their parents. In E. Shanas & G. F. Streib (Eds.), *Social structure and the family.* Englewood Cliffs, NJ: Prentice-Hall.

Sussman, M. B. (1976). The family life of old people. In R. Binstock & E. Shanas (Eds.), *Handbook of aging and the social sciences.* New York: Van Nostrand.

Sussman, M. B., & Burchinal, L. (1972). Kin family network: Unheralded structure in current conceptualizations of famly functioning. In B. L. Neugarten (Ed.), *Middle age and aging.* Chicago: University of Chicago Press.

Sussman, M. B., Cates, J., & Smith, D. (1970). *The family and inheritance.* New York: Russell Sage.

Townsend, P. (1963). *The family life of old people.* Baltimore, MD: Penguin.

Townsend, P. (1976). Integration and family. In R. C. Atchley & M. M. Seltzer (Eds.), *The sociology of aging: Selected readings.* Belmont, CA: Wadsworth.

Treas, J. (1975). Aging and the family. In D. S. Woodruff & S. E. Birren (Eds.), *Aging: Scientific perspectives and social issues.* New York: Van Nostrand.

Troll, L. E. (1971). The family of later life: A decade review. *Journal of Marriage and the Family, 33,* 263–290.

Troll, L. E., Miller, S. J., & Atchley, R. C. (1979). *Families in later life.* Belmont, CA: Wadsworth.

Troll, L., & Smith, J. (1976). Attachment through the life span: Some questions about dyadic relationships in later life. *Human Development, 19,* 156–171.

Wake, S. B., & Sporakowski, M. J. (1972). An intergenerational comparison of attitudes toward supporting aged parents. *Journal of Marriage and the Family, 34,* 42–48.

Watson, J. A., & Kivett, V. R. (1976). Influences on the life satisfaction of older fathers. *The Family Coordinator, 25,* 482–488.

Watson, W. H. (1982). *Aging and social behavior: An introduction to social gerontology.* Monterey, CA: Wadsworth.

Willmott, P., & Young, M. (1960). *Family and class in a London suburb.* London: Routledge and Kegan Paul.

Wilkening, E. A., Gurrero, S., & Ginsberg, S. (1972). Distance and intergenerational ties of farm families. *Sociological Quarterly, 13,* 383–396.

4

Husband and Wife Networks

Beth B. Hess
Beth J. Soldo

For gerontologists, marital status is a bit like the weather—everyone comments on it, but surprisingly little research specifies the mechanisms whereby older couples typically enjoy material and interpersonal advantages over the nonmarried. In large part, this is because many of the benefits of the married state are self-evident: the still-married are likely to be younger than other old people and to have higher incomes, better health, and assured companionship. For these reasons alone, married persons would be expected to display relatively higher levels of physical functioning, morale, life satisfaction, and whatever gerontologists measure as indicators of well-being.

Many of these positive outcomes are predictable since most of the still-married in later life are true survivors—both spouses would not be alive if they did not enjoy superior health or health care, and they would not have remained in a first marriage had they not jointly weathered the vicissitudes of five or more decades of togetherness. By that time many couples will have separated or divorced, and the less healthy will have succumbed to death or been institutionalized. While a relatively small number reaches their 40th anniversary and the less adaptable members of their current cohort of older couples will have remarried upon the death of a spouse or after a divorce (a rarity among today's elderly), the great majority—7 of 10 married older persons—are in their one and only marriage. Our population of interest, then, consists of the slim majority (53%) of persons age 65 and over who, in 1980, were married and living with their spouse, and thus, in principle, were available as supports to one another in the final stage of the life course.

We shall first delineate the population of interest, then describe the crucial characteristics of long-lived marriages, noting the implications for practice and public policy. The limited research literature on espousal supports will be critically examined, concluding with a discussion of the theoretical and methodological issues that face gerontologists in the decades ahead.

Older Married Couples: How Many?

The vast majority—approximately 95%—of Americans now age 65+ have been married at least once (U.S. Bureau of the Census, 1981a). However, because the remarriage rate does not compensate for marital disruptions caused by death and divorce, only slightly over half of those reaching 65 are still married and living with a spouse. An additional 2% are married but not living with their spouse, most likely as a result of institutionalization. In 1980, there were almost 150,000 older "persons of the opposite sex sharing living quarters (POSSLQs)," mostly with partners of approximately the same age (U.S. Bureau of the Census, 1981a). Since our concern in this chapter is with couples and not marriedness per se, we would have liked to include these couples in the analysis but the necessary data are not available. Thus, unless otherwise noted, the population under study is the 12.7 million older Americans living with their spouse in a noninstitutional setting.

Ages of Partners

In two out of three elderly intact marriages, both partners are 65 or older. The number of such couples has grown rapidly, from 3.5 million in 1970 to over 5 million in 1980 (Glick, 1979; U.S. Bureau of the Census, 1982), largely due to enhanced life expectancy at all ages, and to the low incidence of divorce among current cohorts of elderly. The number of couples in which only one spouse is 65+ has remained fairly stable over the past decade at a little over 3 million (U.S. Bureau of the Census, 1982), and in most instances the younger spouse will reach age 65 within five years.

Despite the romantic appeal of the myth of "May–December" marriages, such couples are exceedingly rare. In the future, however, there are off-setting trends, for example, the average difference in the age of spouses at first marriage has steadily narrowed throughout this century (from over five to under two years); but second and higher order marriages are likely to be characterized by wider than average differences in age, including women marrying younger men (Presser,

1975). Since about half of all marriages contracted today are expected to end in divorce at some point, in the years to come more people will enter old age married to persons either much younger or older than themselves, while partners in first marriages will be of almost the same age.

This matter of age differences does have important consequences for espousal support in old age. In most older marriages today, the spouses simultaneously confront physiological and other age-related changes with shared attitudes and values that have been shaped by the same cohort influences. At the same time, in cases of long-term illness, the advanced age of the caretaking spouse may compromise the dyad's capacity for independence, particularly if a traditional division of labor on the basis of gender has characterized the marriage (Dono et al., 1979).

Marital Status Differences

It has become a cliché to preface any demographic discussion of the elderly with the somber warning that "the older population is far from being homogeneous," yet this observation is perhaps nowhere more relevant than in describing the marital status of the elderly. Table 4.1 indicates that there are substantial differences by age and sex in the probability of being married at older ages. At ages 65–74, 8 out of every 10 men are married and living with their spouse, as are close to 68% of those 75+. In contrast, fewer than half of women aged 65–74 are married, and only 22% of those at 75 and over are (see Table 4.1).

Since similar proportions of older women and men had never married or were divorced, the converse of the sex difference in the proportions married is the probability of being widowed. Older widows outnumber widowers by a factor of five, reflecting the greater life expectancy of women. For example, at age 65, the average years of life remaining, in 1978, was 18.4 for women compared to 14 years for men. In addition, older men are eight times more likely than older women to remarry (Treas & Van Hilst, 1976). Not only do older men have a larger pool of potential mates to select for remarriage, including women considerably younger than themselves, but they may also be more motivated to remarry than are their female counterparts. Troll (1971) has suggested that the comparatively higher remarriage rate for older men could reflect their lack of other supportive primary group ties to absorb the nurturant role tasks of the dead wife. In contrast, an older divorced or widowed woman will find very few

TABLE 4.1. Marital Status of the Noninstitutionalized Population 65 Years of Age and Older in 1980 by Age: United States

Sex and Marital Status	Percentage Distribution	
	65–74 yr.	75+ yr.
Women		
Total (in 1,000s)	8,549	5,411
Percent	100.0%	100.0%
Married[a]	48.1	22.1
Not married	51.9	77.9
Single	5.6	6.4
Widowed	40.3	67.9
Divorced[b]	9.6	3.5
Men		
Total (in 1,000s)	6,549	3,234
Percent	100.0%	100.0%
Married[a]	79.4	67.7
Not married	20.6	32.3
Single	5.5	4.4
Widowed	8.5	24.0
Divorced[b]	6.6	3.9

[a]Includes only those married and living with spouse.
[b]Includes those married but living apart from spouse, the vast majority of whom are separated.
Source: U.S. Bureau of the Census. (1981a). Current Population Reports, Series P-20, No. 365, *Marital Status and Living Arrangements: March 1980.* Washington, DC: U.S. Government Printing Office.

potential partners for remarriage in the appropriate age bracket and little encouragement to marry someone very much younger than herself. When older women do remarry, it is likely to be at a younger age than men with similar marital histories (Espanshade, 1982).

The result of these trends in life expectancy and in the sociocultural determinants of remarriage is the striking sex differential in the probability of living with a spouse in the later years—a difference with important implications for the size and scope of supportive networks upon which older women and men can draw.

In summary, slightly more than half of all elderly are living with a spouse, typically of similar age, and most are in their first marriage. Very few older persons will marry, divorce, and remarry for the first time after age 65. Three out of four marriages that do take place among persons 65+ involve widowed men and women (Brotman,

1982), and it has been suggested that the commitment of spouses in these recent marriages may be weaker than that of long-time partners if the need for chronic care arises (Dono et al., 1979). Yet, as most of the data to be discussed in the remainder of this chapter indicate, typically it is better to have a spouse than none at all.

Older Couples and Their Marriages

Living Longer

The benefits of the married state appear to be greater for men than for women—at least with respect to mortality. Indeed, in the case of homicide, married women are at greater risk than the nonmarried. Most of the sex and marital status differences in mortality rates do become attenuated with age, that is, being widowed, divorced, or separated has its strongest deleterious effect on men and women aged 25–34, and its weakest effects on those age 65+ (Gove & Tudor, 1973b).

The differential preservative effect of marriage also is apparent in data on life expectancy in old age, where the relative advantage of being married is greater for men than for women. Looked at another way, recent data on survival after widowhood illustrates the extreme vulnerability of men without wives: on average, the mortality rate for widowers was 28% higher than for age-peers still married—and 60% higher for men age 55–65—while no such effect was observed for women over the 12 years of the study (Helsing, Szklo, & Comstock, 1981).

In part, the impact of widowhood on women is buffered by their having a much larger group of status peers from which to construct a supportive network, and in part by their well-socialized capacity for intimate friendships across the life course (Hess, 1979). Conversely, because men (at least today's older cohorts) often lack the practical skills for maintaining a household, as well as being without alternative primary group supports, they are likely candidates for remarriage—or for premature death.

Staying Healthier

At the most general level, differences in morbidity rates parallel those for mortality, with married persons enjoying better health than the nonmarried, as measured by fewer acute and chronic conditions, less restriction on activity, and shorter hospital stays. Divorced and separated elderly have the highest morbidity rates, followed by the widowed, with the never-married closest to the married in health status. Verbrugge (1979) has suggested that women's higher morbidity rates reflect their greater sensitivity to changes in their marital status, but not to the extent of engaging in death-producing behaviors. Since for both men and women, the differences between married and never-married are minimal, it appears that the key factor in health status is the loss of a spouse and not simply the absence of one.

These variations in morbidity by sex and marital status can be accounted for, in part, by differences in *illness behavior*; that is, women and married persons are more likely to reduce activity and to see a physician when ill than are men in general or anyone without domestic responsibilities or someone to monitor their health (Verbrugge, 1979). Indeed, Verbrugge (1982) argues that sex differences in perceiving and reporting illness may account for the enhanced life expectancy of women and the married; that is, taking steps to reduce the impact of illness ultimately enhances survivorship.

Feeling Better

Data on mental health also indicate that the married are better off than the nonmarried, and that the relative advantage to men is greater than to women (Bernard, 1972; Gove & Tudor, 1973a; Veroff, Douvan, & Kulka, 1981). Such findings, along with those on morbidity and mortality, have led Jessie Bernard (1972) to contrast "his" and "her" marriages, entailing different risks and payoffs for the partners, but generally favoring the husband. In later life, however, many of these differences between partners diminish, undoubtedly as a result of all of the selective factors that winnow out unhappy marriages and the least healthy partners. It is appropriate, therefore, to examine more closely the quality of marriage among older couples.

The Quality of Marriages in Later Life

One of the most consistent findings in the field of family research is the relatively high level of marital satisfaction expressed by older couples—often hailed as comparable to that of persons in the earliest years of marriage. And why not? In terms of family composition, older couples who are also parents have survived the period of lowest

satisfaction—when adolescents are in the household and companion-
ate activities are at their most inhibited (Miller, 1976). In contrast, the
empty nest is experienced as liberating, with a new calm descending
on the household.

The high level of marital satisfaction of older couples is also due in
part to many unsuccessful marriages having been terminated by divorce or separation. Moreover, those who have endured economic
hardship have lower life expectancy than the more affluent, so that
many poor and unhappily married individuals will no longer be alive.
For such time-related reasons, then, the still-married are selected for
adaptability, health, and economic stability (Spanier, Lewis, & Cole,
1975).

Historically, too, there are reasons to expect that older couples
will not express dissatisfaction. Today's elderly population contains
the last of those foreign-born, traditionally oriented marriage partners
who are likely to stay together out of duty and religious obligation,
regardless of the quality of the relationship. Resignation, lowering of
expectations to fit reality, and a lack of viable alternatives may lead to
self-reports of satisfaction.

Last, there are the social-psychological effects of duration in the
role; that is, the longer one's relationship, the more the partners have
invested in "side bets" (Becker, 1961), the more salient the relationship
to self-identity, and therefore, the more difficult to disengage or to
admit failure. This inertia factor may be as important as adaptability in
explaining the data. The outcome of all of these processes is a population of older married couples whose relationships have withstood
many decades of personal and historical change, and who are the
healthier and more affluent survivors of their marriage cohort.

As one might expect, there are also patterned differences by
gender in both the level and components of marital satisfaction. Not
surprisingly, wives are more sensitive than husbands to changes in
family structure—feeling more constrained in their life space by the
presence of offspring, but also more relieved by the launching of their
last child (Hagestad, 1980). Compared to men, women are more
affected by the quality of their marriage in terms of its contribution to
overall feelings of happiness, although for most men marriage contributes more to global happiness than any other activity including work
(Glenn, 1981; Glenn & Weaver, 1981). Taking into account the importance of marital status to the health and longevity of men discussed
earlier in this chapter, it appears that just being married is crucial for
men, while being happily so is for women.

Marital Supports in Older Couples

Having established the many preservative effects of the married state, we now examine the specific supports exchanged by partners. These supports are typically classified as (1) material, (2) affectional, and (3) caregiving in the sense of providing assistance in daily tasks.

Material Supports

Because they are likely to be younger, with one spouse still in the labor force, and with assets that have not yet been depleted, older married couples enjoy a level of economic well-being higher than that of nonmarried elderly. But even controlling for age, the married have an economic advantage, probably as a function of higher life-time earnings and accumulated assets, including the family residence (Henretta & Campbell, 1976).

The material superiority of the married, then, reflects the past economic history of the couple and the advantageous characteristics carried into later life, including physical well-being. But the financial security of married women may not last through an extended widowhood. Unless her husband has specifically arranged for continuation, a private pension may cease upon his death. Most older widows today are totally dependent on Social Security survivor's benefits averaging about $400 a month.

Nonetheless, while she is married, the older woman is likely to be protected from poverty. For example, in 1980, when over 15% of all older persons were officially defined as "living below the poverty level," this percentage dipped to under 10% for married persons, and rose to almost 28% in female-headed households (U.S. Bureau of the Census, 1981b).

Another material advantage enjoyed by the married elderly is privacy. Even at the extremes of old age and in the presence of long-term disability, older couples are more likely than the nonmarried to live in a household by themselves and to own their dwelling unit. In 1978, less than 2% of married old people shared their home with another person or resided in the home of another (Mindel, 1979). In contrast, higher proportions of the nonmarried share their living quarters, live in rented dwellings, and reside in the home of a relative (U.S. Bureau of the Census, 1979). In part because of their more secure housing tenure, older couples are less likely than their nonmarried counterparts to have relocated recently, although geographic mobility rates are quite low for all elderly.

Affectional Supports

Perhaps the most obvious advantage of marriage is the stable companionship provided by a spouse. Much has been written of the role of confidant as a buffer against loneliness and disorientation (e.g., Lowenthal & Haven, 1968) and of social support systems or "convoys" as protectors of health and sanity (e.g., Cobb, 1979; Kahn, 1979). In one highly regarded longitudinal study, the single most powerful predictor of survival over a nine-year span was embeddedness in a social network (Berkman & Syme, 1979). Few support systems will be as predictable as one provided by a spouse. Yet this, too, is not without some risk.

Older men are more likely than women to have lost the company of workmates through retirement, disability, migration, or death. When asked about their best friend, older husbands typically name their wives. The wives, however, are most likely to nominate adult offspring or female age-peers. As a consequence, widowed men are doubly bereft—they have lost both helpmate and confidante, which may explain their special vulnerability to illness and death. Conversely, the widowed woman is unlikely to be entirely devoid of close friends (but see Lopata, 1979, with respect to elderly ethnic widows in the inner city).

For both men and women, however, the companionship of a spouse is a crucial interpersonal resource, even if the relationship appears conflicted or distant. At the minimum, a spouse is an "accustomed other." If the couple have been together for 40 or more years, we can assume that each has come to define a "self" in relation to the other, so that just being together confers an authenticity to each partner's identity. However, as Cuber and Haroff (1963) noted some time ago, happy marriages are not all alike; couples become habituated to particular interaction styles and find some satisfaction in the sheer predictability of their relationship, however difficult it may appear from outside. Still, many long-lived marriages will also continue to be characterized by exchanges of affection and sexual gratification.

Precisely because human identities are socially constructed, we are compelled to look to others for verification of our essential lovableness. Having our existence authenticated is not enough; we must also know that we are worthy of affection. This is the need that so often binds us to others in relatively permanent unions. The never-married, in contrast to the widowed, divorced, or separated, have cultivated alternative sources of affection, approval, and self-validation throughout their lifetimes and consequently also display relatively high levels of happiness in old age—not as high as marrieds but higher than the formerly married.

Married persons have an obvious advantage over the nonmarried in the maintenance of sexual relations in old age. Trustworthy data on sexual behavior have been hard to acquire until quite recently, and especially so from older persons socialized in an era of less openness about such topics. Two recent comprehensive reviews of the relevant literature (Ludeman, 1981; Weg, 1982) however, agree on many points: that older people are not asexual; that men, married or not, were apt to report sustained interest and activity; that older couples' sexuality was largely determined by their past patterns; and that the husband was most responsible for discontinuing sexual activity.

Caregiving

As important as companionship, exchange of affection, and sexual gratification may be throughout a marriage, old age brings special challenges to the relationship through illness and disability and the consequent need of the healthier partner to provide care for the other. Although the health-care problems of the elderly are much more likely to be chronic than acute, the approach to long-term care built into both Medicare and Medicaid is based on the medical model of technology-intensive care for acute, tractable illness. In contrast, long-term care, by definition, involves labor-intensive, personal care supportive of a wide range of daily functions. Meeting long-term care needs requires flexibility and dedication, but not usually professional training. As often as not, the indirect aspects of long-term caregiving, including its affective component, are just as important as direct care services, particularly for older persons experiencing declines in functional capacities. Thus, the family, as the premier primary group, is particularly well suited to providing for the chronic care needs of the elderly.

A growing body of research evidence now testifies to the family's substantial involvement in long-term caregiving (Brody, 1978; Brody, Poulshock, & Mascioshi, 1978; Callahan et al., 1980; Shanas, 1979b; Shanas et al., 1968). Recently released data from the Home Care Supplement to the 1979 Health Interview Survey, presented in Table 4.2, demonstrate once again the dependency of the frail elderly on the informal support network of family, friends, and neighbors. Nearly 90% of the elderly with functional health limitations rely, in whole or in part, on informal caregiving. In the vast majority of these

TABLE 4.2. Sources of Nonmedical Care Assistance for the Noninstitutional Population 65 Years of Age and Over with Functional Limitations, by Marital Status: 1979 (Base numbers in 100s)

Source of Assistance	Percentage Distribution		
	Total 65+ Home Care[a] Population	65+ Married[b] Home Care Population	65+ Unmarried Home Care Population
No assistance received	2.3%	2.8%	1.8%
Informal care providers only	72.6	75.6	69.7
Relatives within same household only	38.6	52.3	30.0
Relatives/friends outside household only	23.1	8.3	31.4
Relatives/friends in and outside household	10.9	15.0	8.3
Formal care providers only	9.2	4.9	11.6
Formal and informal care providers	15.9	16.5	15.3
Total	100.0% (5724)	100.0% (2068)	100.0% (3656)

[a]The "home care population" includes those who stay in bed all or most of the time and/or need help with one or more ADL activities (walking, going outside, toileting, bathing, dressing, eating, and transferring) and/or need help with instrumental activities (cooking, shopping, doing chores, and handling money) and/or need assistance with a bowel/bladder device.

[b]Includes only those married and living with spouse.

Source: Tabulations from the 1979 Health Interview Survey, Home Care Supplement, prepared by the Center for Population Research under subcontract to the Urban Institute for DHHS, Office of the Assistant Secretary for Planning and Evaluation, Contract No. HHS-100-80-0158, 1979.

cases, informal care providers are unassisted by community service programs. It also is important to note that those in the informal support network provide care services to older relatives without compulsion or compensation, even though the time required for caregiving is frequently the equivalent of a full-time job (Newman, 1976).

Columns two and three of Table 4.2 contrast the informal and formal service utilization patterns of married and unmarried elderly in the community. The married elderly have, by definition at least, the potential for a live-in caregiver. In fact, for the married long-term care population in the community, the most likely primary caregiver is the spouse (Crossman et al., 1981; Shanas, 1979b). Hence, it is not surprising that 75% more married than unmarried elderly with functional health limitations rely *exclusively* on care services produced within their own households. Older impaired and married persons also are more likely than their unmarried counterparts to command a broader informal support network both within and outside of their own households. While unmarried disabled elderly are nearly three times as likely to be totally dependent on formal service providers (e.g., home health aides or visiting nurses), married and unmarried elderly seem to have almost an equal chance of mixing informal and formal services to sustain themselves outside of a nursing home.

Not only is informal caregiving pervasive, it is also effective in deterring nursing home admissions. By merging data collected in the 1977 Health Interview Survey with those obtained in the 1977 National Nursing Home Survey, Weissert, Scanion, & Unger (1981) have assembled a unique data base that provides nearly complete coverage of the long-term care population. These data, reproduced in Table 4.3, indicate the particular effectiveness of espousal caregiving in preventing or deterring nursing home placement. Even at the extremes of old and functional disability, the institutionalization rate of married elderly is about half that of either the never-married or the previously married, most of whom are likely to have had recourse to adult children caregivers. Palmore (1976) reaches similar conclusions from an analysis of nursing home admissions in a 20-year panel study.

Prior research demonstrates that dependent elderly living with their spouse have a comparatively low chance of tapping into the network of formal community services. Frail elderly living with others, most often adult children, however, are the least likely to consume community services in the current, constrained long-term care service market (Soldo, 1983). These data suggest two alternative explanations of the relationship among type of caregiver, level of need, and use of community services. Because espousal caregivers are themselves often elderly and struggling with their own functional declines, they may find it more necessary than adult children to recruit outside caregivers to reduce their care burden. This interpretation, the "limited capacity" hypothesis, is certainly consistent with the findings cited above.

The competing hypothesis, however, takes account of the cross-sectional nature of the data. Adult children may be less likely than spouses to turn to community services simply because they are more likely to opt for an institutional solution to the long-term care needs of

TABLE 4.3. Rates of Institutionalization Among Elderly with Extreme ADL Dependencies, by Marital Status and Age: 1977[a]

	Percentage Residing in Nursing Homes		
Marital Status	65–69	70–74	75+
Married	22.6%	23.9%	41.3%
Once married	38.3	60.6	75.9
Never married	[b]	55.9	78.1

[a]Data from the merger of the 1977 Health Interview Survey and the 1977 Nursing Home Survey.
[b]Number of cases fewer than 2,500.
Source: Table 8 in Weissert, E., Scanlon, W., & Unger, A. (1981). Estimating the Long-Term Care Population: National and State Prevalence Rates and Selected Characteristics. Working Paper 1466-11, The Urban Institute, Washington, DC, under Contract No. HHS-100-80-0158 to DHHS, Office of the Assistant Secretary for Planning and Evaluation.

older relatives. The possibility of a differential tolerance threshold finds support in the works of Cantor (1981) and Soldo and Myllyluoma (1982). Using very different data, both studies report that spouses are more frequent caretakers of impaired elderly than are adult children. One implication of the "differential tolerance" hypothesis is that spouses are willing to do almost anything, including reluctantly admitting service providers into their own homes, to prevent the nursing home admission of their lifelong companion. The extremely frail elderly residing in the homes of offspring or other kin are a self-selected remnant of their cohort and may be less functionally impaired than spouses. Adult children who continue to provide care under such extreme circumstances may resemble spouse caregivers in their commitment, while also having the personal resources, particularly the stamina and energy, to provide chronic care unassisted by community providers.

To explore these hypotheses, we reexamined the existing literature on caregiving burden, although the conclusions of most such studies need to be accepted cautiously since the use of local nonprobability samples is commonplace. There is little doubt that attending to the unrelenting chronic care demands of a frail older person places a substantial burden on his or her caregiver and that these demands vary directly with level of need. A sense of social isolation, frustration, and disruption of daily life are experienced by all caregivers, regardless of their relationship to the recipient (Zarit, Gatz, & Zarit, 1981). The differential tolerance hypothesis implies, however, that the perceived caregiving burden is not determined solely by the level of need or even the social, psychological, or financial impact of caregiving.

Recently Mindel and Wright (1982), drawing on the principles of exchange theory, have proposed a three-dimensional model in which caregiver satisfaction is a consequence of the interaction among (1) the dependency needs of the carereceiver, (2) characteristics of the caregiver, and (3) the context in which care is given. Although caregiver satisfaction and perceived burden are not wholly overlapping constructs, this model is a useful framework for organizing a discussion of tolerance thresholds.

Dependency Needs

As noted above, the frail elderly cared for at home by spouses are generally more impaired than those cared for by other relatives or friends. In Cantor's study (1981) the average number of instrumental tasks with which spouses assisted was 7 while the number for adult children was 5.4 and for other relatives and friends, 4.0 and 2.7, respectively. The greater the impairment, of course, the fewer social roles available to the older dependent person and the lower the level of social activity. The more impaired elderly may also have fewer opportunities for reciprocity (Fengler & Goodrich, 1979), and this may eventually undermine their morale. Although it is impossible to sort out the causal direction, the satisfaction and morale of caregiving and -receiving spouses tend to covary together (Fengler & Goodrich, 1979). It also is highly probable that some degree of psychological difficulty overlays the physical dependencies of the severely impaired. Caregivers report that it is harder for them to cope with mental problems than with physical ones. In sum, the existing literature overwhelmingly indicates that objective burdens shouldered by spousal caregivers are greater than those of other relatives or friends.

Caregiver Characteristics

In considering the ways in which the caregiver's characteristics contribute to subjective burden perceptions, it is necessary to distinguish factors that facilitate caregiving from those that are likely to inhibit it. Clearly the caregiver's own functional health limitations will exacerbate the degree of difficulty experienced in performing caregiving tasks if not the extent of perceived burden. Although the demands of caregiving should, over time, select out caregivers with serious health problems, spouses who provide care are more likely than other relatives who provide care to have moderate needs for assistance themselves (Cantor, 1981; Soldo & Myllyluoma, 1982). Even if not chronically disabled, the elderly spouse will experience difficulty in providing direct assistance simply because of the reduced functional capacities associated with aging (Crossman, Landon, & Barry, 1981; Fengler & Goodrich, 1979; Rathbone-McCuan, 1976).

There are also important sex differences in the capacity to care for a disabled spouse. Since wives are typically younger than their husbands, they can, in most cases, perform caretaking tasks for a longer period of time than can their male counterparts. Among younger relatives, it is the women of the family who overwhelmingly assume the caregiving role, reflecting the still-strong cultural perception of tending the ill as "women's work." In old age, however, espousal obligations appear to supercede gender-based norms regulating the division of household labor, and older men with disabled wives become the caretakers, with varying degrees of comfort in an unaccustomed role. If the marriage had been previously characterized by rigid gender-role allocation of tasks, the caregiving husband may have a heightened perception of burden, compared to both women in general and men whose marriages involved a more egalitarian division of expressive and instrumental responsibilities.

Caregiving Context

Compared to adult children who provide personal care, espousal caregivers appear to be free of competing demands that would tend to increase caregiver dissatisfaction. Very few older caregiving spouses work or have childrearing obligations or concerns about sustaining other close relationships. Fengler and Goodrich (1979) noted, however, that spouses who do work or who have responsibilities to others are particularly susceptible to "role overload."

The perceived caregiving burden of spouses is also affected by characteristics of their long-standing intimate bonds. Existing research strongly suggests that the closer the caregiver–carereceiver relationship, the greater the impact of impairment on everyday life and consequent emotional strain. The very qualities in the marriage that lead to a heightened sense of caring also exacerbate the trauma of caregiving.

Lastly, in comparison to adult children, elderly spouses have fewer resources to ease the burden of caregiving. Their incomes are typically much lower, with a smaller discretionary component than for younger persons. As the social world of both the disabled and the caregiver contracts and outside activity is reduced, contacts with friends and neighbors diminish. Although adult children may periodically provide respite care, there is usually no one else in the household of the spouse to assist with the daily provision of direct care.

It is quite clear, then, that spouses, in contrast to other caregivers, are more likely to maintain an extremely impaired older person with fewer mediating resources, and at great personal costs. When "burnout" occurs, it is typically a reaction to cognitive impairments, incontinence, or care demands that interrupt the caregiver's sleep night after night. Nonetheless, spouses will continue to resist institutional placement for a longer period of time than will nonspouse caregivers, regardless of the level of disability of the recipient. Only when all physical and emotional resources are depleted will the caregiving spouse entertain the idea of a nursing home alternative (Crossman et al., 1981).

It seems clear that spouses have a substantially higher tolerance threshold than other caregivers. It is not currently known, however, whether spouses and other types of caregivers progress through similar stages of adaptation. The sequence may involve denial, empathy and acceptance (including suppressing one's own needs), anger, and finally a self-assertion phase wherein they acknowledge their own independent existence. Spousal caregivers may move through these states at a slower rate than other caregivers or their adjustment and resolution process may differ in content as well as timing. Additional research is needed not only to ascertain why the tolerance threshold for spouses, on average, is higher than that of other caregivers but also to identify and explain differences among spousal caregivers in their threshold for caregiving. It is reasonable to hypothesize, for example, that spouses whose marital history has been emotionally "bumpy" will initiate institutional placements at lower levels of debility than those whose relationship with the dependent spouse has been relatively fulfilling.

From all the foregoing, it should be clear that while the disabled elderly typically benefit from being cared for by a spouse, the experience may not always have beneficial outcomes for the caregiver. Burnout is only one possible drawback of the married state in old age. In the next section we shall briefly note other potential dysfunctions.

Penalties of Marriage

In general, the research literature has focused on variations in the relative advantage of the married and to the sex differential in benefits. No one has seriously suggested that nonmarried old people are better off than their married counterparts. But we should not gloss over the possibility that under some circumstances, for some couples, there are clear drawbacks to having a spouse. Ironically, these conditions are often created by presumably beneficial public policies, as in the case of disentitlement.

Disentitlement

The United States is unique among modern industrial nations in its reluctance to provide universal access to health and welfare services. Service eligibility is most often based upon "means" tests, whereby the potential recipient must prove to be without any other means of purchasing care. In many cases, then, the presence of a spouse could affect access to delivery systems. Under the most rigorous criteria, married couples will seldom qualify, especially if it can be claimed that the healthier spouse could remain in the labor force. As it is, among the married elderly poor, where the wife is much younger than her impaired spouse, the couple may be required to deplete all their resources (savings accounts and other accumulated assets, with the exception of equity in a home) before becoming eligible for Medicaid, in effect pauperizing the healthier partner. It is perhaps ironic that the couples who have undoubtedly had the hardest time remaining together should be penalized for their remarkable accomplishment, but such are the consequences of means testing in a politically mean climate.

Plugging into the System

In still other instances, a spouse may serve—unwittingly—to isolate a needy partner from potential sources of care. Persons utilizing one social welfare program are often drawn into the complete array of services. However, the initial contact remains problematic; that is, many more are eligible than actually apply for entitlements. Today's elderly are especially reticent claimants, given their strong commitment to values of self-reliance and their lack of experience in negotiating bureaucracies (Moen, 1978). But these are cohort-specific traits that may not inhibit incoming cohorts of elderly who have grown up with the expansion of such programs. Initial contact, however reluctant, is typically made by a social worker or adult offspring on behalf of a nonmarried elder, so that the older person becomes aware of and often benefits from a range of services. Aging married couples are the least likely recipients, either from lack of need or because of the inability of a spouse to admit "failure" by making contact with the social service network. Thus, being married may actually reduce the opportunity to receive needed services. In other cases, it will be the healthier spouse who can link the couple to outside sources of assistance, although espousal referrals are relatively uncommon.

Isolation

The tendency to rely solely upon a spouse may ultimately have negative consequences. Cut off from kin and community, the couple can drift into pathological states without corrective inputs from outside their closed system. Just as for younger couples, mutually reinforced misrepresentations (*folie à deux*) become the operative reality. Then when authentic mental or physical conditions develop, as is likely, the couple cannot make accurate appraisals and seek necessary help.

At another behavioral extreme, espousal abuse in old age is most likely to occur where the couples are relatively isolated socially and when one severely impaired partner makes unmeetable demands upon the other. Although very few systematic studies have been conducted on older abuse in general and almost nothing on that between elderly spouses, available estimates suggest that espousal abuse accounts for between 15 and 20% of reported cases (see O'Rourke, 1981, for a comprehensive review; Block & Sinnot, 1979; Hickey & Douglas, 1981). Most abusive behavior occurs between caregiving relatives and extremely ill and/or disorientated elders and involves psychological rather than physical acts. Often the abuse is a matter of neglect and ignorance rather than malevolence.

Research Needs

If the field of gerontology itself is to come of academic age, researchers must outgrow reliance on correlational analysis of data from flawed samples, in which the techniques bear little logical relationship to the research questions. The criticism could easily be extended to most research on family relationships, where a lack of correspondence between concepts and their measurement raises questions of internal validity. Too often, sophisticated statistical methods have outstripped the full understanding of their implications. At this time, it seems to us that the most pressing needs—at least in studies of relationships—are these: (1) processual models that allow for life-course contingencies; (2) measures that refer to the unit under study rather than the component parts, and (3) more sophisticated longitudinal designs.

Processual Models

All too often, studies of marital functioning are based on but a few observations and the results of bivariate correlational analysis. But the correlates of marital quality, whether synchronic or diachronic, do not tell us much—except by inference—of the processes involved in producing any given outcome. It is the *intervening contingencies* that should command research interest not only for epistemological reasons but also for evaluating or targeting the effects of public policy. It is while couples are adjusting to the normal as well as extreme vicissitudes of aging that intervention programs can have the greatest impact; if inaugurated too early, resources are dissipated; if too late, they may be wasted. Figure 4.1 suggests the type of analysis we have in mind.

Appropriate Units of Analysis in the Study of Relationships

All too often, researchers use individual measures rather than ones that refer to *dyad*, a different level of sociological reality from the individual characteristics of the husband and wife. Dyads have consonance or dissonance, a division of labor, shared definitions of reality, negotiating styles, and coping tactics that are the outcome of interaction and, therefore, cannot be captured by data on individuals. Even if both partners are interviewed in a study, the information often is not combined to produce a variable that is descriptive of the couple. We need conceptual models that allow us to predict something about both the dyad and its constituent parts, as illustrated in Figure 4.2.

Longitudinal Designs

Our objection to cross-sectional analysis is quite different from the usual critique based on the potential incomparability of cohorts. Rather, following our call for processual models, we would emphasize the salience of the intervening period between measurements. To

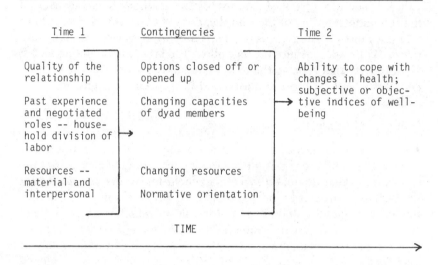

FIGURE 4.1: Processual model

measure the unit only at one or even two points in time may obscure the importance of factors that compress or lengthen a process. That is, cross-sectional studies cut into a process that is of varying length in each case, and it may be precisely the *variability* over time (e.g., how long before institutionalization) that is of greatest interest.

A second crucial shortcoming of cross-sectional designs also reinforces our emphasis on process and unit measures. When researchers have data from only one period in time the temptation to infer the quality of an earlier state of the relationship is often irresistible. The assumption that a given end state must be the product of a particular condition and path, while theoretically plausible, obscures the reality of convergences and crossovers of causes and outcomes. For example, if a wife is successfully coping with her husband's illness at home, we might impute such traits as reciprocity to the relationship, and assume that at some prior time the couple had mutually arrived at a commitment to caring and equity. But the end state could as easily have resulted from any one of several earlier conditions, even an unhappy marriage in which the wife now enjoys her power over the spouse or seeks to amend for past lapses out of fear of eternal damnation.

Conversely, relationships characterized by high levels of mutuality at Time 1 may not be able to survive the impact of extreme disability and actually fare better under conditions of institutionalization.

Conclusions

We began with a brief demographic overview and ended with a relatively complex illustration of the possible outcomes for the married elderly. In a sense, the structure of this chapter represents its major message: between the abstract numbers and the realities of aging there are innumerable contingencies, not all of which can be captured by the theories and methods currently employed in social gerontology. As sociologists, however, we cannot resist a few generali-

	Wife Segregated	Wife Shared
Husband Segregated	A Traditional	B Mixed Wife Angry
Husband Shared	C Mixed Husband Frustrated	D Modern

FIGURE 4.2: Example of dyadic model

zations. First, and not surprisingly, it is typically better to be married
than not to be married in old age. Whatever it takes to make life
comfortable, the married have more of it: income, primary group ties,
sexual access, companionship, residential privacy, adequate nutrition,
physical and mental health. The marital dyad support system is associated with a number of positive outcomes, particularly for husbands—longer life, lower morbidity, higher standard of living, greater
life satisfaction, and home-based care when disabled. The potentially
negative outcomes of the married state are due largely to exogenous
factors such as bureaucratic and policy decisions that are amenable to
change.

Marriage partners provide material, affective, and instrumental
support for one another. Again, there are sex differences in the effects
of such benefits; many studies of morale in old age have found that the
satisfaction of married women correlates most directly with the economic security provided by a spouse, while that of men is linked to the
nonmaterial supports received from a wife. The most important of
these is undoubtedly caregiving in case of illness. The great majority of
disabled elderly are cared for at home, by a spouse or adult offspring.
Wives are more likely than husbands to assume this task, even controlling for age and degree of disability. An examination of recent data on
caregivers found important differences between spouses and other
relatives in their utilization of community-based services and available
resources. Types of caregivers appear to have different "tipping
points" at which demands of the task overwhelm capacities to meet
these needs.

Finally, we offer several recommendations for enhancing our
knowledge base, with an emphasis upon processual models and con-
tingency equations. There is not much more to be learned from the
localized, small-scale, cross-sectional, nonprobability convenience
samples that constitute the bulk of gerontological research. Of course,
it is always easy to tell others how to conduct their research and very
difficult to find the funding or to spend the time and energy needed to
produce appropriate data. We hope that this chapter will stimulate
renewed interest in making that effort.

References

Becker, H. S. (1961). Notes on the concept of commitment. *American Journal
of Sociology, 66*, 32–40.
Berkman, L. F., & Syme, S. L. (1979). Social networks, host resistance, and

mortality: A nine-year follow-up study of Alameda County residents. *American Journal of Epidemiology, 100,* 186–204.

Bernard, J. (1972). *The future of marriage.* New York: World Publishing Co.

Block, M. R., & Sinnot, J. D. (Eds.). (1979). *The battered elder syndrome.* University Park, MD: University of Maryland Center on Aging.

Brody, E. M. (1978). The aging of the family. *The annals, 438,* 13–27.

Brody, S., Poulshock, W., & Mascioschi, F. (1978). The family caring unit: A major consideration in the long-term support system. *The Gerontologist, 18,* 556–561.

Brotman, H. (1982). *Every ninth American: An analysis for the chairman of the Select Committee on Aging.* House of Representatives, Washington, DC: U.S. Government Printing Office.

Callahan, J. J., Diamond, L.D., Giele, J. Z., & Morris, R. (1980). Responsibility of families for their severely disabled elders. *Health Care Financing Review, 1,* 29–48.

Cantor, M. H. (1981). *Factors associated with strain among family, friends and neighbors caring for the frail elderly.* Paper presented at the 34th Annual Meeting of the Gerontological Society of America, Toronto, Canada.

Center for Population Research. (1979). Health interview survey: Home care supplement. (Contract No. HHS-100-80-0158). Washington, DC: The Urban Institute for DHHS, Office of the Assistant Secretary for Planning and Evaluation.

Cobb, S. (1979). Social support and health through the life course. In M. W. Riley (Ed.), *Aging from birth to death.* Boulder, CO: Westview Press.

Crossman, L., Landon, C., & Barry, C. (1981). Older women caring for disabled spouses: A model for supportive services. *The Gerontologist, 21,* 464–470.

Cuber, J. F., & Haroff, P. B. (1963). *The significant Americans.* New York: Appleton.

Dono, J. E., Faibe, C. M., Kail, B. L., Liwak, E., Sherman, R. H., & Siegel, J. (1979). Primary groups in old age: Structure and function. *Research on Aging, 1,* 403–433.

Espanshade, T. J. (1982). *Marriage, divorce, and remarriage from retrospective data: A multiregional approach.* Paper presented at the Annual Meeting of the Population Association of America, San Diego, CA.

Fengler, A., & Goodrich, W. (1979). Wives of elderly disabled men: The hidden patients. *The Gerontologist, 19,* 175–183.

Glenn, N. D. (1981). The contribution of marriage to the psychological well-being of males and females. *Journal of Marriage and the Family,* 161–168.

Glenn, N. D., & Weaver, C. N. (1981). The contribution of marital happiness to global happiness. *Journal of Marriage and the Family,* 161–168.

Glick, P. (1979). The future marital status and living arrangements of the elderly. *The Gerontologist, 19,* 301–309.

Gove, W. R., & Tudor, J. F. (1973a). Adult sex roles and mental illness. *American Journal of Sociology, 78,* 812–835.

Gove, W. R. (1973b). Sex, marital status, and mortality. *American Journal of Sociology, 79,* 45–67.

Hagestad, G. O. (1980). *Role change in adulthood: The transition to the empty nest.* Unpublished paper cited by L. K. George, role transitions in later life. Monterey, CA: Brooks/Cole.

Helsing, K. J., Szklo, M., & Comstock, G. W. (1981). Factors associated with mortality after widowhood. *American Journal of Public Health, 71,* 802–809.

Hanushek, E. A., & Jackson, J. E. (1977). Models with discrete dependent variables. In *Statistical Methods for Social Scientists,* chap. 7. New York: Academic Press.

Henretta, J. C., & Campbell, R. T. (1976). Status attainment and status maintenance: A study of stratification in old age. *American Sociological Review, 41,* 981–992.

Hess, B. B. (1979). Sex roles, friendship, and the life course. *Research on Aging, 1,* 494–515.

Hickey, T., & Douglas, R. L. (1981). Mistreatment of the elderly in the domestic setting: An exploratory study. *American Journal of Public Health, 71,* 500–507.

Kahn, R. L. (1979). Aging and social support. In M. W. Riley (Eds.), *Aging from birth to death.* Boulder, CO: Westview Press.

Lopata, H. Z. (1979). *Women as widows: Support systems.* New York: Elsevier-North Holland.

Lowenthal, M., & Haven, C. (1968). Intimacy as a critical variable. *American Sociological Review, 33,* 20–30.

Ludeman, K. (1981). The sexuality of the older person: Review of the literature. *The Gerontologist, 21,* 203–208.

Miller, B. C. (1976). A multivariate developmental model of marital satisfaction. *Journal of Marriage and the Family, 38,* 643–657.

Mindel, C. H. (1979). Multigenerational family households: Recent trends and implications for the future. *The Gerontologist, 5,* 456–463.

Mindel, C. H., & Wright, R. (1982). Satisfaction in multigenerational households. *The Journal of Gerontology, 37,* 483–489.

Moen, E. (1978). The reluctance of the elderly to accept help. *Social Problems,* 293–303.

Newman, S. (1976). *Housing adjustments of older people: A report of findings from the second phase.* Ann Arbor, MI: Institute for Social Research.

Newman, S. J. (Nov. 1980). *Government policy and the relationship between adult children and their aging parents: Filial support, Medicare and Medicaid.* Paper presented at the Annual Meeting of the Gerontological Society of America, San Diego, CA.

O'Rourke, M. (1981). *Elder abuse: The state of the art.* Boston: Legal research and services for the elderly.

Palmore, E. (1976). Total chance of institutionalization among the aged. *The Gerontologist, 16,* 504–507.

Presser, H. B. (1975). Age differences between spouses: Trends, patterns and social implications. *American Behavioral Scientist, 19,* 190–204.

Rathbone-McCuan, E. (1976). Geriatric day care: A family perspective. *The Gerontologist, 16,* 517–521.

Shanas, E. (1979a). Social myth as hypothesis: The case of family relations of old people. *The Gerontologist, 19,* 3–9.

Shanas, E. (1979b). The family as a social support system in old age. *The Gerontologist, 19,* 169–174.

Shanas, E., Townsend, D., Wedderman, D., Friis, H., Milno, P., & Stehouwer, J. (1968). *Old people in three industrial societies.* New York: Atherton Press.

Soldo, B. J. (1983). Income services for dependent elderly: Determinants of current use and implications for future demand. Washington, DC: The Urban Institute, working paper 1466–30.

Soldo, B. J., & Myllyluomo, J. (1983). Caregivers who live with dependent elderly. *The Gerontologist, 23,* 605–611.

Spanier, G. B., Lewis, R. A., & Cole, C. L. (1975). Marital adjustment over the family life cycle: The issue of curvilinearity. *Journal of Marriage and the Family, 37,* 263–275.

Townsend, P. (1965). The effects of family structure on the likelihood of admission to an institution in old age. In E. Shanas & G. F. Streib (Eds.), *Social structure and the family: Generational relations.* Englewood Cliffs, NJ: Prentice Hall.

Treas, J., & Van Hilst, A. (1976). Marriage and remarriage rates among older Americans. *The Gerontologist, 16,* 132–136.

Troll, L. E. (1971). The family of later life: A decade review. *Journal of Marriage and the Family, 33,* 263–290.

U.S. Bureau of the Census. (1978). Current Population Reports, Series P-23, No. 77, *Perspectives on American husbands and wives.* Washington, DC: U.S. Government Printing Office.

U.S. Bureau of the Census. (1979). Special Studies Series P-23, No. 85. *Social and economic characteristics of the older population: 1978.* Washington, DC: U.S. Government Printing Office.

U.S. Bureau of the Census. (1980). Current Population Reports, Series P-60, No. 130. *Characteristics of the population below the poverty level: 1979.* Washington, DC: U.S. Government Printing Office.

U.S. Bureau of the Census. (1981a). Current Population Reports, Series P-20, No. 365. Marital status and living arrangements: March 1980. Washington, DC: U.S. Government Printing Office.

U.S. Bureau of the Census. (1981b). Current Population Reports, Series P-60, No. 127. Money income and poverty status of persons and families in the United States: 1980 (Advance Data). Washington, DC: U.S. Government Printing Office.

U.S. Bureau of the Census. (1982). Current Population Reports, Series P-20, No. 371. Household and family characteristics: March 1981. Washington, DC: U.S. Government Printing Office.

Verbrugge, L. (1979). Marital status and health. *Journal of Marriage and the Family, 41,* 267–285.

Verbrugge, L. (1982). Women and men: Sex differences in mortality and health of older people. In M. W. Riley, B. B. Hess, & K. Bond (Eds.),

Aging in society: Selected reviews of recent research. Hillsdale, NJ: Lawrence Erlebaum Associates.

Veroff, J., Kulka, R. A., & Douvan, E. (1981). *Mental health in America: Patterns of help-seeking from 1977 to 1976.* New York: Basic Books.

Weg, R. (Ed.). (1982). *Sexuality in the later years: Roles and behavior.* New York: Academic Press.

Weissert, W., Scanion, W., & Unger, A. (1981). Estimating the long-term care population: National and state prevalence rates and selected characteristics. Working paper 1466-11, The Urban Institute, Washington, DC.

Zarit, J., Gatz, M., & Zarit, S. (1981). *Family relationships and burden in long-term care.* Paper presented at the 34th Annual Meeting of the Gerontological Society of America, Toronto, Canada.

Zarit, S. H., Reever, K. E., & Bach-Peterson, J. (1980). Relatives of the impaired elderly: Correlates of feelings of burden. *The Gerontologist, 20,* 649-655.

5

The Role of Siblings as Family Caregivers

Victor G. Cicirelli

Any discussion of the social support networks of the elderly in today's society would be incomplete without some consideration of the role of the brothers and sisters of elderly individuals in providing help. Most people can readily bring to mind an instance of elderly siblings who minister to each other's needs in later years. Just as readily, most people can recall an elderly person who has little or no contact with a sibling or who is actually estranged. Obviously, the relationship of most elderly people with their siblings is somewhere between these two extremes. An examination of existing research findings can provide a basis for delineating sibling roles in later life and for promoting the inclusion of siblings in the family support system of the elderly.

The nature of the sibling relationship itself can be explored by considering three separate aspects of this question: Do most elderly have living siblings? What is the proximity of the elderly to their siblings? What is the quantity and quality of contact among elderly and their siblings? Each of these questions will be explored in the following text.

Do Most Elderly Have Living Siblings?

While the sibling relationship is typically one of very long duration, the increase in mortality rates with increasing age means that many people will have lost one or more siblings through death by the time they reach the latter part of the life span. The percentage of elderly with at least one living sibling has been reported by various authors as 85%

(Shanas et al., 1968), 93% (Clark & Anderson, 1967), and 78% (Cicirelli, 1979). Since approximately 10% of elderly were born into families where they were the only child, it is clear that the great majority of those who originally had siblings still had a living sibling in old age. Cicirelli (1979) also reported data on the number of living siblings reported by each individual. Elderly aged 60–69 had a mean of 2.88 living siblings, while the mean was 2.18 for those in the 70–79 age range and 1.08 for those aged 80 and over. These three groups originally had 4.6, 4.9, and 4.2 siblings, respectively. Nevertheless, even those elderly who are over age 80 are likely to have a living brother or sister.

Do Elderly Have Siblings Living Nearby?

If older people are to receive (or exchange) help from their siblings on a regular basis, they must be near enough to make this kind of help feasible. (While proximity is most important for tangible forms of help such as homemaking or home health care, it can be argued that it is also a factor in less tangible forms of help such as emotional support. Although emotional support can be extended from a distance via telephone or letter, it is given more easily when there is close proximity.) Geographic distance has frequently been taken as an approximation of the proximity of two individuals. However, the same geographic distance may have different psychological meanings to different individuals depending on such things as their age, health, physical mobility, income level, available means of transportation, travel time and costs, the nature of competing activities, and lifelong habits of travel for the individuals concerned. Thus, visiting a sibling who lives across town may seem like a much greater distance psychologically to one person than visiting a sibling a hundred miles away seems to another person. Similarly, geographic distance provides only a partial indicator of the feasibility of telephone contact between siblings. Beyond the local calling zone, long distance charges to any point in the nation frequently are less than charges for calls within the same state. On the average, however, geographic distance can provide an indication of whether a sibling is close enough to make a helping relationship feasible.

Rosenberg and Anspach (1973) presented a strong argument for the position that for a sibling relationship to be feasible the siblings should at least live within the same city. In their sample of blue-collar elderly over age 65 in an Eastern major metropolitan area, 49% reported a living sibling within the same city. (See Cicirelli, 1980a, for a fuller discussion of the Rosenberg and Anspach data on sibling proximity.) In a study of 300 elderly in a small Midwestern city who had a mean age of 73.8, Cicirelli (1979) reported that 26% of the siblings with whom the elderly respondents had the most contact lived within a hundred miles. In another study (Cicirelli, 1980b) of adults ranging in age from 29 to 72, proximity data were obtained in regard to all living siblings. Overall, 36% of the siblings lived within the same city as the person interviewed, and 56% lived within a hundred miles. Since proximity was not correlated with age, these figures are applicable to the young-old group represented in the sample. They do not differ greatly from the proximities reported for the elderly group. Thus, one can conclude that somewhat over half of the elderly's siblings live within a hundred miles, but perhaps only a quarter of them are to be found in the same city.

What is the Quantity and Quality of Contact of Elderly with Their Siblings?

While sibling proximity can provide only a gross indication that siblings are near enough to have an active relationship, a better marker of the kind of relationship that exists is provided by measures of the quantity and the quality of contact between siblings.

Contact

Contact between elderly siblings has most often been measured by the frequency of visiting, telephoning, and letter writing. In studies dealing with the elderly in the United States, Denmark, and Great Britain, Shanas et al. (1968) found that 34% of elderly men and 43% of elderly women saw a sibling at least once a week, while 39% of women and 44% of men saw a sibling at least once a month. In a more recent study in Chicago, Bild and Havighurst (1976) found that the percentage of elderly people who reported visiting with a sibling weekly or more often varied from 17 to 30% among seven subsamples representing different residential neighborhoods. Rosenberg and Anspach (1973) reported that 47% of their sample over age 65 saw a sibling weekly or more often; they also reported that the frequency of sibling visiting declined from middle adulthood to old age. However, this decline is difficult to interpret since it appears to be confounded with sibling mortality. Cicirelli (1979) found that 17% of the elderly in his sample saw the sibling with whom they had the most contact at least once a week, while 33% saw that sibling at least once a month.

Siblings who see each other more frequently also tend to telephone each other more frequently (Cicirelli, 1980b), with the correlation between visiting and telephoning 0.61 for a middle-aged to elderly group. Among the elderly, frequencies of visiting and telephoning were about the same (Cicirelli, 1979). Frequencies of writing were in general quite low, especially among the elderly men. Letter writing seemed to be used as a means to keep in touch by those who did not visit or telephone, while visiting and telephoning appeared to be complementary parts of a more intensive pattern of contact between siblings. At the extreme of contact, 2% of the elderly group lived with a sibling and only a few had no contact of any kind with a sibling. If one were to characterize the typical level of contact between elderly siblings, it would be that of visiting several times a year and telephoning several times a year. If one were to judge by amount of contact alone, the relationship between elderly siblings cannot be described as a close one for the majority of sibling pairs.

Quality of Relationship

What then can be said about the quality of the relationship between elderly siblings? A number of authors (Allan, 1977; Atchley, 1977; Cicirelli, 1979; Cumming & Schneider, 1961; Farber, 1966; Manney, 1973) regard the feelings of closeness and affection between siblings as more important indicators of the relationship than judgments based on the amount of contact alone. Elderly people tend to feel closer to their siblings than to any other relatives except their own children and perhaps their spouses. Where the elderly have never married, or are childless, divorced, or widowed, they may feel especially close to their brothers and sisters.

Cicirelli (1979, 1980a, 1981, 1982b) investigated the quality of the relationship between siblings among elderly over 60 years of age. Of those who had at least one living sibling, 53% reported feeling "extremely close" to the sibling with whom they had the most contact, while another 30% felt "close." Only 5% reported feeling not close at all. These elderly people named a sister as the sibling to whom they felt "closest" more frequently than a brother, with the sister–sister bond closest of all. This closeness of the sister–sister bond has been noted by other researchers (Adams, 1968; Cumming & Schneider, 1961). Also, middle-born siblings were named more frequently than first-born or last-born siblings as the sibling to whom the elderly person felt closest. Although this finding may simply be an artifact of the greater number of middle-born children in large families (the mean number of siblings born into the family of origin of the elderly was 4.6), it is certainly consonant with the reputedly greater sociability of middle-born children.

Value consensus is another aspect of the relationship between siblings which is indicative of the fundamental closeness of the relationship. Among middle-aged adults, Adams (1968) found that 45% reported a high degree of value consensus with siblings, while Cicirelli (1980b) reported 49% with high consensus. The consensus among the elderly and their siblings was higher (Cicirelli, 1979), with 68% agreeing either completely or about most things.

Cicirelli (1980b, also unpublished data) has investigated compatibility of the relationship between siblings in middle age and old age. Among the elderly, 88% reported that they got along very well with their siblings, 74% reported gaining considerable or very great satisfaction from the sibling relationship, 74% reported that their siblings took an interest in their activities, and 68% felt that they could discuss intimate topics with their siblings. However, only 30% talked over an important decision with a sibling before making the decision; 70% did so only rarely or never. Looking at the responses to these items, it seems that most elderly people tend to feel a global sense of closeness and compatibility with siblings while a smaller proportion is able to share intimate details of their lives and still fewer consult with siblings about important decisions. (One can speculate that the decrease in proportion of siblings in the latter cases may be due to distance or perhaps a reticence to disclose feelings and personal problems, which is typical of many in the older generation.)

Rivalry between siblings is an aspect of the sibling relationship which has received great attention from psychologists of the psychoanalytic tradition. During childhood and adulthood, rivalry has been found to be greater among brothers than for other sibling sex combinations. Rivalry for cross-sex pairs was least of all (Adams, 1968; Form & Geschwender, 1962; Sutton-Smith & Rosenberg, 1970). Whether sibling rivalry continues in old age has been frequently questioned. Troll (1975) regarded rivalry as being expressed subtly in later life, with the sibling being used as a standard of comparison for the individual's own activities. Laverty (1962) found that feelings of rivalry were reactivated in certain situations in old age. Allan (1977) felt that sibling rivalry dissipated or mellowed by later life. Cicirelli (1980b, also unpublished data) looked at several possible manifestations of rivalrous behavior between elderly siblings. Some 90% never argued with their sibling or did so only rarely, while the remaining 10% did so only occasionally when they were together. Only 6% reported that their siblings ever tried to "boss" or dominate them in family matters occasionally or more often. Only 8% reported any feelings of competition with their elderly siblings, and that occurred only rarely. Few reported any incidence of jealousy, hostility, hypercriticism, insensitivity to feelings, or snobbishness in their relationship with elderly siblings. Some 86% reported having no conflicts of any kind with siblings, another 10% reported only rare conflicts, and only 4% had more frequent conflicts. Conflicts, when they occurred, seemed to revolve around the criticism of one sibling's lifestyle by the other and an attempt to tell the other what to do. There was, however, some indication that conflict could be expected to increase if the siblings were to live together once again. Although 65% expected only rare conflict or none at all under such circumstances, 20% expected that living together would result in occasional conflict, 8% expected frequent or continual conflict, and 6% expected conflict so severe that it would never work. Thus, for as many as a third of the elderly, sibling conflict could be evoked under proper circumstances. This suggests that the low sibling rivalry reported in old age may be a function of diminished contact. When siblings see each other infrequently, it may be easier for them to relate to each other in a harmonious way.

Changes with Age

The question of how the relationships with siblings change with increasing age has been a matter of some interest (Cicirelli, 1980a; Riley & Foner, 1968; Troll, 1971; Troll, Miller, & Atchley, 1978). Problems of sibling mortality make it difficult to interpret data from existing studies. Further, there have been no longitudinal studies of sibling relationships in later life. Cicirelli (1980b, and unpublished data) found that elderly subjects, when asked to compare feelings of closeness with siblings to closeness at earlier points in their lives, felt closer at present than they did as children, as young adults, during childrearing years, or when their parents were still living. Cross-sectional data from various age-groups are presented in Table 5.1 and tend to bear out the retrospective judgments. Feelings of closeness increase from adulthood into old age. Table 5.1 also includes means for measures of sibling compatibility and sibling conflict. Like closeness, sibling compatibility increased with increasing age. However, conflict with siblings declined over the decades from ages 30 to 90. There was a significant age effect in the analyses for all three measures of the sibling relationship, with a significant linear trend in every case.

TABLE 5.1. Closeness, Compatibility, and Conflict with Siblings for Six Age Groups in Adulthood and Old Age (Means and Standard Deviations)

Age-group	Closeness		Compatibility		Conflict	
	Mean	SD	Mean	SD	Mean	SD
30–39	2.81	0.97	16.44	5.03	4.62	2.31
40–49	2.87	0.84	16.96	4.21	4.23	1.97
50–59	3.03	0.91	16.58	4.80	3.89	1.34
60–69	3.00	0.94	17.49	4.70	3.71	1.13
70–79	3.12	0.85	17.34	4.97	3.62	1.24
80–89	3.28	0.89	19.16	4.56	3.64	1.29

Note. F-tests for the effect of age were significant at the .05 level of significance in analyses for each of the three variables (df = 5,417). Table derived from data in an earlier report (Cicirelli, 1980b) and unpublished data.

Another recent study (Ross, Dalton, & Milgram, 1980) has explored sibling relationships in late adulthood and old age. Conclusions were based on clinical interviews conducted in small group settings. Most felt that their closeness to siblings increased as they grew older. Especially noteworthy was a reported increase in closeness among cross-sex pairs. Most people were able to identify one of their siblings as the one to whom they felt "closest." Most of those interviewed viewed their closeness to siblings as having its origins in the family life of childhood. Achieving a close relationship (if it had been disrupted) was regarded as highly important. Indeed, the sibling relationship in old age seemed to be accorded a particular salience, as if through contact with siblings the individual could reactivate the closeness of early family life. Both the shared memories and shared family histories were regarded as important reasons for the value placed on sibling relationships in later life. Ross, Dalton, and Milgram (1980) probed sibling rivalry in a similar study, and reported a much higher incidence of rivalrous feelings than had been reported in other studies. Some 71% reported experiencing rivalrous feelings with a sibling at some point in their lives, most generally in childhood and adolescence. However, only 45% considered this rivalry to be still active in the adult years; where rivalry was still active, there appeared to be a continuation of unsatisfactory sibling interaction patterns from earlier years. The incidence of rivalrous feelings may have been as high as it was because of stimulation to self-disclosure in the clinical group setting. Also, no

distinctions were made as to whether the rivalrous feelings reported
were serious or trivial in nature. Nevertheless, even though they found
a higher incidence of rivalry, Ross et al. (1980) noted a decline in
rivalry into adulthood and old age. The value which older people
place on the renewal and repair of sibling relationships can account for
the successful resolution of much earlier rivalry.

Theoretical Bases

Two theoretical positions have been advanced (Cicirelli, 1981, 1982a)
in explanation of sibling relationships in later life—attachment theory
and substitution theory. In attachment theory (Bowlby, 1979, 1980;
Troll & Smith, 1976), the early bond between mother and child comes
to be extended to others in the family interactional system of childhood. Feelings of attachment may be generalized from attachment to
the mother, or they may arise through mutual reinforcement of one
another's needs (e.g., social needs) in the early years. The elderly
subjects of Ross et al. (1980) saw the roots of their closeness to siblings
in their childhood experiences as members of close families, thus
lending support to such a view. Sibling contacts in later life, even when
relatively infrequent, may be important in reevoking feelings of belonging from early childhood. Their salience may be a response to the
threat which death of parents and their own aging poses to the bond of
attachment.

Substitution theory (Cumming & Schneider, 1961) holds that
when a relationship is lost, the relationship with another tends to be
substituted for the missing relationship. Thus, following loss of a
parent or a spouse, a closer relationship with a sibling can help to
substitute for the lost loved one and to fill the void which remains. A
sister may take over many of the family roles of a deceased mother, or
a brother may fulfill some of the duties of a sister's lost husband. As
people grow older, their relationships may thus come to assume
greater psychological importance through their substitution for other
relationships which have been lost.

Reviewing the evidence regarding the quality of the sibling relationship in later life, for most the relationship is one characterized by
great closeness of feelings, consensus of values, compatibility of the
relationship, and little feeling of rivalry. Nevertheless, the relationship
for any given sibling pair can range from extraordinary closeness and
loyalty (Bank, 1979) to total apathy or even great hatred. Troll et al.
(1978) also emphasized that human relationships are complex and both
positive and negative feelings can exist at the same time.

What Types of Help Do Siblings Provide Each Other?

One important part of sibling relationships throughout life is the help and support which siblings can provide for one another. In old age this help can take a variety of different forms. It may include serving as a confidant, giving advice, aiding in decision making, boosting morale, and help with homemaking, shopping, home repairs, transportation, or finances. A few interview studies have reported that siblings of the elderly are generally ready to give aid in time of trouble, although their help may be called for only on rare occasions (Allan, 1977; Cicirelli, 1979; Cumming & Schneider, 1961). Help of this kind can be viewed as auxiliary help, or help within the framework of the substitution hypothesis. Townsend (1957) has provided examples of extensive help provided by an elderly sibling following the loss of a spouse.

Cicirelli (1979, and unpublished data) investigated the extent of help which elderly people received from their siblings. In one part of the study, the elderly subjects named the kin members from whom they received the most help for 16 different areas in which help or services could be given. For most elderly, as might be expected, their children were the primary sources of help.

Cultural norms are that most help within families is exchanged in a vertical direction between parents and children, and not in a collateral direction. However, some 7% of all elderly interviewed reported turning to a sibling as a primary source of psychological support. (Psychological support was considered to include such things as serving as a confidant, cheering up spirits, and willingness to help in a crisis.) Smaller percentages of elderly regarded a sibling as a primary source of help with reading materials, business dealings, social and recreational activities, protection, and help with homemaking. More surprising, when the data were examined separately for different age-groups of elderly, siblings were regarded as more important sources of help in all of the above areas as people grew older. When the elderly subjects of the study were asked about which family member they would desire as a primary source of help in the future, from 5% to 7% named a sibling as the desired helper for 8 of the 16 types of help studied. These percentages seem small, but it should be remembered that they refer only to the case where the sibling is seen as the primary source of a given type of help. If occasional and supplementary help from siblings had been considered in the study, the contribution of siblings would surely have been much greater. Indeed, some 60% of the elderly regarded their siblings as a source of support. Most felt that their siblings were ready to help if they were needed, and that if a crisis came they would call on their siblings. The majority reported that they felt better after talking to siblings and that siblings helped them in the adjustment to aging. (This may seem somewhat surprising in view of the fact that smaller percentages of elderly reported sharing intimate details of their lives or talking over decisions with siblings as a source of psychological support. It is likely that shared intimacies and decisions play only a small part, at best, in psychological support between siblings.)

Silverstone and Hyman (1982) advocate that an elderly person's siblings be included in a "family task force" to plan a course of action when that person becomes dependent or there is a crisis situation where the family must take action. Certainly, at the very least, the elderly siblings can provide the viewpoint of a contemporary in the situation and may be more aware of the individual's needs and desires than adult children would be. In other cases, siblings can provide respite care, look after the individual's business affairs and other interests, and provide needed psychological support.

Overall, then, it can be said that siblings of the elderly seem to feel an obligation toward each other. However, in the usual course of events, help between elderly siblings is at a low level with the possible exception of psychological support and help with social and recreational activities. The role of elderly siblings in the support system appears to be that of "standing ready" should the primary lines of help from spouse and adult children be lost or prove insufficient. The elderly individual appears to count on this potential source of help, increasingly so with advancing age.

What Are the Antecedents of Helping Patterns Between Elderly Siblings?

Since most research into the antecedents of helping behavior has been concerned with adult children's support to elderly parents or with family support in general, any discussion of antecedents of helping patterns between elderly siblings must rest largely on reasoning by analogy from existing findings. Many of these findings have been discussed elsewhere in this volume and will only be mentioned here: notions of exchange theory, extensiveness of existing mutual aid and socialization patterns prior to illness or crisis (Sussman, 1965), an attachment model of helping (Cicirelli, 1980b), and helping as an aspect of solidarity (Bengston, Olander, & Haddad, 1976) in which helping behavior is seen as a function of the dependency needs of the elderly person, residential propinquity, sense of responsibility, and sex linkage.

Cicirelli (1982a) investigated variables leading to psychological support among elderly siblings, using a path model based on attachment theory in which siblings' feelings of attachment were viewed as leading to attachment behaviors and in turn to sibling help. Sibling conflict (rivalry) and sibling obligation were also hypothesized to be precursors of attachment behavior and sibling help. Results indicated that feelings of attachment had the strongest influence on sibling help in the area of psychological support, while attachment behaviors had a smaller effect. Sibling conflict, which was low in old age, had no effect, while sibling obligation had a very weak negative effect. Thus, it was concluded that help to siblings rested primarily on close feelings of attachment between them.

Finally, two antecedent variables should be mentioned which are particularly pertinent to the topic of sibling help. The first, based on substitution theory (Cumming & Schneider, 1961), is the unavailability of help from those more directly obligated to provide support (spouse or adult children). There is some evidence indicating that siblings step in to help following the death of a spouse (Townsend, 1957; Troll, 1971), or that sibling relationships (including sibling help) are more important to those who have never married or who are childless (Cicirelli, 1979, and unpublished data). The second antecedent variable that bears mentioning is concerned with the resources of the elderly sibling who might wish to provide help. If he or she is ill or physically handicapped, helping anyone else may be impossible. Or a sibling who desires to help may have little money or other resources for use in providing help. When the sibling lives at a distance, this may provide a real barrier to helping. Also, the individual may have competing obligations which come first except in an extreme crisis, such as those to a job, spouse, and children or grandchildren. In such cases, help to a sibling may be minimal or nonexistent.

What Are the Consequences of Sibling Relationships to the Well-being of the Elderly?

There is some research to indicate that good sibling relationships are important to the older person. Cumming and Henry (1961) noted the improved morale of elderly with living siblings. Sibling relationships are seen as having a positive value for the individual (Ross et al., 1980), since siblings share early memories of family life and a shared emotional bond. If the life review is indeed an important task of later life, siblings can serve as a valuable source of information should memory become dimmed.

Cicirelli (1980c) found that those elderly persons who had greater frequency of contact, closeness of feeling, and value consensus with siblings were more likely to have an internal locus of control. It was theorized that the individual's efforts at social interaction were reinforced by relationships with siblings, providing satisfaction of affective and other needs. By instigating rewarding interactions with siblings, the individual maintains a greater sense of efficacy in everyday life. Through such a mechanism, close sibling relationships in later life can enable the elderly person to feel in greater control of events and to feel more motivated to act to improve conditions for themselves. In another study (Cicirelli, 1977), the problems and concerns of the elderly were found to depend on sibling relationships. Elderly men who had more sisters had a greater sense of emotional security in life. For elderly women, sisters were associated with stimulation and challenge to maintain social activities, skills, and roles in life. Siblings may also perform valuable pioneering functions (Bank & Kahn, 1975) for each other, serving as role models for successful aging, widowhood, bereavement, and/or retirement.

Due to the egalitarian nature of sibling relationships, when help is needed it may be easier to accept from a sibling than from some other source. (In some cases, a bitter sibling rivalry may make help from a sibling all but impossible to accept, but data indicate that most rivalry has dissipated by old age.)

What Are the Current Research Priorities in This Area?

Since research into sibling helping relationships in old age has been quite limited thus far, there remain many questions which should be investigated. Most important of these is the general question of determining the most important antecedent variables of sibling help. Several have been suggested here as likely to be predictors of helping behavior, but systematic research is needed. If those factors leading to sibling help are understood, ways of promoting and maintaining sibling help can be devised.

Second in order of priority are those questions revolving around the process of helping itself. How and when help is elicited or initiated, how it is given and received, and the reactions of giver and receiver all need to be understood.

Third, the role of sibling help within the larger system of family support for the elderly should be determined. We need to know when help from siblings is needed or desired and what its strength is in comparison to help from other family members. The amount of sibling help as revealed by existing studies does not seem great, yet it may assume greater importance in relation to help from other sources. Also, siblings may perform functions other than giving active help. They may serve in advisory or resource functions to other family members, interpreting their elderly sibling's needs and desires to adult children (or other helpers) or counseling them on how best to help. They may stimulate adult children or other helpers to take action, or they may act as watchdogs to see that their sibling is being taken care of properly.

From what we have learned thus far, sibling help may be limited in amount. Nevertheless, siblings do appear to fulfill important and valuable functions in old age. It is a topic which deserves further study.

References

Adams, B. N. (1968). *Kinship in an urban setting.* Chicago: Markham Publishing Co.

Allan, G. (1977). Sibling solidarity. *Journal of Marriage and the Family, 39,* 177–184.

Atchley, R. C. (1977). *The social forces in later life* (2nd ed.). Belmont, CA: Wadsworth.

Bank, S. (1979). *Hansels and Gretels: A study of extremely loyal sibling groups.* Paper presented at the annual meeting of the American Psychological Association, New York.

Bank, S., & Kahn, M. D. (1975). Sisterhood-brotherhood is powerful: Sibling subsystems and family therapy. *Family Process, 14,* 311–337.

Bengston, V. L., Olander, E., & Haddad, A. (1976). The generation gap and aging family members: Towards a conceptual model. In J. F. Gubrium (Ed.), *Time, self and roles in old age.* New York: Behavioral Publications.

Bild, B. R., & Havighurst, R. J. (1976). Family and social support. *The Gerontologist, 16,* 63–69.

Bowlby, J. (1979). *The making and breaking of affectional bonds.* London: Tavistock Publications.

Bowlby, J. (1980). *Attachment and loss. Vol. III. Loss: stress and depression.* New York: Basic Books.

Cicirelli, V. G. (1977). Relationship of siblings to the elderly person's feelings and concerns. *Journal of Gerontology, 131,* 309–317.

Cicirelli, V. G. (May, 1979). *Social services for the elderly in relation to the kin network.* Report to the NRTA-AARP Andrus Foundation.

Cicirelli, V. G. (1980a). Sibling relationships in adulthood. In L. W. Poone (Eds.), *Aging in the 1980's.* Washington, DC: American Psychological Association.

Cicirelli, V. G. (Dec. 1980b). *Adult children's views on providing services for elderly parents.* Report to the NRTA-AARP Andrus Foundation.

Cicirelli, V. G. (1980c). Relationship of family background variables to locus of control in the elderly. *Journal of Gerontology, 35,* 108–114.

Cicirelli, V. G. (April 2–5, 1981). *Interpersonal relationships of siblings in the middle part of the life span.* Paper presented at the 1981 Biennial Meeting of the Society for Research in Child Development, Boston, MA.

Cicirelli, V. G. (Aug. 23–27, 1982a). *An attachment model of sibling helping behavior in old age.* Paper presented at the 90th Annual Convention of the American Psychological Association, Washington, DC.

Cicirelli, V. G. (1982b). Sibling influence throughout the lifespan. In M. E. Lamb & B. Sutton-Smith (Eds.), *Sibling relationships: Their nature and significance across the lifespan.* Hillsdale, NJ: Lawrence Erlbaum Associates.

Clark, M., & Anderson, B. (1967). *Culture and aging.* Springfield, IL: Charles C. Thomas.

Cumming, E., & Henry, W. (1961). *Growing old.* New York: Basic Books.

Cumming, E., & Schneider, D. (1961). Sibling solidarity: A property of American kinship. *American Anthropologist, 63,* 498–507.

Farber, B. (1966). Kinship and family organization. New York: Wiley.

Form, W. H., & Geschwender, J. A. (1962). Social reference basis of job satisfaction: The case of manual workers. *American Sociological Review, 27,* 228–237.

Laverty, R. (1962). Reactivation of sibling rivalry in older people. *Social Work, 7,* 23–30.

Manney, J. D. (1973). *Aging.* Office of Human Development, HEW.

Riley, M. W., & Foner, A. (1968). *Aging and Society. Vol. 1. An inventory of research findings.* New York: Russell Sage Foundation.

Rosenberg, G. S., & Anspach, D. F. (1973). Sibling solidarity in the working class. *Journal of Marriage and the Family, 35,* 108–113.

Ross, H. G., Dalton, M. J., & Milgram, J. I. (Nov. 1980). *Older adults' perceptions of closeness in sibling relationships.* Paper presented at the 33rd Annual Scientific Meeting of the Gerontological Society, San Diego, CA.

Shanas, E., Townsend, P., Wedderburn, D., Friis, H., Milhoj, P., & Stehouwer, J. (1968). *Older people in three industrial societies.* New York: Atherton Press.

Silverstone, B., & Hymen, H. K. (1982). *You and your aging parent* (rev. ed.). New York: Pantheon Books.

Sussman, M. B. (1965). Relations of adult children with their parents in the United States. In E. Shanas & G. Strieb (Eds.), *Social structures and the family: Generational relations*. New York: Prentice-Hall.

Sutton-Smith, B., & Rosenberg, B. G. (1970). *The sibling*. New York: Holt, Rinehart, and Winston.

Townsend, P. (1957). *The family life of old people: An inquiry in East London*. Glencoe, IL: Free Press.

Troll, L. E. (1971). The family of later life: A decade review. *Journal of Marriage and the Family, 33,* 263-290.

Troll, L. E. (1975). *Early and middle adulthood*. Monterey, CA: Brooks/Cole.

Troll, L. E., Miller, S., & Atchley, R. (1978). *Families of later life*. Belmont, CA: Wadsworth.

Troll, L. E., & Smith, J. (1976). Attachment through the lifespan: Some questions about dyadic bonds among adults. *Human Development, 19,* 156-170.

6

Extended Kin as Helping Networks

Barbara Shore

The general fiction that older persons in the United States are alone, with no family or other supports, is not upheld by the research that has been done in this area. Many researchers point out that older persons do have considerably more family and extended ties than the popular myths and conventional wisdom suggest.

Data belie the stereotype that families are alienated from older persons (Shanas, 1979a, 1979b). The older person's first source of help is almost always family (a spouse, an adult child, a sibling) or friends and neighbors.

It is difficult to document the actual extent of informal help. Available studies are consistent in indicating that the elderly receive extensive informal help, however, and have been documented by Eustis, Greenberg, and Patten (1984).

Family Helpers

Relatives are likely to provide help before friends, and of relatives, a spouse, if available, is likely to provide the most help; then an adult child will be called upon, usually a daughter or daughter-in-law. Shanas (1979a) found that older men are more likely to receive care from their spouses, while older women are more likely to receive care from children living in or outside of the household. This difference is related to women's longer average life expectancy, and the greater chance of widowhood. Shanas (1979b) also notes that "a principle of substitution" seems to occur for elderly with no adult children. That is, other relatives, such as siblings, nieces, and nephews, take on the roles and responsibilities of children. It is also important to note that women comprise the majority of informal caregivers. These generalizations seem to be confirmed repeatedly by research studies (Shanas, 1979a; Johnson, 1979; Community Council of Greater New York, 1978; Lewis, McLauchlan, & Cantor, 1981). It has also been shown in at least one study that respondents report having only one helper, although additional helpers may be available if the current helper were to become incapacitated or unavailable (Eustis et al., 1984).

There seems to be far more natural reliance on family members for help than on friends. In fact, one demonstration project undertaking to pay family and friend helpers has had difficulty obtaining volunteers who are friends. Friends, however, may play a key role as a backup system (Community Council of Greater New York, 1978) and may serve an important role for older persons living alone who have few or no living relatives.

Many kinds of services are provided informally to functionally impaired older persons. A spouse can take over all or most home maintenance functions as well as serve as a home health aide helping with personal care such as bathing and dressing. The spouse may even provide some services usually performed by a nurse (perhaps under the tutelage of a public health or home nurse). The services most frequently provided by adult children, other relatives, or friends are social and emotional support and the tasks or chores that make it possible for the older person to maintain a separate residence, such as shopping, providing transportation, and unusual or heavy household chores. Relatives often give needed items as gifts and may give money as well.

The direction of support and giving is not all toward the older generations, except perhaps for the very old and impaired. Older persons seek to maintain reciprocity, and even persons 80+ responding in a national poll by Louis Harris and Associates reported giving their children and grandchildren gifts (86%), helping out in the case of illness (57%), helping with money (38%), fixing things around the house (20%), and other contributions (National Council on the Aging, 1974). However, a survey such as this is likely to miss the severely impaired elderly and to exclude institutionalized persons.

Other functions performed by family and friends relate to obtaining and using formal services (Shanas, 1979a; Sussman, 1976). Usually a spouse or adult child, with the older person or alone, seeks out available services such as home care or a nursing home. In cases of severe impairment or a domineering family member, this process may exclude the older person, possibly disallowing what consumer rights the individual may be able to exercise. The family or friend helper often continues to relate to the formal service provider throughout the older person's receipt of services. In addition, help from family and friends continues as a complement to formal services. How this occurs in part relates to the type of service being received.

The help of family and friends is therefore complementary to each type of care. Litwak (1965) has defined the complementarity generically, positing that informal helpers are better at providing emotional support, linkage, nontechnical, and idiosyncratic or emergency tasks, whereas formal caregivers offer routine and technical services.

Litwak's research found that the extended family form exists in modern urban society among middle-class families, that extended family relations are possible in an urban society, that geographical propinquity is an unnecessary condition of these relationships, and that occupational mobility is unhindered by the activities of the extended family. Some of the extended family activities include advice, financial assistance, temporary housing, and similar assistance given during such movement.

The evidence indicates, then, that the isolated nuclear family expected to emerge in modern industrial nations simply has not come to pass. Three- and four-generation family units who interact with and assist each other frequently in a variety of different circumstances seem the most common pattern.

Types of Help

Sussman and Burchinal found that a variety of help patterns exist between family members including the exchange of services, gifts, advice, and financial assistance. Moreover, the exchange of aid among family members flows in a variety of different directions including from parents to children and vice-versa, among siblings, and less frequently from more distant relatives. Financial assistance, apparently, more often flows from parents to children.

Social activities of family units are also a source of emotional support for family members. Many family sociologists believe that the difficulty of developing satisfactory primary relationships outside of the family in urban areas makes the extended family even more important to the individual. The extended family interaction and assistance pattern found in this country carries with it a system of satisfaction and support for older family members.

The protective function of the family, as it looks after all its members, is still one of its more useful and integrating aspects. While some of the support functions for older members of the society have been shifted off of the famly and onto the government (such as retirement income), the family still provides many and often the most crucial services for its older members.

The family still provides a very personal, primary, and immediate response to the needs of its elder members. While government services are important to America's elders, it is doubtful that it could ever replace vital family support functions.

There is, however, ambiguity in the findings. Evidence of extended family support is not as strong as that of immediate family support. Lopata (1978) found that "the hypothesis predicting an active modified extended family network functioning in American metropolitan centers, with exchanges of support from separate households, is not supported for any relatives other than children" (p. 362). This, however, does not obviate the existence of the modified extended family.

The University of Connecticut has done an excellent summary of some of this data. They note some of the knowledge and gaps (1982). In 1978, the Census Bureau reported that 30% of those 65 and older live alone (U.S. Special Committee on Aging, 1980). It is also estimated that there are 4.5 million childless elderly persons (E. Brody, 1978). Reports do indicate, however, that most elders have at least one significant other.

Substantial data also reveal that social supports from the family significantly delay the institutionalization of its older members (E. Brody, 1980; S. Brody, Poulshock, & Masciocchi, 1978; O'Brien & Wagner, 1980; Townsend, 1965). A comparison of demographic characteristics of frail elderly living in the community and those living in institutions strongly supports this contention. A disproportionately large number of older institutionalized elderly have no spouse and/or children (E. Brody, 1978; Townsend, 1965). Those with few relatives on hand find it more necessary to enter an institution (Townsend, 1965).

The literature suggests that approximately twice as many disabled older people reside at home as in institutions of any kind (E. Brody, 1978). O'Brien and Wagner (1980) believe that the availability of informal supports beyond the immediate family has a similar effect.

Cantor and Johnson's (1979) sample survey of New York City elderly indicated that only 4% did not have a significant other. Kaplan, Fleisher, and Regnier (1979), however, found that 28% of a sampled population had no significant others. The considerable discrepancy in these figures exemplifies the need for further investigation.

Another significant finding is articulated by Stanley Brody et al. (1978, p. 558): "differential levels of functional ability did not predict placement of chronically ill/disabled elderly in institutions or in the community. The most critical factor was living arrangement, primarily in the form of living with spouse and/or with children."

But what of the families who maintain their elderly in the community or their homes? The data supports the statement that they "strive to delay the institutionalization of the parent at considerable costs to themselves" (Robinson & Thurhner, 1979, p. 592). Stress of family members has increasingly become a concern of gerontologists. The U.S. Special Committee on Aging (1980) estimates that one in four families with whom an older person lives prior to admission experiences considerable stress before placement. Although evidence of change is available (Robinson & Thurhner, 1979), historically women usually have been the primary care providers for elders (E. Brody, 1978; Conklin, 1980). It can be agreed even today that they provide the most care and experience stress with this role more so than do men. Robinson and Thurhner (1979, p. 592) found that, "consistent with other studies, stress also resulted when the caretaking relationship was experienced as confining . . . as the child became more involved in performing services for the parent, and particularly when the child felt he had to always be available, the situation became problematic."

Further evidence of the family role in caring for very impaired old people is found in an official report to the Congress by the Comptroller-General of the United States (1977). Using a Cleveland, Ohio, sample, the researchers found that 14% of the elderly living at home were greatly or extremely impaired and were getting care at home the equivalent of that in institutions. They concluded that at all impairment levels family and friends provide 50% of the services received by old people and over 70% of the services received by the impaired.

Little (1982) reports on comparative international data for family support. This study highlights the varied nature of the extended kin as helping networks.

What about the silent majority of old people who are not significantly impaired? Here the attention of Shanas and other researchers has focused on evidence of interaction, such as the visiting patterns of old people and their adult children. Shanas (1979a) reports that more than half of old persons with surviving children had seen one of their children either the day they were interviewed or on the day before that. Three of every four persons with children saw one of their children during the week preceding the interview; only about one person in 10 had last seen one of their children more than a month before the interview.

When children were not seen during the previous week, about 4 of every 10 saw a brother or sister or other relative. About 13 of every 100 old people have no surviving children. For these persons there is some evidence that brothers, sisters, and other relatives tend to substitute for a child (Shanas, 1979, Tables 5 and 6).

Urban aged, according to Mahoney, appear to be less assisted and more socially isolated. This fits with other findings. A study of personal time dependency (PTD) in New York City defined the concepts as "the state of dependency requiring time-consuming help from another person." The researchers found that the PTD elderly and their families were predisposed to depression, with depression warranting clinical attention occurring in at least one in eight cases of elderly persons with PTD, and in one in four households in which a PTD person resides. For this highly dependent group, formal support personnel (nurses, aides, home helpers) provided about 15% of primary support services, and daughters, spouses, and other family members about 77%. There was little assistance from friends.

Further evidence of the role of the family and informal support in caring for a low-income inner-city New York sample is reported by Cantor and Johnson (1978). Two-thirds had immediate kin defined as "functional," either because they were co-resident or because they were in regular contact. Another 18% had kin, either a sibling or another relative. Only 15% were without at least one functional kin, and these were more apt to receive both affective and instrumental support from friends and relatives. Only 14% of the entire sample lacked visible informal supports.

Baum and Baum (1980) have reported in their studies of the role families play in the lives of elderly persons. Spouses and children seem to be in the foreground of the family network, but other relatives have some part in old age. In line with previous comments about "old preferring old" for intimacy, there is some evidence that involvement with relatives of one's own generation is strengthened in old age (Cumming & Schneider, 1961). But the breakdown into separate units with separate destinies which occurred at marriage is not really bridged again. Depending partially on proximity, contacts increase but never reach the frequency and regularity of those with children. It is only among those who never married that the sibling tie seems to persist unbroken, so that living together or at least keeping in regular touch and exchanging services is common. Single siblings can and sometimes do provide services to one another in a manner somewhat comparable to that of married couples. Unfortunately, brothers and sisters as family-intimacy options do not seem to be easily available to those who have married, even when the marriage has subsequently been dissolved. There also is the possibility as in other same-generation pairing patterns of losing even close sibling ties through death.

"Social class" applies to a number of different situations, and it appears that the closest extended family ties were in the lowest socio-economic groups (Sussman, 1976). Here, parents and children and often other relatives were more likely to live together or at least to remain in very close proximity. Poorer families apparently depended much more on one another for both economic and social support and were reluctant to leave the common neighborhood.

Minority Groups

In this country, there are many racial minorities and white ethnic groups, but knowledge of their family patterns is so far very limited (Kalish & Moriwaki, 1973). Some recent work has been done on the largest racial minority, the blacks, and we shall confine our remarks about subcultural variation to them. Statistics show that elderly black households were much less likely (67%) than elderly white households (83%) to contain only two persons. Four times as many elderly black families as white (20% versus 5%) had a child of 18 or younger in the home (Hendricks & Hendricks, 1977, p. 268). Thus, older blacks were less likely to be living as a couple alone, and their households were much more likely to encompass a broad age span.

Studies show more reliance on an extended kin system of a type somewhat different than that found for whites (Hirsh, Kent, & Silverman, 1972; Jackson, 1972a,b; Shimkin & Shimkin, 1975). The black family recognizes bilateral descent with more loosely related spouses and is centered on representatives of the oldest living generation. Affective ties are, however, concentrated on the matrilineal base so that younger descendants live either with or near the wife's mother. The emphasis on the female line is probably partly because black women are even more likely than white women to live longer than men, and partly because the greater economic participation of black women compared with white females during adult life has persisted for many more years. A relatively high degree of family connectedness of the black aged has been found on all socioeconomic levels, and the model of relations between older parents and children is one of parity or equality. Despite the greater emphasis on linearity, however, black elderly also expressed preference for intimacy at a distance, and family cohesion seemed to diminish among the economically more affluent. Thus, women, working-class persons, and blacks place less stress on independent living, but the overriding theme continues to be fairly consistent.

The Extended Family

There is further confirmation from empirical studies that the demise of the extended family has been greatly exaggerated (Adams, 1970; Troll, 1971). Interaction among kin remains quite frequent, with reciprocal provision of services, and people still consider their kinship ties important, even in the absence of residential proximity. It does not appear that urban life necessarily results in family deterioration or the replacement of kin ties by friends, neighbors, or voluntary associations.

The extended family has become more geographically dispersed, has lost its occupational importance, and no longer exercises rigid authority. Kin relations have become more open and voluntaristic. But family ties remain important in fulfilling social and emotional needs and providing a wide range of services. Even young people agree that people should maintain contact with families (Hill, 1970), and an ideology of "taking care of one's own" persists among younger cohorts, though they allow other social institutions to take major responsibility (Sussman, 1976).

Why has the extended family continued to play important roles in modern society? A combination of affection, general obligation, and long-term reciprocal commitments results in a "positive concern" for the well-being and activities of kin (Adams, 1970), because of which family ties tend to be more persistent than friendships, more narrowly based on sociability and similarity. How many of our friendships from college survive for 10 or 20 years? When we do develop "positive concern" about friends, we often say the person is "like a sister" or "like a father." This mutual interest keeps family ties alive over the years and across the distances which separate people. These family ties are sustained through ceremonies and holidays—weddings, funerals, christenings, Christmas, Passover, etc.

Modernization has not entirely stripped the extended family of its functions. For example, the first source of aid during illness or disasters is more likely to be the family than formal community agencies, which are still not a preferred source of help (Hill, 1970; Quarantelli, 1960). Family assistance is not considered welfare, but stems instead from a long history of reciprocity. Mobility need not reduce family ties, since a dispersed family can aid individuals who move (Litwak, 1960). Litwak and Szelenyi (1969) suggest that the extended family has survived because modern communication and a monetary economy allow the family to communicate and exchange services without face-to-face interaction. Neighbors can be of immediate assistance because of their proximity. Friends provide a reference group and consensus-based sociability. The virtue of the family is the long-term commitments and reciprocity which are built up. In addition, the extended family offers a network of interpersonal relationships to compensate for or replace ties which are missing or lost, for those who are single or widowed, for example. Thus, the aged can at least potentially be enmeshed in a complex family network of affectional ties and reciprocal assistance.

The evidence thus suggests that extended kin are available to elderly persons in much greater numbers than has been supposed. The kin that are available are of two types: same-generation and cross-generation. The same-generation network support system is composed of sisters, brothers, cousins, and so on and is often the immediate support in a neighborhood or housing community. In many neighborhoods, the basic network that exists is a crisscrossing of extended family relationships that provide a place and a set of supports for the persons involved.

The cross-generational experiences are often found when nieces, nephews, younger cousins, and grandchildren have been treated as substitute children over some time. The connections are often strong, as when "Aunt May" is viewed as a quasi-grandparent or as a comfort when stresses and tensions with parents are too great, or when the parenting experience is shared between several family members, as often occurs in an extended family (Shore, 1984). The supports and assistance that are provided are interesting and varied. However, they fall into the categories of other types of help unneeded and unused by older persons' emotional support and tangible services.

The antecedents appear to be strong family ties and connections that have been present over time. Since these patterns are often the crucial difference between survival and despair, the importance of these ties, and our understanding of them, is clearly increasing, in direct relationship to the increase in our aging population.

Social Networks

Informal, nonfamilial, and voluntary relationships of older people provide an important source of cultural meaning, social definition and value, personal identity, and emotional security. Social networks of older people are fundamental aspects of their everyday lives that involve a great deal of their time, energy, and activity. They are central to understanding the very nature and character of the social and social-psychological processes of aging. As childrearing and occupation recede in importance and as retirement or reduced work approaches, the importance of such networks as social support and mental and bodily health maintenance grows appreciably.

There is a surprising lack of research on the role of siblings and other close relatives throughout the life span. Of all human relationships, those between siblings have the longest duration, and the majority of people over age 70 have one or more living siblings. Yet little information is available on the quality and the nature of sibling relationships in youth or later life (Cicirelli, 1980; see also Chapter 5 herein). There is some evidence that actual contact decreases between elderly siblings, but most still report that they feel close to a brother or sister. Relationships tend to be especially durable between same-sexed siblings, and sisters in particular. In fact, a sister will often take on the role of mother with the death of the female parent. Many elderly people end their lives living with a sibling, but no information is available on how such arrangements develop or progress. Certainly, this area has rich research potential for those interested in close attachment over the life cycle.

Some final observations on the future of the family network are in order. It is easy to underestimate the strength of family networks. After all is said and done, they persist in the face of institutions and norms that "result in treating people as commodities rather than human beings" (Sussman, 1976, p. 238). If the society is to accommodate increasing numbers of elderly individuals in a humane, healthy way, we must investigate the potential of the family for care of the aged. Perhaps the family network should be supported by services and economic incentives under contractual arrangements between the government, institutions, and families. Money now channeled through institutions might go directly to families instead, and the growth of mobile services for patients living at home might be encouraged or directly subsidized. In the long run, this approach could cut hospital costs substantially. Paraprofessionals could be used more widely. Families might, with appropriate community support, provide special facilities in their homes. Contracts with individual families could provide for the nurturance, intimacy, and privacy older people require, as well as health care, physical rehabilitation, and economic relief. Benefits could be transferred through tax write-offs, property tax waivers, and low-cost loans for renovating or building independent quarters for the older person. Further, specific care and therapeutic services from established agencies might be made available to the family.

Sussman (1976) urges that removing sacrifice and deficit living from the linkage between elderly people and their families will engender a modern version of filial responsibility. Dependence need not create the mutual sense of guilt and neglect that can develop when "filial piety" is taxed to the breaking point. The alternatives currently available so often result in unsatisfactory or even disastrous situations that suggestions such as institutional support for the family deserve serious consideration.

References

Adams, B. (1970). Isolation, function, and beyond: American kinship in the 1960's. *Journal of Marriage and the Family, 32,* 575–597.

Anderson (Eustis), N. N., Patten, S. K., & Greenberg, J. N. (1980). A comparison of home care and nursing home care for older persons in Minnesota. Minneapolis: Hubert H. Humphrey Institute of Public Affairs and the Center for Health Services Research, University of Minnesota.

Baum, M., & Baum, R. C. (1980). *Growing old: A societal perspective.* Englewood Cliffs, NJ: Prentice-Hall.

Brody, E. (July 1978). The Aging of the Family. *The Annals of the American Academy,* 13–27.

Brody, E. (June 15, 1980). *Institutions and alternatives.* Lecture presented at the Gerontology Forum '80.

Brody, S. J., Poulshock, W., & Masciocchi, C. F. (Dec. 1978). The family caring unit: A major consideration in the long-term care support system. *Gerontologist, 18*(6), 556–561.

Cantor, M. H., & Johnson, J. L. (Nov. 1978). *The informal support system of the "familyless" elder—who takes over?* Paper presented at the 31st Annual Meeting of the U.S. Gerontological Society, Dallas, TX.

Cantor, M. H., & Johnson, J. L. (Dec. 1979). Neighbors and friends. *Research on Aging, 1*(4), 434–463.

Cicirelli, V. (1980). Sibling relationships: A life span perspective. In L. W. Poon (Ed.), *Aging in the 1980's.* Washington, DC: American Psychological Association.

Community Council of Greater New York. (1978). *Dependency in the elderly in New York City.* New York: Author.

Comptroller-General of the U.S. Report to the Congress. (Dec. 30, 1977). Home health—the need for a national policy to better provide for the elderly. Washington, DC: U.S. Government Printing Office (HRD-78-19).

Conklin, C. (Nov. 1980). Rural community care-givers. *Social Work, 25*(6), 495–496.

Cumming, E., & Schneider, D. M. (1961). Sibling, solidarity: A property of American kinship. *American Anthropologist, 63,* 498–507.

Eustis, N. N., Greenberg, J. N., & Patten, S. K. (1984). *Long term care for older persons: A policy perspective.* Monterey, CA: Brooks/Cole.

Hendricks, J., & Hendricks, C. D. (1977). Aging in mass society, myths and realities. Cambridge, MA: Winthrop.

Hill, R. (1970). Family development in three generations. Cambridge, MA: Schenkman.

Hirsch, D., Kent, D. P., & Silverman, S. L. (1972). Homogeneity and heterogeneity among low-income negro and white aged (pp. 484–500). In D. P. Kent, R. Kastenbaum, & S. Sherwood (Eds.), *Research planning and action for the elderly: The power and potential of social sciences.* New York: Behavioral Publications.

Jackson, J. J. (1972a). Comparative life styles and family and friend relationships among older black women. *Family Coordinator, 21,* 477–485.

Jackson, J. J. (1972b). Marital life among aging blacks. *Family Coordinator, 21,* 21–27.

Johnson, C. L. (Nov. 1979). *Impediments to family supports to dependent elderly: An analysis of the primary caregivers.* Paper presented at the Annual Meeting of the Gerontological Society, Washington, DC.

Kalish, R. A., & Moriwaki, S. (1973). The world of the elderly Asian American. *Journal of Social Issues, 29*(2), 187–209.

Kaplan, B. H., Fleisher, D., & Regnier, V. (Nov. 29, 1979). *Helping networks.* Paper presented at the 32nd Annual Scientific Meeting of the Gerontological Society, Washington, DC.

Lewis, M. S., McLauchlan, W. G., & Cantor, M. (1981). *Impact on informal supports of the entrance of the formal organization on a homemaker population.* New York: Center of Gerontology, Fordham University.

Little, V. C. (1982). International symposium: The family as a source of support for the elderly. *The Gerontologist, 22,* 108.

Litwack, E. (1965). Extended kin relations in an industrial democratic society. In E. Shanas & G. Streib (Eds.), *Social structure and the family: Generational relations.* Englewood Cliffs, NJ: Prentice-Hall.

Litwak, E. (Winter 1959-60). The use of extended family groups in the achievement of social goals: Some policy implications. *Social Problems, 7,* 177–187.

Litwak, E., & Szelenyi, I. (1969). Primary group structures and their functions: Kin, neighbors, and friends. *American Sociological Review, 34,* 465–481.

Lopata, H. (May 1978). Contributions of extended families to the support systems of metropolitan area widows. *Journal of Marriage and the Family*, 355–384.

Mahoney, K. (Nov. 1977). *A national perspective on community differences in the interaction of the aged with their adult children.* Paper read at the 30th Annual Meeting of the U.S. Gerontological Society, San Francisco, CA.

National Council on the Aging. (1974). *The myth and reality of aging.* New York: Author.

O'Brien, J. E., & Wagner, D. L. (Feb. 1980). Help seeking by the frail elderly: Problems in network analysis. *Gerontologist, 19*(1), 78–83.

Quarantelli, E. (1960). A note on the protective function of the family in disasters. *Marriage and Family Living, 22,* 263–264.

Robinson, B., & Thurhner, M. (Dec. 1979). Taking care of aged parents: A family cycle transition. *Gerontologist, 19*(6), 586–594.

Shanas, E. (1979a). The family as a social support system in old age. *The Gerontologist, 19,* 169–174.

Shanas, E. (1979b). Social myth as hypothesis: The case of the family relations of older people. *The Gerontologist, 19,* 3–9.

Shimkin, D. B., & Shimkin, E. M. (1975). *The extended family in United States black societies: Findings and problems.* Unpublished paper, Department of Anthropology, University of Illinois, Urbana-Champaign.

Shore, B. K. Current research, in process (1984).

Sussman, M. B. (1976). The family life of old people. In R. H. Binstock & E. Shanas (Eds.), *Handbook of aging and the social sciences* (pp. 218–243). New York: Van Nostrand Reinhold.

Sussman, M. B., & Stroud, M. W. (1959–1964). *Studies in chronic illness and the family* (unpublished paper, Western Reserve University and Highland View Hospital), pp. 1–25.

Townsend, P. (1965). On the likelihood of admission to an institution. In E. Shanas & G. F. Streib (Eds.), *Social structure and the family: Generational relations.* Englewood Cliffs, NJ: Prentice-Hall.

Troll, L. (1971). The family of later life: A decade review. *Journal of Marriage and the Family, 33,* 263–290.

U.S. Special Committee on Aging. (May 1980). *Future directions for aging policy: A human services model.* Comm. Pub. No. 96-226.

University of Connecticut, School of Social Work, Career Training Program on Aging. (1982). *Social work and the elderly: The growing challenge.* Storrs, CT: Author.

Part III
Community Relations

7

The Role of Friends and Neighbors in Providing Social Support

George R. Peters
Marvin A. Kaiser

Introduction

In this chapter we examine the role played by friends and neighbors in providing support to older people. The importance of friendship, neighboring, and confidant relationships as elements in the broader array of social supports available to the elderly has great currency in more recent gerontological research and practice. Moreover, such social supports are now emphasized in public policy regarding the elderly. We shall first discuss briefly the emergent research, practice, and policy interest in friendship and neighboring. We then examine friendship and neighboring as components of social support systems. We summarize what is currently known about friendship and neighboring in old age. Finally, we examine gaps in our knowledge and suggest further avenues of research.

The literature on friendship broadly conceived is not extensive. During the 1950s and 1960s social psychologists conducted a number of studies on interpersonal choices in small group settings, with particular emphasis upon the use of sociometric techniques. To a large extent, these studies were conducted within laboratory settings, focused on a narrow domain of questions, and were almost exclusively oriented to younger adults who were typically students. In relative terms, more is known about friendship among children and college students than about adult friendships (see Berscheid & Walster, 1969; Lindzey & Byrne, 1969). As a consequence, findings on the friendship relations of adults are scattered, are frequently lacking rigorously developed conceptual frameworks, and offer only adjunctive considerations to the interests of researchers. With notable exceptions (e.g., Kutner et al., 1956) studies of friendship during this period and through the early 1960s did not deal extensively with friendship in old age. Concerted efforts by a large number of researchers to understand friendship in the later years and across the life cycle began to emerge in the middle 1960s and has continued to the present.

To be sure, friendship and neighboring in the later years have long been viewed as valued forms of relating to others and as important social resources irrespective of sex, ethnicity, religious belief, geographic locale, social class, economic situation, or educational background. Whether intuitively or in terms of the scanty data provided by early studies, involvement with friends and neighbors has been recognized as a source of emotional support and intimacy necessary to psychic well-being. Friendship and neighboring are prevalent forms of social intercourse in which pleasure and enjoyment are experienced, and implicit networks through which people exchange services, assistance, information, and advice which far exceeds the capacity or ability of existing formal service agencies to provide regardless of how humanitarian their mission. Friendship and neighboring also serve as important adjuncts to the family as providers of services, emotional support, and intimacy, but in a form not always available within family settings. Beyond these considerations, friendship and neighbor relations in old age can provide an important mechanism for social integration into the community and the broader society. To illustrate, in times of loss or crisis friends and neighbors often provide not only support but a continuing link to the community. When the crisis is past, friends and neighbors can be of invaluable assistance in helping individuals to reestablish former community involvements or form new ones.

Nonetheless, despite the recognized implicit value of such ties, friendship and neighboring generally, and particularly in old age, have been largely treated as residual categories until recently. That is, they were studied, if at all, to aid in the understanding of other social roles and relationships such as kinship or work, or significant life events such as widowhood or retirement. Friendship and neighboring as components of informal systems available in varying degrees to older people are now of interest to researchers, policymakers, and practitioners alike.

Social Policy, Social Research, and Informal Support Systems

In part, the heightened interest in informal support systems is a response to the demand for information as a basis for policy formulation. More substantively, it reflects the development of social network analysis both as a methodology and as a conceptual framework for problem formulation. Friends and neighbors, along with kin, comprise principle elements of informal social networks. The delineation, description, and analysis of these networks, and the ways in which they intersect in the lives of older people as well as the examination of their outcomes for individual well-being, has become a major research thrust.

The present emphasis upon friendship and neighboring, along with other social support elements, then, represents a convergence of substantive research concerns and policy issues. The so-called graying of America with all its implications for the economic, social, and political structures of American society has confronted policymakers with a set of issues and questions heretofore addressed in piecemeal fashion, if at all. Now it is not possible to ignore policy issues pertaining to an aging America. Thus, questions about our ability and willingness as a society to support an aging population, the manner and mechanisms for providing such support, and the extent to which the society and its communities have obligations to older citizens for ensuring maximally feasible independent lifestyles and making provisions for well-being in the later years have become pressing issues at all levels of government.

Public agencies and their programs, while necessary components of the support system for elderly persons, are not sufficient to respond to the manifold needs of older Americans. The economic, social, psychological, and political constraints of formal support systems and the reticence of many older people to use them reflect and rest upon certain value orientations endemic to American society. Strong orientations toward minimizing governmental involvement and regulation in individual affairs, maximizing local input and control over matters pertaining to citizen well-being, opposition to social welfare, the importance of volunteerism and community participation, and the right of individuals to live independent lives are espoused—even if not always acted upon—by people of all ages, including older Americans.

Thus, for pragmatic economic, social, psychological, and political reasons, as well as in recognition of the value bases upon which such pragmatic reasons rest, policymakers have refocused on the informal support system of kin, friends, neighbors, and community-based volunteer groups as resources essential to providing support to the elderly. The informal system did not have to be created since it was already in existence and, in fact, predated most available formal service systems. For policymakers key questions concern how and in what ways such informal systems function to provide assistance to its older members. It has become important to identify points of intersection and divergence between formal and informal systems for purposes of finding areas in which one as opposed to the other, or both together, provide a more effective response to needs. Not as fully recognized an issue by policymakers, but implicit nonetheless, is the fact that formal and informal systems are differently structured, often exist for different purposes and reasons, and typically function in quite different ways. Thus, the question of conflict between the demands, expectations, and constraints of the two systems have become relevant for policymakers and practitioners. It is from researchers that answers to such questions are sought.

For their part, researchers have begun to vigorously address such questions but have found that information from earlier studies either had serious methodological and conceptual problems or often were inadequate to directly apply to the questions being raised. Thus, much work was necessary in regard to conceptualizing friendship and neighboring, developing methodologies and techniques of measuring dimensions of these relationships, and developing data bases sound enough to allow for generalizing results. In large part, this preparatory work continues.

The convergence of policy and research interests is fortunate in the sense that inducements for expanding knowledge and understanding friendship and neighboring among adults must increase. However, the interests and needs of researchers and policymakers are seldom identical. For example, policymakers want and need rapidly acquired, easily accessible, and fairly straightforward answers that provide a basis for and ease the dilemmas of decision making. Researchers are often uneasy about such requests or frequently unable to honor them since data necessary to reliably answer such questions are nonexistent or inadequate or contains apparent or real inconsistencies requiring further examination before valid conclusions can be drawn.

Friends and Neighbors as Components of the Informal Support System

Despite the caveats just presented and particularly with the development of social network analyses, the contours of informal support systems are now being delineated and the importance of informal ties in the everyday lives of older people better understood. In particular, the special role played by friends and neighbors is becoming apparent. This in no way negates the importance of governmental agency and organizational roles in the provision of entitlements and services necessary to well-being in old age. Indeed, as Cantor (1979) points out, most available information supports the theory of shared functions between formal organizations and primary groups. Most simply stated, the theory posits that, because of their different structures, formal bureaucratic organizations and informal groups such as kin, friends, and neighbors respond to different types of problems, but that both are necessary components of the social support system. Litwak and his colleagues who initially delineated the theory of shared functions argue effectively that given their different structures and the nature of the tasks they perform, formal and informal support systems are complementary and must function together if the welfare of older people is to be realized (Dono et al., 1979; Litwak, 1965; Litwak & Figueira, 1968; Litwak & Meyer, 1974). There is reason to believe, however, that the formal and informal support systems do not always intersect in an effective fashion. Several studies (O'Brien & Wagner, 1980; Wagner & Keast, 1981; Ward, Sherman, & LaGory, 1984) suggest that informal support group ties may inhibit rather than enhance access to needed services from formal support systems. Litwak (1970) suggests that ideally the two systems should operate at some midpoint of social distance close enough to cooperate but not so close as to conflict.

Following Cantor (1979), "the social support system is broadly defined as including those informal and formal functions and services which enable an older person to remain independent in the community" (p. 441). Such supports span the arena of assistance and aid from basic entitlements provided through social policy and services rendered by bureaucratic organizations through more personal help received from family, friends, and neighbors. To be effective a support system must respond to three types of needs: socialization, conducting the tasks of daily living, and assisting in times of need.

Dono et al. (1979) and Cantor (1979) argue that informal supports from kin, friends, and neighbors are most appropriate in situations involving unpredictable and idiosyncratic need, where fast and flexible decision making is involved, or where knowledge based on everyday socialization and intimate interaction is the more useful. Formal organizations are best able to handle tasks requiring the application of technical knowledge uniformly and impartially to large aggregates of people. Formal systems, by legislative action and through their agen-

cies and organizations, determine basic entitlements and deliver services in the areas of income maintenance, health, housing, safety,
education, and transportation. Informal support systems are ready
sources of support in providing more personal aid, meeting individualized needs involved in crisis assistance and help during illness, and
with the tasks of daily living, tension reduction, and socialization.

Kin, friends, and neighbors comprise the informal support system
by providing affective and instrumental assistance which enhances the
ability of the older person to live independently in the community.
However, as Cantor (1979) points out, merely having one or more of
these supports does not necessarily guarantee that older people will
receive support from those around them. Thus, it is necessary to add
the proviso that kin, neighbors, and friends actually function in the
capacity of support givers by being available and involved in ongoing
relationships with older persons so as to make meaningful support a
possibility.

Further, it is important to recognize that in terms of their structure
and the nature of tasks performed, the three types of informal support
given may differ from one another. A substantial number of studies
document the ways in which informal support groups differ structurally (e.g., Adams, 1967; Babchuk, 1965, 1978; Cantor, 1979; Dono
et al., 1979; Hoyt & Babchuk, 1983; Litwak & Szelenyi, 1969; Muir &
Weinstein, 1962; Ward et al., 1984). Such structural differences provide the basis for defining the three types of informal support systems.

Kinship ties are more or less permanent relationships governed to
some degree by ascription, inevitably associated with a sense of obligation—whether moral or legal and whether honored or not—and
based on long-term commitment. The characteristics produce what
Adams (1967) calls positive concern. In contrast, friendship ties are
characterized by voluntary involvement, affective bonds, and consensus. Friends may, and frequently do, develop a strong and long-lived
sense of commitment to one another. However, such commitment
rests more upon the continued willingness of the friends to commit to
one another than upon the sense of obligation engendered by blood
ties. Neighborhood ties resemble friendship in many respects, but
require residential proximity and are more likely than either kin or
friend ties to be characterized by short-term commitment. As will be
seen, neighbors may in fact be friends, but this is not necessarily the
case for all neighbors. More typically, neighbors develop friendly
relations more characteristic of acquaintanceships in which congenial-
ity and helpfulness are expected behaviors mutually beneficial to all
involved.

Although there is general agreement on the defining components of friendship and neighboring just provided, the treatment of these relationships in research suffers from some rather serious problems. In comparative terms more is known about the more easily quantifiable and to some extent more superficial aspects of friendship such as frequency and scope of interaction with friends and neighbors than is understood about the content of friendships—that is, what subjective meanings does friendship have for people and for the researcher—and their significance in the lives of older people. For example, it is particularly important to understand how friendship patterns change as people age. We know something of this, but hardly with the depth, breadth, and precision required either for theory building or practical applications (e.g., Hess, 1971; Riley, Foner, Hess, & Toby, 1969; Shulman, 1975). Much more needs to be known about the qualitative dimensions of friendship in old age. A number of studies, for example, suggest the importance of confidants in the lives of the elderly (Babchuk, 1978; Lowenthal & Haven, 1968; Powers & Bultena, 1976; Strain & Chapple, 1982). We do not yet comprehend to what extent, under what conditions, and in regard to what issues friends and neighbors are selected as confidants. Some studies indicate that not all friends are confidants and that relations with confidant friends may have quite different significance for the person than relations with nonconfidant friends (Babchuk, 1978; Strain & Chapple, 1982). But exactly how relations differ with confidant friends, friends who are close but are not confidants, and people who are less intimate yet considered friends is not yet well understood.

Researchers have not been consistent in their techniques of gathering information on friendships. Some ask questions about friends, others about close friends, and still others about the most intimate of friends. Unfortunately, there has been a tendency in the literature to treat these different catgories of friendships as synonymous. In some studies respondents are queried about all friends, while in others information is gathered on a number of friends specified by the researcher. With some exceptions (e.g., Cohen & Rajkowski, 1982; Shulman, 1975), information on friendship and neighboring is obtained from the respondent only. Thus, it is difficult to assure the accuracy of respondent reports or to know whether relationships with friends and neighbors are reciprocated. In the main, current research focuses on dyadic friendships rather than on delineating the entire network of friendships and neighboring relations a person has. Until full network analyses are accomplished, it will be difficult to assess precisely how friends and neighbors support one another (Cohen &

Rajkowski, 1982). It is important to keep these considerations in mind as the literature on friends and neighbors as support givers is reviewed below.

Considerable evidence suggests that informal support groups are not readily substitutable for or interchangeable with one another (Babchuk, 1965, 1978; Blau, 1973; Dono et al., 1979; Gordon, 1977; Hoyt & Babchuk, 1983; Litwak & Szelenyi, 1969; Rosow, 1967). Although the matter is hardly a simple one, and there are exceptions to the generalizations which follow, it appears empirically that the kinship group is best able to handle nontechnical tasks involving long-term commitments, for example, planned care during a prolonged illness (Sussman, 1965). Neighbors seem best prepared to provide assistance of a nontechnical sort which requires fast or immediate action or entails close proximity so that fairly close and continuous surveillance is possible. Thus, neighbors are both available and present to assist in emergencies or to keep an eye on the house, listen for the telephone, or check in during an illness with an ease and facility typically not possible for kin and friends residing outside the immediate neighborhood (Dono et al., 1979). Friends are generally similar to one another in characteristics such as age (Adams, 1967; Riley & Foner, 1968), life status and role (Blau, 1961; Rosow, 1967), and sex and socioeconomic status (Booth & Hess, 1974; Powers & Bultena, 1976; Rosow, 1967). Because of these similarities, friends share a repertoire of common experience and often are living through similar role changes. Such bonds make friends valuable aids in the learning of new and altered roles and in the relinquishment of old ones (Dono et al., 1979; Hess, 1972; Rosow, 1967). Given that friendships are consensually based and are maintained with fewer obligatory or choice constraints than are either kinship ties or neighbor relations, it follows that friends should be an important source of affective and emotional support that exceeds legitimate claims on neighbors and does not carry the obligatory demands of kinship.

While it is true that informal support groups are structurally different, seem to be more effective in the performance of particular tasks, and are generally nonsubstitutable, there is also evidence of overlap between them (Dono et al., 1979). Cantor (1979), for example, suggests that in highly dense urban areas older people tend to be neighborhood-bound and functional friends most frequently live in the neighborhood, thus producing a blurring of the distinctions made between neighbors and friends. Other research suggests that people make distinctions among kin in terms of shared intimacy (Hoyt & Babchuk, 1983) and that some kin are, in fact, selected and identified as friends (Bultena, Powers, Falkman, & Frederick, 1971; Laumann,

1966; Shulman, 1975; Verbrugge, 1979). There are often cases of long-lived friendships in which the friends actually think of one another as being like relatives and not just as friends (Adams, 1967; Ballweg, 1969). Moreover, there are certainly frequent incidents of kin residing in the neighborhood and actually functioning as a neighbor to an older person. Indeed, such findings have led some researchers to suggest that kin and friendship ties are becoming structurally more similar and, as a consequence, to some degree more interchangeable (Adams, 1967).

The tendency for relations to overlap with one another has been called role "multiplexity" (Boissevain, 1974; Boissevain & Mitchell, 1973; Fischer et al., 1977; Verbrugge, 1979). The term recognizes that in contemporary American society some ties with intimates are limited and unidimensional while others are characterized by the coexistence of two or more roles—for example, being identified both as a relative and a friend (Hoyt & Babchuk, 1983). While this does not deny the recognized conceptual usefulness of distinguishing support roles played by kin, friends, and neighbors, it is a reminder that real-life situations of older people may be more complex and diverse than the typology of three networks performing specific tasks might suggest.

These considerations have led to the development of two major models for understanding how informal support systems operate in the lives of older people (see Cantor, 1979). The task-specific model proposed by Litwak in his theory of shared functions emphasizes the nature of the task and the differential structural characteristics of support groups. The hierarchical-compensatory model posited by Cantor (1979) argues that support giving rests more upon the primacy of the relationship of the support giver to the elderly person than upon the nature of the task. The model postulates an ordering in the selection of support givers such that among the elderly kin generally are the preferred sources of support followed by significant others such as friends and neighbors, and only then by formal organizations. When the preferred element is absent, other groups operate in a compensatory fashion as replacement. As will be seen, both models have received empirical support.

Friendship and Neighboring in Old Age

While the focus of this chapter is on friendship and neighboring among the elderly, we do not divide the chapter into sections which treat separately these two components of the informal support system. Much of the literature fails to distinguish the two types of relationships in any systematic fashion. Moreover, as was suggested above, in real life, the two roles often overlap so that it is frequently difficult to divide the two roles in any meaningful fashion. This is particularly so for older people. It is not suggested that all neighbors are friends and clearly not all friends are neighbors. But it does indicate that there are friendly relations existing between older people and those neighbors with whom they engage in exchange and from whom they receive assistance.

Contrary to earlier conceptions and concerns about the isolated older person who, because of the disengagement process, was presumably experiencing traumatic role losses, it appears that the large majority of older people maintain ties with friends and neighbors well into later life and that few older people are isolated (Babchuk, 1978; Riley & Foner, 1968; Rosow, 1967). Moreover, numerous studies on diverse older populations show that interaction with friends and neighbors is frequent (Arling, 1976; Babchuk, 1978; Cantor, 1979; Powers & Bultena, 1976; Shanas, 1962; Townsend, 1957). There are a number of variables which influence the maintenance of friendship relations in old age and frequency of interaction with friends. Principle among these are age and sex of the older person, although age probably reflects the impact of other conditions generally associated with growing older. Neighbors move away, friends die, declines in health which typically accompany advanced old age may limit the mobility of the individual thereby also reducing abilities to remain active with friends and neighbors or to make new friendships. Lowered financial resources can reduce opportunities for interaction with friends. Marital status, living arrangements, and place of residence are also related to friendship and neighboring activities.

The numbers of friends reported by older people varies from study to study. The range can be from as few as two or three friends on the average (Babchuk, 1978) to everyone in the community (Philblad & Adams, 1972). There are both substantive and methodological reasons for such variation. Thus, size of community, rural–urban locale, and ethnic and personal differences in determining what constitutes a friend help to explain some of the variation. For example, respondents in the Philblad and Adams study were residents of a small, rural Missouri town where there exist both an opportunity and an expectation to know and maintain friendly relations with all community members, at least in public statements. Although data on ethnic group definitions of friendship and of older members of ethnic communities is lacking, the work of Creecy and Wright (1979), Sterne, Phillips, and Rabushka (1974), Jackson and Wood (1976), and Hawkins (1978) suggests that black elderly may hold a looser conception of what constitutes a friend, and that their life conditions combined with this conception render many black elderly incapable of keeping friendships intact.

Researchers have not always been consistent or precise in their methods of obtaining information on friendshp. Thus, depending on how questions are asked, friends may refer to people with whom one maintains friendly relations, very close friends, confidante friends, or functional friends. Obviously, variations in methods employed will produce differences in results. Thus, while it is impossible to draw a definitive conclusion on the numbers of friends older people have, it is reasonably safe to conclude that the majority of older people maintain a small core of very intimate friends and a larger number of contacts which are friendly in nature, and that few older people are isolated from contacts with friends. Interestingly, this pattern is not greatly different than that reported for younger adult populations (Babchuk, 1965).

The close friendships of older people are typically stable, long-term relationships (Babchuk, 1978; Shulman, 1975). It is not unusual for older people to identify as friends persons met in childhood or early adulthood with whom they have maintained close ties over the years. There is a tendency for certain kinds of friendship to persist even when friends are no longer in close proximity (Babchuk & Bates, 1963; Hess, 1971). At the same time older people do make new friendships (Riley & Foner, 1968). The ability to make new friendships depends upon available opportunities. Some older people report fewer opportunities for making new friendships (Shanas, 1962; Townsend, 1957) while others report greater opportunities (Martel & Morris, 1960; Zborowski & Eyde, 1962). Hess (1972) points out that the very young and very old are severely restricted in the distances they can cover to recruit or maintain friendships. Thus, limitations on mobility and separation from contexts for meeting and making new friends—for example, work, voluntary associations—can reduce greatly the likelihood of forming new relationships. This, of course, emphasizes the importance of existing friendships for older people and the impact that disruptions of such friendships can have.

Older people in their advanced years (the old-old) are less likely than other old people to visit friends and neighbors frequently (Babchuk, 1978; Blau, 1961; Hunter & Maurice, 1953; Riley & Foner, 1968), although a minority report more participation (Riley & Foner, 1968; Shanas, 1962; Smith, 1966). It is likely that such results do not reflect the effects of age per se but rather the impact of other variables associated with aging. Principle among such variables are declines in health status or financial security and consequent reductions in mobility. The literature is consistent in pointing to the negative effect of poor health on the maintenance of interaction with friends and neighbors (Arling, 1976; Babchuk, 1978; Clark & Anderson, 1967; Hunter & Maurice, 1953; Lowenthal & Boler, 1965; Riley & Foner, 1968; Shanas, 1962; Tallmar & Kutner, 1969). Similar results are found for financial security (Blau, 1961; Kutner et al., 1956; Lawton & Simon, 1968; Shanas, 1962). Health status has two effects upon the maintenance of friendship and neighboring relationships. First, the capacity of the person to engage in activities with friends lessens. That means that whatever activities are shared must take into account the older person's condition and increasingly requires initiation by the friends or neighbors. Moreover, the older person becomes more dependent upon the immediate environment for the formation and maintenance of friendship and neighboring activities (Hess, 1972; Lawton & Simon, 1968). Second, the nature of the relationship itself is altered. Thus, exchanges and the provision of support which had earlier been negotiated and reciprocal become more unidirectional, where neighbors and friends assume greater responsibility for the provision of emotional support and assistance with the activities of daily life. Financial insecurity also contributes to the dependence of the older person on others and prevents individuals from participating fully in activities.

Sex Differences in the
Friendship Behavior of Older People

A number of studies report differences between older men and women in regard to their friendship relations. The differences are concerned less with merely having friends and neighbors and visiting with them than with the relative intimacy of the ties which are formed. Indeed, men and women alike say that their friends and neighbors are important to them and that they do things with and for one another, and the numbers of men and women who report having no friends and neighbors are roughly equivalent. Men tend to report a wider range of social contacts than women, but women are more likely to have intimate friends in later life. Men more often than women report never having had an intimate friend and in old age are less likely than women to replace a relationship that has been terminated. For women, friendships are more stable, long-lived, and intense (Arth, 1962; Babchuk, 1978; Blau, 1961; Booth, 1972; Booth & Hess, 1974; Cantor, 1979; Lowenthal, Thurner, & Chiriboga, 1975; Moss, Gottesman, & Kleban,

1976; Powers & Bultena, 1976; Rosenkaimer, Saperstent, Ishikazi, & MacBride, 1968; Rosow, 1967; Strain & Chappell, 1982). Whereas men rely most heavily on their marriage and spouse for emotional intimacy (Blau, 1973; Haas-Hawkings, 1978; Huyck, 1976; Lowenthal & Haven, 1968; Rosenkaimer, Saperstent, Ishikazi, & MacBride, 1968; Rutzen 1977; Trela & Jackson, 1976), women seem to have a greater affinity for intimate friendships and a wider range of intimate social contacts outside the immediate family (Hess, 1979; Powers & Bultena, 1976).

Hess (1979) suggests that gender variations in friendship patterns reflect the differential life expectancy and marriage age of men and women. At older age levels the proportion of men with a living spouse far exceeds that of women. Thus, in part, men simply may have the advantage and luxury of a spouse who is present and with whom intimacies may be shared. However, throughout adulthood women seem to be more prone to sharing intimacies with friends than do men. This suggests that variations in friendship patterns may be an expression of differences in sex-role socialization. Drawing upon the work of numerous scholars, Hess (1979) argues that the American male socialization experience emphasizes sociability and friendliness, characteristics compatible with adult male occupational roles, but deemphasizes expressions of intimacy and the disclosure of highly personal matters. Females, on the other hand, are encouraged to be specialists in human relations, a role which emphasizes the receipt and transmission of highly personal communications, sensitivity to others, and frequent intimate disclosures. Such characteristics, it can be argued, are highly functional to female adult roles. As a result, men tend to be less accurate perceivers of others and less responsive to subtle emotional cues. Women, on the other hand, are trained to excel in precisely these attributes.

To be sure, such observations are highly general and hardly apply to all men and women in American society. To the extent that they are valid, however, they provide a framework for understanding the gender variations in friendship patterns. As Hess (1979) suggests, men, because of their tendency to focus upon the marriage and spouse for intimacy, may experience greater trauma if that relationship is disrupted, despite the fact that they may have had a wider range of social involvements throughout their lives, because they lack the reservoir of close interpersonal relations characteristic of women. Women's expertise in personal relations allows them more flexibility in constructing social support networks, in replacing relationships which are lost, and ultimately in maintaining a more functional set of resources to deal with the vicissitudes of old age.

The Neighborhood and Friendship

The neighborhood or immediate residential environment is an important resource for the formation of friendships among older people (Arling, 1976; Cantor, 1979; Carp, 1966; Clark & Anderson, 1967; Rosenberg, 1967, 1970; Rosow, 1967; Schulman, 1975). Moreover, length of residence in a neighborhood is positively related to having friends in the neighborhood (Langford, 1962; Riley & Foner, 1968). Some studies (Langford, 1962; Youmans, 1962) suggest that ties with friends are fewer and less likely in large cities than in smaller communities, but Cantor's (1979) work on the inner-city elderly in New York City indicates that having friends in the neighborhood is not unusual in urban areas. Indeed, she argues that, with the exception of those in the higher socioeconomic strata, older people in the city tend to be neighborhood-bound.

Hess (1972) provides two reasons for the prominence of neighborhood friendships in the lives of older people. First, growing older can restrict the distances individuals can travel to recruit or maintain friendships. This would be particularly true for those who lack financial resources or who have health and mobility problems. Thus, the immediate neighborhood becomes a key place for the formation of friendships. Second, older people, because they typically reside in their neighborhood for long periods of time, simply have had greater opportunity to establish friendships, particularly "old" and close friendships in their immediate environment.

To conclude that the neighborhood or local community is the sole source of friendships for older people would be inaccurate. Indeed Schulman (1975) reports that neighbors as intimate friends comprise only a portion of the close friendships that people have. Work by Babchuk and his colleagues (1965, 1978; Babchuk & Bates, 1963) and Hess (1971) suggests that people, including the aged, typically include as friends others who are no longer in close proximity. These are often long-lived friendships which in the minds and reports of respondents represent close and abiding ties despite the fact that distance does not permit frequent or face-to-face interaction and exchange. Moreover, other contexts such as work, voluntary associations, and the church also provide places and opportunities for the formation of friendships, regardless of the place of residence of the friends.

Two additional points are relevant in this context. First, we have focused here on neighbors as friends, and perhaps as close friends. Obviously, most people will not name all neighbors as friends, much less close friends, despite the fact that they may be on friendly terms with their neighbors. Some neighbors may have little to do with one

another or possibly actively dislike one another. Being on friendly
terms may range from merely speaking to one another when meeting
to exchanging or providing assistance on a regular basis. The pool of
all neighbors then is likely to be greater than the number of neighbors
with whom one is friendly, which is greater than the number of
neighbor-friends. Thus, as with other relationships, including kin ties
(Hoyt & Babchuk, 1983), selective processes occur which determine
who will be chosen from among the pool of eligibles for exchanges or
assistance whether instrumental or affective. It is this type of reasoning
that led Cantor (1979) to introduce the concept of functionality of
support givers. For Cantor, a functional neighbor is one whom the
respondent knows well and interacts with in one or more instrumental
or affective ways. A functional friend is one whom the respondent sees
at least monthly and is in phone contact with at least weekly. Her data
show that restricting the definition of support givers in this way reduces the counts of friends and neighbors who ostensibly are available
for aid and assistance. On the other hand, having at least one functional significant other may in most cases be sufficient to meet the
needs of everyday living.

Second, that neighbors may become friends and even very close
friends emphasizes the fact that roles overlap and that multiplex relationships are fairly frequent (Verbrugge, 1977). Thus, despite the
distinctions between friends and neighbors made earlier, there is often
behaviorally a blurring of the two roles (Cantor, 1979).

Homogeneity in the Selection of Friends

Adult friendships are highly homogeneous in social and demographic
status, attitudes, interests, and intelligence (Barnes, 1954; Berkun &
Meeland, 1958; Curtis, 1963; Ellis, 1957; Friedmann, 1966; Gans, 1962,
1967; Greer, 1956; Hess, 1972; Kahl & Davis, 1955; Laumann, 1966,
1973; Lawton & Simon, 1968; Lazarsfeld & Merton, 1964; Messer,
1965; Richardson, 1940; Riley & Foner, 1968; Rosow, 1967; Suttles,
1968; Verbrugge, 1977; Zander & Havelin, 1960). The tendency toward homogeneity in friendship selection seems to reflect the operation of two interrelated processes. First, people whose lifestyles, preferences, beliefs, social roles, and life situations are similar are more
likely to be in the same place at the same time than people who are
dissimilar in such characteristics. This is particularly so in regard to
residential patterns, meaning that neighbors will share many similar
attributes. Beyond residential patterns, however, all things being equal,
opportunities for meeting others who are similar are maximized. Sec-

ond, as Adams (1967) points out, consensus is an important defining characteristic of friendship. Since consensus is more likely among status similars than among status dissimilars, this principle should result in high status homogeneity in friendships (Verbrugge, 1977).

For older people the availability of age-peers as potential friends is an issue that has received attention in the literature. Age similarity among friends means that the friends are likely to share a range of role experiences, sequences, and changes which provide an important basis for cementing relationships. Age similarity also means belonging to the same cohort—that is, having lived through the same historical era, having been reared in similar socialization and educational contexts, and having confronted many common historical events and changes. Taken in combination, opportunity structure, consensus, similar role experiences, and common cohort membership make it highly likely that older people will tend to name as friends other older people.

Available evidence indicates that friendships occur often, though by no means exclusively, among age-peers (Hess, 1972; Powers & Bultena, 1976; Riley & Foner, 1968). One study shows that nearly 40% of people 65 years and older say that most of their friends are the same age as themselves (Batten et al., 1966). Several studies show that if other older people are available and accessible, there is a tendency to name those people as friends and to participate more actively with those friends (Messer, 1966; Rosenberg, 1967; Rosow, 1967). Having age-peers as friends declines somewhat among the old-old because friends die (Riley & Foner, 1968). However, this is to some extent dependent upon the availability and proximity of other older people for purposes of making friends. Rosenberg (1967), for example, reports that as the mean age of the people in the neighborhood rises, older people are increasingly likely to have at least one age-peer as a friend, but decreasingly likely to have some younger friends. On the other hand, older people do have younger friends (Batten et al., 1966; Langford, 1962; Powers & Bultena, 1976; Rosenberg, 1967; Verbrugge, 1977). Cantor (1979) in a recent report found that over half the friends named by her urban elderly respondents were younger people. Thus, it would appear that age-mates are likely to be a part of the network of friendships of older people, but that younger people are also a part of that network.

There are several problems with existing data that preclude drawing a definitive conclusion on age homogeneity in friendship choices among the elderly. First, the majority of studies have been conducted in urban settings. Whether similar patterns exist in smaller communities is not known. Second, with exceptions (e.g., Verbrugge, 1977), the emphasis in many studies has been upon neighbor-friends rather than the full range of possible friendship choices. Third, it is not always specified what is meant by "younger" when respondents report having younger friends. More to the point in this regard is how friendships with age-mates and with younger people differ in content and meaning to older people. Unfortunately, few if any studies have directly addressed this issue. We have noted elsewhere in this chapter that the friendships of older people tend to be long-lived and fairly stable. This would indicate that the age of the friendship rather than the ages of the friends may be as important a variable in understanding friendships among the elderly as merely determining the extent to which friends are age homogeneous.

Friends and Neighbors as Confidants

Friends and neighbors can and often do play an important part in the lives of older people by serving as a confidant, or someone the older person can talk to about himself/herself or his/her problems. A confidant relationship is special in that it involves a level of trust and sharing not typical in more casual relationships. In that sense, to learn about the types and nature of confidant relations the older person has means to tap more intimate and meaningful dimensions of interaction with significant others that surpass analyses of frequency and score of interactions and their concomitants. Indeed, there is evidence that the presence of a confidant is related to high morale and good mental health. Confidants also act as buffers to lessen anxiety and tension when social roles are lost or to insulate individuals from stressful life events (Brown, 1980; Lowenthal & Haven, 1968; Moriwaki, 1973; Strain & Chappell, 1982).

    Older people generally have at least one confidant (Cantor, 1979; Jonas, 1979; Strain & Chappell, 1982; Tigges, Cowgill, & Habenstein, 1980), although there are aged people who do not have and possibly never have had intimate ties and seemingly do not experience low morale (Lowenthal & Haven, 1968). Several studies suggest that about one in five older people report having no confidants (Cantor, 1979; Jonas, 1979; Strain & Chappell, 1982).

    As might be expected, kin, and particularly immediate family members—spouse and adult children—are most often mentioned as confidants, but friends are also named as people with whom confidences are shared. While others—for example, doctors, ministers, nurses—may serve as confidants, they do so only infrequently (Strain & Chappell, 1982). Available data suggests that the selection of confidants is

distributed most frequently among spouse, child, and friend (Babchuk, 1978; Lowenthal & Haven, 1968; Powers & Bultena, 1976; Strain
& Chappell, 1982). At least one study (Babchuk, 1978) indicates that
older people are not likely to confide in others much younger than
themselves.

When taking all confidants into account, it appears that women
are more likely than men to have a confidant and to name someone
outside the immediate family as a confidant (Babchuk, 1978; Powers &
Bultena, 1976; Strain & Chappell, 1982). There is some reason to
believe that sex differences in confidant relations may reflect differences in marital status. Thus widowed males seem least likely to have a
confidant within or outside of the family (Strain & Chappell, 1982). As
reported earlier, men are more likely than women to name their
spouse as confidant, and often the sole confidant (Babchuk, 1978;
Lowenthal & Haven, 1968; Powers & Bultena, 1976; Strain & Chappell, 1982). Some studies suggest that married people are more likely
to have confidants than the unmarried and particularly those who have
always been single (Babchuk, 1978; Lowenthal & Haven, 1968; Powers
& Bultena, 1976), while others report no significant differences by
marital status (Strain & Chappell, 1982). One recent study (Kohen,
1983) indicates that the widowed report greater contact or confiding
behavior in informal relationships than the married. The likelihood of
having a confidant seems to decline with age (Babchuk, 1978; Lowenthal & Haven, 1968). Babchuk (1978) reports that persons of higher
social class status are more likely to have confidants than those who are
lower in social class status. Kohen (1983) finds that as income declines,
reliance upon family and friends as confidants increases. While people
can and do have more than one confidant, it appears that the mere
presence or absence of a confidant is more critical to the well-being of
the individual than the numbers of such persons (Strain & Chappell,
1982).

As noted above, friends too are named as confidants by older
people. On the average, older people who have confidant friends
report having either one or two such relationships (Babchuk, 1978;
Cantor, 1979), although a minority name considerably more. Available
data are mixed in regard to the proportions of older people who name
confidant friends. The range seems to be between 30–40% (Cantor,
1979; Strain & Chappel, 1982) and around 60% (Babchuk, 1978). Differences in percentages reported probably reflect variations in sampling
frame and methodologies employed. For example, Babchuk's sample
was somewhat younger in age than either Cantor's or Strain and
Chappell's, and his use of aided recall techniques to elicit a full enu-

meration of confidant friends may have produced a somewhat more complete listing of such friends. What is important is that friends with some degree of regularity provide support to many elderly.

As with the confidants of older people in general, sex, marital status, age, and social-class differences have been observed among their confidant friends. Unfortunately, not enough studies have been conducted to allow firm conclusions. Nonetheless, there is evidence that women more often than men have confidant friends (Babchuk, 1978; Hess, 1979; Powers & Bultena, 1976). Strain and Chappell (1982) and Kohen (1983) do not find such differences. However, Kohen (1983) reports that women are more likely than men to use confidant friends as a resource. Babchuk (1978) reports that persons who have been single for most of their lives are the least likely to have confidant friends, but there are few differences between married, widowed, and divorced or separated individuals in this regard. Strain and Chappell (1982) find that the single/separated/divorced are significantly more likely to name confidant friends than married persons, while the widowed are between extremes. Kohen (1983) does not find differences in numbers of confidant friends by marital status, but does show that the widowed more than the married report greater contact and confiding behavior with friends. In part, variations in results may highlight methodological differences employed rather than substantive disagreements. For example, it is possible that combining single individuals with separated and divorced people, as Strain and Chappell did, may mask precisely the differences which Babchuk reports.

Babchuk (1978) and Lowenthal and Haven (1968) report that the likelihood of having confidant friends declines with advancing age. For Lowenthal and Haven this was not evident until the older person was in his/her 70s. For Babchuk the decline in naming confidant friends occurred somewhat earlier. In any event, such results do suggest that the ability to maintain a confidant friendship declines as age increases. Whether this is because old and trusted friends become incapacitated or die or move away, or the older person experiences declines in health and mobility which decrease opportunities for maintaining the relationship, or life conditions cause the person to turn to other confidants—for example, family members—is not known. While the amount of data is limited, it appears that the generally reported wider range of friendship patterns among the higher socioeconomic groups does not hold in regard to confidant friends. Lower- and working-class people do name confidant friends (Babchuk, 1978; Lowenthal & Haven, 1968).

The empirical literature on friends as confidants is sparse, but nonetheless tantalizing. On the one hand, one recognizes the significance of confidant friends for older people. On the other hand, we do not yet understand precisely how and in what ways confidant friends are significant. Do confidant friends, for example, serve a different function than confidant kin for older people? Some evidence suggests that confidant friends do not act as substitutes for confidant relations with a spouse or children (Strain & Chappell, 1982). If this is so, what, if anything, does having confidant friends add to the reservoir of confidant relations that the older person has, to his/her needs for intimacy in relationships, and to the quality of life of the older person? Are there specific types of issues or problems about which the older person is more likely to turn to friends than to other confidants? What are the differences, if any, in the frequency of interaction between the various types of confidants and respondents? Are confidant friends likely to be old friends or do new friends also serve as confidants? If confidant friends are lost, with what frequency are they replaced? What effect does health of either the confidant or the elderly individual have on the relationship? Further research is needed to clarify relationships between age, sex, marital status, and ethnic and social-class variations and confidant relationships in old age.

Friends and Neighbors as Support Givers

A substantial body of literature attests to the salience of the family as a source of affective and instrumental support across the life cycle, particularly in old age (Adams, 1967; Bell & Boat, 1957; Bott, 1971; Cantor, 1979; Hochchild, 1973; Philblad, Hessler, & Freshley, 1975; Powers & Bultena, 1974; Rosow, 1967; Shanas, 1979; Stephens & Bernstein, 1984; Stoller & Earl, 1983; Sussman, 1953, 1965, 1977; Sussman & White, 1959). At the same time, friends and neighbors also provide assistance to elderly people in times of need or crisis, help with nonpersonal tasks of daily living, and give affectional support (Arling, 1976; Atchley, 1980; Bott, 1971; Cantor, 1979; Dono et al., 1979; Langford, 1962; Lowenthal & Robinson, 1976; Philblad et al., 1975; Rosenmayr & Kockeis, 1962; Rosow, 1967; Shanas, 1962; Stephens & Bernstein, 1984; Stoller & Earl, 1983; Townsend, 1957; Youmans, 1962). Help from friends and neighbors tends to supplement rather than substitute for or compete with family assistance and, as Lowenthal and Robinson (1976) suggest, may serve to lessen the burden of care on the family.

The large majority of noninstitutionalized elderly report that they either do carry out or are capable of performing the activities of daily living and of personal care themselves (e.g., Stoller & Earl, 1983). Shanas (1979) estimates that only 5-10% of all noninstitutionalized elderly require some home care, and that about 80% of such care is provided by family and friends. Thus, that many studies report low percentages of the elderly receiving help from neighbors and friends should not be surprising given the apparent vitality of the majority of the aged. However, many older people report needing occasional help with one or more tasks, or sometimes needing help in emergencies. Typically, assistance when needed is desired in regard to chores around the house or yard, shopping, or borrowing items—not money—rather than in areas of personal care or health matters. Those who seek aid from neighbors and friends in personal care or health matters are usually the older, more frail, or impaired elderly or those for whom the health problem is fairly sudden and is likely to be short term. Whether in areas of tasks of everyday living, personal care, health matters, or emergencies, older people state a preference for help from their spouse—if present, family members—particularly their children, and then neighbors and friends, in that order (see Cantor, 1979; Kohen, 1983). Only infrequently are formal organizations named as a preferred support giver, although one study of a relatively wealthier, younger, and more mobile sample of elderly reports a tendency to choose helpers from formal organizations over primary group members (Lebowitz, Fried, & Madaris, 1973).

Much of the social support literature emphasizes the amount and kind of support older people receive from significant others. Given that most elderly people are capable of and do continue to live independent lives, and that only a minority of those outside of institutions require more intense care or assistance, it is perhaps more relevant to determine how older persons are involved in systems of exchange within their informal social networks. Indeed, there is evidence that assistance and support received from significant others is reciprocated (Cantor, 1979; Stephens & Bernstein, 1984; Youmans, 1962). Reciprocation, of course, varies by type of support and the ability of the older person to reciprocate. For example, the older person is often not in a position to reciprocate assistance with transportation, but can often provide help to a friend or neighbor in times of illness. The issue of reciprocation in support exchanges between older people and their friends and neighbors needs further examination since much of the available data in the area focuses upon support provided to the older person and may thereby produce an unwarranted image of dependency among the elderly.

It is difficult to draw a definitive conclusion on the extent to which older people turn to friends and neighbors for assistance and support. This is so for several reasons. First, the ways in which questions on support and assistance are asked vary from study to study. Thus, some researchers inquire about preferred sources of help while others seek responses to actual help patterns. In some studies responses to sources of assistance and support refer to family, neighbors, and friends as providers relative to one another, while in other studies each support group is treated as a potential provider in its own right. Different studies use different listings of areas in which support might be provided. Questions about the support process are often vaguely worded or stated in such general terms that they lack the kind of specificity that would allow persons to respond in ways relevant to their own experience. Second, the samples of older people studied vary greatly, making comparisons of results difficult. Third, the researcher's unit of analysis may differ so that research results sometimes refer to percentage of older people receiving assistance, sometimes to the percentage of relationships with friends and neighbors in which help is received, and sometimes to percentages of support networks in which aid is exchanged. The unit of analysis used can lead to different conclusions. Schulman(1975), for example, points out that while exchanges of goods, services, and support occur only in about 25% of all relationships, the large majority (75%) of all networks involve at least one such exchange. Thus, it would appear that older people select conclusions. Schulman (1975), for example, points out that while exchange assistance and support.

Keeping in mind the caveats just mentioned, it is clear that friends and neighbors are an important source of affectional support to older people (e.g., Cantor, 1979; Stephens & Bernstein, 1984). This is implied if not explicitly stated by studies that show the importance among older people of interaction with friends to life satisfaction and morale (Arling, 1976; Haas-Hawkings, 1978; Lee & Ihlinger-Tallman, 1980; Philblad & Adams, 1972; Wood & Robertson, 1978). However, not all studies find a positive relationship (e.g., Lemon, Bengston, & Peterson, 1972; Smith & Lipman, 1972). It has been suggested that inconsistencies in research results may be caused by the uses of quantitative rather than qualitative measures of social interaction (Strain & Chappell, 1982). Indeed, the confidant literature discussed earlier seems to indicate more reliable relationships between qualitative measures of relationships and morale and life satisfaction. The point here is that friends as confidants, by virtue of the nature of that role, find themselves providing affectional support whether by serving as sympathetic listeners or by providing advice. Friends and neighbors are a frequently used source of support when the older person is worried or when bad things happen (Kohen, 1983) or as a relief for loneliness (Cantor, 1979). It is in the area of socialization and the provision of day-to-day companionship that friends and neighbors play a highly significant role.

Friends and neighbors can assist in times of emergency and in regard to health-related tasks. As with other areas of support, older people say they would prefer to or would likely rely on family most in these circumstances. Indeed, there is a wide range of percentages of how many older persons would or do turn to friends or neighbors when such problems arise (see, e.g., Cantor, 1979; Langford, 1962; Rosow, 1967; Shanas, 1962; Stoller & Earl, 1983). The extent to which older people would turn to or utilize friends as supports in emergencies or in regard to health problems ranges from less than 10% to more than two-thirds of those sampled. There is reason to believe that such variations may reflect more the approach of researchers than true incidence rates. Thus, the capacity of any given primary group to provide support will always depend upon the nature of the task and the elements which characterize the relationship between the older person and his/her support groups. Dono et al. (1979) suggest that researchers have not always been sensitive to basic dimensions which differentiate primary groups and thus make them more or less ready sources of support to older people. Dimensions such as proximity, long-term commitment, size and resources, and degree of affectivity are particularly important since they will bear strongly on the relative ability of any given primary group to provide assistance on any given task and the likelihood of the older person's using them. For example, neighbors seem best prepared to respond effectively to emergencies involving a short time frame but requiring close proximity. Friends can provide effective support over a somewhat larger time period and in situations in which proximity is less crucial. Family members are best prepared to respond to long-term problems in which proximity is a less important concern (Dono, et al., 1979; Litwak & Szelenyi, 1969). One area in which older people are unlikely to turn to any informal support group for help is in the area of financial assistance (e.g., Cantor, 1979; Rosow, 1967). This is also the one area in which formal organizations are viewed as appropriate supporters (Cantor, 1979).

It is in the area of the tasks of daily living that friends and neighbors are less likely to be mentioned by older people as sources of support. This may merely reflect the relative good health and vitality of the majority of older Americans. Thus, even if some help would be desirable, they are able to accomplish most everyday tasks by themselves and do so. It may be, however, that the way in which questions are asked produces an underestimation of the extent to which older people and their friends and neighbors exchange services and help. By being asked questions in the context of receiving support, the older respondent may neglect to mention, whether consciously or not, incidents of borrowing and lending and exchanging other forms of minor assistance—for example, help in starting a stubborn lawnmower—which typically occurs among neighbors regardless of age.

Looking to friends and neighbors as sources of support varies by the nature of the task, the availability and proximity of family members, length of residence in a neighborhood, marital status, and health status. As was indicated above, friends and neighbors are particularly important support givers in the areas of socialization, day-to-day companionship, and responding to short-term emergencies (Cantor, 1979). Elders turn to friends and neighbors for assistance when family members—particularly the spouse or children—are not available (e.g., Cantor, 1979; Dono et al., 1979; Stoller & Earl, 1983). Depending upon friends and neighbors for help is more likely among the widowed (Stoller & Earl, 1983) and the childless (Cantor, 1979). The impaired elderly tend to rely on friends and neighbors more than those whose health status is good or those who have a spouse or children available for assistance (Stoller & Earl, 1983). Length of residence in a neighborhood increases the likelihood of receiving help from friends and neighbors. Many years of common neighborhood residence allows for the emergence of affectional patterns and mutually understood commitments which enhance the provision of support (Stoller & Earl, 1983).

In summary, the majority of older people continue to live relatively independent lives, they receive help from friends and neighbors, although reported percentages are not always great, their exchanges with friends and neighbors are often reciprocal, and there appears to be an order of preference among the elderly regarding whom they rely upon for help. These considerations have implications for further research on informal support systems. It may be useful to couch questions about support in exchange terms in which reciprocation is at least recognized as a possibility rather than focusing upon assistance received by the elderly. Such an approach could provide a more accurate picture of the extent to which older people do receive help from friends and neighbors, since it would not carry the negative connotation of dependency. Being more sensitive to the basic dimensions of informal support groups and to the fact that difficult types of aid may require groups with different dimensions (Dono et al., 1979) is necessary if we are to understand the conditions under which particular significant others are approached for assistance and how the principle of preference as opposed to the realities of life interact in the choice of support givers. Since the way in which questions on support provision are asked can affect responses to those questions, careful attention must be paid to how questions are worded, to the wording being consistent with the researchers' intent, and to the researchers' intent being made explicit in published reports. In particular, it is important to avoid the use of vaguely worded questions, questions which are so general that it is difficult to ground them in experience, or items that encourage the respondent to stress one type of support group over another (Dono et al., 1979). Much work needs to be done which clarifies how the provision of support varies by age, sex, marital status, health status, place and length of residence, living arrangements, social class, and the like.

Summary and Implications

Friendship and neighboring have been viewed as valuable sources of emotional and instrumental social support for older people, despite the fact that substantial research on these relationships is fairly recent. The increased recognition of the significance of friendship and neighboring as social supports represents a convergence of research and policy concerns.

The growth in numbers and proportions of the elderly in American society has led policymakers and practitioners to examine the support role played by friends and neighbors in the lives of older people. The realization that formal support systems are inadequate to respond to the needs of older people for economic, social, and psychological reasons has led to a refocus of attention on informal support systems.

Partly in response to demands for information from the policy arena, but also because of an increase in substantive interests in social network analyses, research on family, friends, and neighbors as elements in the informal support systems of older people has grown substantially. As a result, the outlines of informal support systems have begun to be delineated and the importance of such systems to the well-being of older people much better understood in their own right as well as with regard to how they intersect with formal support systems.

Despite continuing problems of conceptualization and.the lack of consistency in the approaches researchers have taken in studying informal support groups, there is general consensus on the defining components of family, friendship, and neighboring relationships. It is recognized that the three types of informal support groups differ structurally and that, given such differences, they may be appropriate in providing support on different types of tasks. The roles of support givers may often be multiplex, or overlap, so that it is not always possible or realistic to completely differentiate the activities of family members, friends, and neighbors. Two major models for understanding how informal support groups function in the lives of older people have been proposed. The task specific model developed by Litwak emphasizes the nature of the task as it relates to structural characteristics of the family, friendship, and neighbor groups as providers of support. Cantor's hierarchical compensatory model postulates that support giving depends more upon the primacy of the support giver to the elderly person than upon the nature of the task. Elderly people typically prefer particular support givers—usually kin—and turn to other sources of support when the preferred support giver is not available. There is empirical support for both models.

The literature suggests that the majority of older people are not isolated from friends and neighbors and that interaction with friends and neighbors is frequent. Unfortunately, much of what is known about friendship and neighboring derives from studies which emphasize more easily quantifiable aspects of such relationships such as frequency and scope of social interaction. Only recently have attempts been made to examine the more qualitative and subjectively meaningful components of friendship and neighboring. Numbers of friends and neighbors and interaction with them appear to correlate negatively with variables such as age, health status, and financial status. The majority of older people maintain a small core of intimate friends and a larger number of people with whom they have friendly contacts.

The friendship and neighboring relations of older people are generally stable and long term. However, older people do make new friendships. Men and women alike report that friends and neighbors are important to them. Men tend to have a wider range of social contacts, whereas women are more likely to maintain more intimate ties with friends. Thus, older women may have greater flexibility than older men in replacing relationships which are lost, including the loss of a spouse.

Neighborhood friends appear to assume a prominent place in the lives of older people. However, friends outside the neighborhood are frequently named. As with adults generally, the friendships of older people tend to be homogeneous in terms of social and demographic characteristics, attitudes, values, and interests. While there is a tendency toward age homogeneity in the friendships of older people, they frequently have younger friends.

Most older people have at least one confidant, a relationship that involves intimacy and sharing. While immediate family members are most often named as confidants, friends too are often cited. Having a confidant is related to good morale and positive mental health and may provide an important buffer in times of crisis.

While the literature confirms the importance of the family as a source of support, friends and neighbors clearly are also supportive of older people. Most older people report that they are capable of caring for themselves, belying an image of dependency in old age. Moreover, many of the support exchanges between older people and their neighbors and friends are reciprocal. It is clear that friends and neighbors are an important source of affectional support for older people. The extent and type of instrumental support varies by the nature of the task, proximity, commitment, and degree of affectivity existing between the older person and the support groups.

Implications for Further Research

Over the past decade or so our understanding of the significance of friends and neighbors in the lives of older people has increased markedly. Nonetheless, a number of issues and research questions need to be addressed if a fuller grasp of the support roles of friends and neighbors is to be realized.

A key issue concerns the way in which friendship is conceptualized. There continues to be some ambiguity in defining what is meant by friendship (Cohen & Rajkowski, 1982; Paine, 1969; Shames, 1981). In part, criticism directed at current conceptualizations is epistemological. One criticism is that current conceptualizations tend to remain at the level of abstract generality rather than grounding them in the real-life experiences of older people. Thus, while defining terms like consensus, voluntary involvement, and affectivity may be useful for researchers, they may bear little resemblance to how older people experience their relations with friends. A second criticism concerns the tendency of many studies to approach friendships as dyadic relationships rather than as social relationships embedded in and reflecting the array of other social relations in which the person is involved. A third criticism refers to the tendency in research to ignore the contexts and cultural and temporal settings in which friendships are formed and exist.

We cannot debate here the accuracy of these criticisms; neither does space allow us to engage in epistemological discussions. Nonetheless, there is an increasing awareness of the need to incorporate such criticism into ongoing work and in the conceptualization of friendship ties. For example, it is now apparent to researchers that easily quantifiable measures of friendship ties such as frequency and scope of interaction are insufficient to tap the richness of such relationships and that strategies for examining more qualitative and subjectively meaningful dimensions of friendship ties must be developed. The development of social network analysis and its application in studies of informal social networks has provided a valuable methodological tool but also a framework for conceptualizing, delineating, and describing the array of social ties, including friendship, that make up the social worlds of people. In the gerontological literature at least, an increasing number of studies of special settings are being conducted which require that attention be paid to contextual issues. Clearly, however, much additional conceptual work is needed before an adequate understanding of friendship relationships will be possible.

There are several other concrete areas in which additional knowledge on relations with friends and neighbors is needed. These were alluded to throughout this chapter but are elaborated here. First, we need to know much more about how friendship patterns change as people age. A number of more specific questions need to be addressed. For example, to what extent and under what conditions do new relationships with friends develop as the older person retires, as his or her spouse dies, or as his or her children and old friends move away? To what degree are continuing friendships and forming new friendships dependent upon joint participation in common activities? What qualitative differences exist between the new friendships that older people form and those friendships of a lifetime that have been disrupted by death? What role do friends and neighbors play in socializing adults to old age? Do older people perceive differences in the meaning, value, and significance of friendships formed earlier in life by comparison to those formed later in life?

Research is needed that separates age from cohort effects on friendship. Speculations derived from available studies suggest that the friendship patterns of the young, middle-aged, and aged differ in regard to the extent to which friendships are fused with other major life roles, complement other roles, and substitute for or compete with the demands of other roles. If such results are valid, it would appear that placement in the life cycle has a powerful effect upon the formation and maintenance of friendship.

We need to know much more about the qualitative dimensions of friendship in old age. What constitutes intimacy in friendship, how do levels of intimacy relate to individual well-being, and to what extent do people vary in their need for intimate ties with friends? The significance of close affective ties for older people has been repeatedly stated in the literature. Beyond knowing something of the broad parameters in which the proposition holds and being able to demonstrate its applicability in times of crisis or stress, little is understood about the conditions, extent, content, and outcomes of intimate friendship relations in the everyday lives of older people.

Much additional information is needed on the structure, composition, and functioning of social support networks and the role of friends and neighbors in such networks. How extensive are these networks and to what extent do they overlap in terms of membership and the content of ties between people? In terms of limited data sources, we are led to believe that life outcomes for people involved in extensive social networks are different than for those not so involved. To what extent and in what specific ways is that so? Under what conditions and in what respects does substitutability occur within social networks? The social networks of older people are typically viewed as a positive resource system. Is involvement in social networks also costly in social and emotional terms? If there are costs for such involvement, what implication might this have for the well-being of older people?

Implications for Policy and Service

Several issues relevant to the formulation of public social policy and service delivery emerge from our discussion of friends and neighbors as components of the informal support systems of older people. Our review of the literature suggests that most older people continue to live independently. Whether vigorous or frail, they maintain ties with friends and neighbors well into old age. Friends and neighbors, along with kin, do provide affective and instrumental support to older people, and frequently the support provided is reciprocated in some fashion. One implication of these data is that it may be inappropriate to view the older person as the sole unit of analysis in planning, assessment, and intervention strategies. Rather, more appropriately the older individual should be considered within the context of his/her informal support network, including neighbors and friends. This is not a fully novel idea. As with the approach suggested in the family systems literature, the older person may be the identified client. However, strategies for assessing need, planning for and providing assistance, and determining points of intervention can only properly and effectively occur by taking into account the availability, viability, and significance, not only of family supports, but of friendship and neighboring supports as well.

There has been a tendency in the gerontological literature on social support systems and in the development of public policy to focus on the older person as the recipient of support. To some extent this has fostered a conception of older people as dependent and aging as a social problem. There is evidence suggesting that most older people reciprocate in some fashion the supports they receive. Thus, older people are recipients of informal supports but they also are providers in this regard. Policymakers, practitioners, and researchers should continue their current emphasis on identifying the contributions that friends and neighbors make to older people. Additionally, increased attention must be given to the affective and instrumental contributions and supports that older people themselves provide within their informal social networks. Approaching informal support networks as systems of exchange in which reciprocity is potentially an important component rather than viewing such networks merely as unidirectional could alter views of the aged as dependent and provide a more accurate appraisal of how informal support systems function in the lives of older people.

Finally, continued effort must be given to developing strategies whereby informal and formal systems can complement and support one another rather than compete or perhaps conflict. It is troublesome to discover that friends and neighbors may hinder rather than facilitate knowledge of and access to needed formal services (Ward et al., 1984). Unfortunately, this finding may be exacerbated by the tendency of public policy and formal service providers to ignore the importance of informal social supports. On the one hand, formal support systems must be designed to supplement and support informal systems, not displace or replace them. On the other hand, ways must be developed that encourage informal support networks to recognize and utilize at appropriate points formal support systems. In regard to the latter point, there are some steps that could be taken in the formulation of public social policy in behalf of older people. Already, some attention has been given to supplementing and enhancing family support systems through such strategies as tax deductions and a variety of in-home support services. Few policy initiatives have focused on the supportive role of friends and neighbors, even though grassroots programs developed at the community level provide useful examples of the direction such policy might take—that is, neighborhood watch programs and volunteer credit banks. It appears that when considering the important role played by friends and neighbors in the lives of older people, policymakers and practitioners might give greater attention to strategies which would recognize, reward in some appropriate fashion, and enhance the support provided to older people by their friends and neighbors.

References

Adams, B. N. (1967). Interaction theory and the social network. *Sociometry, 30*, 64–78.

Arling, G. (1976). The elderly widow and her family, neighbors and friends. *Journal of Marriage and the Family, 38*(4), 757–768.

Arth, M. (1962). American culture and phenomena of friendship in the aged. In C. Tibbets & W. Donahue (Eds.), *Social and psychological aspects of aging.* New York: Columbia University Press.

Atchley, R. C. (1980). *The social forces in later life.* Belmont, CA: Wadsworth.

Babchuk, N. (1965). Primary friends and kin: A study of the association of middle class couples. *Social Forces, 43*, 483–493.

Babchuk, N. (1978–79). Aging and primary relations. *International Journal of Aging and Human Development, 9*, 137–151.

Babchuk, N., & Bates, A. (1963). The primary relations of middle-class couples: A study in male dominance. *American Sociological Review, 28*, 384.

Ballweg, J. A. (1969). Extensions of meaning and use for kinship terms. *American Anthropologist, 71*, 84–87.

Barnes, J. A. (1954). Class and committees in the Norwegian island parish. *Human Relations, 7*, 39–58.

Batten, Barton, Durstine, and Osborn, Inc. (1966). *Report: an investigation of people's feelings on age.* Batten, Barton, Durstine, and Osborn Research Memorandum, unpublished.

Bell, W., & Boat, M. D. (1957). Urban neighborhoods and informal social relations. *American Journal of Sociology, 62*, 391–398.

Berkun, M., & Meeland, T. (1958). Sociometric effects of race and of combat performance. *Sociometry, 21*, 145–149.

Berscheid, E., & Walster, E. H. (1969). *Interpersonal attraction.* Reading, MA: Addison-Wesley.

Blau, Z. (1961). Structural constraints on friendships in old age. *American Sociological Review, 26*, 429–438.

Blau, Z. (1973). *Old age in a changing society.* New York: Franklin Watts.

Boissevain, J. (1974). *Friends of friends.* New York: St. Martin's.

Boissevain, J., & Mitchell, J. C. (1973). *Network analysis: Studies in human interaction.* Paris: Mouton.

Booth, A. (1972). Sex and social participation. *American Sociological Review,* 37, 183–192.

Booth, A., & Hess, E. (1974). Cross-sex friendship. *Journal of Marriage and the Family,* 36, 38–47.

Bott, E. (1971). *Family and social networks.* London: Tavistock.

Brown, B. B. (Nov. 1980). *The impact of confidants on adjusting to stressful events.* Presented at Gerontological Society, San Diego.

Bultena, G., Powers, E., Falkman, P., & Frederick, D. (1971). *Life after 70 in Iowa.* Ames, IA: Sociology Report 95.

Cantor, M. H. (1979). Neighbors and friends: An overlooked resource in the informal support system. *Research on Aging,* 1, 434–463.

Carp, F. M. (1966). *The future of the aged: Victoria Plaza and its residents.* Austin: University of Texas Press.

Clark, M., & Anderson, B. G. (1967). *Culture and aging.* Springfield, IL: Charles C Thomas.

Cohen, C. I., & Rajkowski, H. (1982). What's in a friend? Substantive and theoretical issues. *The Gerontologist,* 22, 261–266.

Creecy, R. F., & Wright, R. (1979). Morale and informal activity with friends among black and white elderly. *The Gerontologist,* 19, 544–547.

Curtis, R. F. (1963). Differential association and the stratification of the urban community. *Social Forces,* 42, 68–77.

Dono, J. E., Falbe, C. M., Kail, B. L., Litwak, E., Sherman, R. H., & Siegel, D. (1979). Primary groups in old age: Structure and function. *Research on Aging,* 1, 403–433.

Ellis, R. A. (1957). Social stratification and social relations: An empirical test of the disjunctiveness of social classes. *American Sociological Review,* 22, 570–578.

Fischer, C., Jackson, R., Stueve, A., Gerson, K., Jones, L., & Baldassare, M. (1977). *Networks and places: social relations in the urban setting.* New York: Free Press.

Friedmann, E. P. (1966). Spatial proximity and social interaction in a home for the aged. *Journal of Geronotology,* 21, 566–571.

Gans, H. (1962). *The urban villagers.* New York: The Free Press.

Gans, H. (1967). *The Levittowners.* New York: Pantheon.

Gordon, M. (1977). Primary-group differentiation in urban Ireland. *Social Forces,* 55, 743–752.

Greer, S. (1956). Urbanism reconsidered: A comparative study of local American metropolis. *American Sociological Review,* 21, 19–25.

Haas-Hawkings, G. (1978). Intimacy as a moderating influence on the stress of loneliness in widowhood. *Essence,* 2, 249–258.

Hawkins, B. (1978). Mental health of the black aged. In L. E. Gary (Ed.), *Mental health: A challenge to the black community.* Philadelphia: Dorrance & Co.

Hess, B. (1971). Amicability. Ph.D. dissertation, Rutgers University.

Hess, B. (1972). Friendship. In M. W. Riley et al. (Eds.), *Aging and society*. New York: Russell Sage.

Hess, B. (1979). Sex roles, friendship, and the life course. *Research on Aging, 1*, 494–515.

Hochschild, A. R. (1973). *The unexpected community*. Englewood Cliffs, NJ: Prentice-Hall.

Hoyt, D. R., & Babchuk, N. (1983). Adult kinship networks: The selective formation of intimate ties with kin. *Social Forces, 62*, 84–101.

Hunter, W. W., & Maurice, H. (1953). *Older people tell their story*. Ann Arbor, MI: Institute for Human Adjustment, Division of Gerontology.

Huyck, M. H. (Oct. 1976). *Sex, gender and aging*. Presented at the Gerontological Society, New York.

Jackson, M., & Wood, J. L. (1976). *Aging in America: Implications for the black aged*. Washington, DC: NCOA Publishing Dept.

Jonas, K. (1979). Factors in development of community among elderly persons in age-segregated housing: Relationships between involvement in friendship roles with the community and external social roles. *Anthropological Quarterly, 52*, 29–38.

Kahl, J. A., & Davis, J. A. (1955). A comparison of indexes of socio-economic status. *American Sociological Review, 20*, 317–325.

Kohen, J. A. (1983). Old but not alone: Informal social supports among the elderly by marital status and sex. *The Gerontologist, 23*, 57–63.

Kutner, et al. (1956). *Five hundred over sixty: A community survey on aging*. New York: Russell Sage Foundation.

Langford, M. (1962). Community aspects of housing for the aged. Research Report No. 5. Ithaca, NY: Center for Housing and Environmental Studies, Cornell University.

Laumann, E. O. (1966). *Prestige and association in an urban community*. Indianapolis: Bobbs-Merrill.

Laumann, E. O. (1973). *Bonds of pluralism: The form and substance of urban social networks*. New York: Wiley.

Lawton, M. P., & Simon, B. (1968). The ecology of social relationships in the housing for the elderly. *The Gerontolgoist, 8*, 108–115.

Lazarsfeld, P. F., & Merton, R. K. (1964). Friendship as a social process: A substantive and methodological analysis. In M. Berger, T. Arl, & C. A. Page (Eds.), *Freedom & control in modern society*. New York: Octagon Books.

Lebowitz, B. D., Fried, J., & Madaris, C. (1973). Sources of assistance in an urban ethnic community. *Human Organization, 32*, 267–271.

Lee, G. R., & Ihlinger-Tallman, M. (1980). Sibling interaction and morale: The effects of family relations on older people. *Research on Aging, 2*, 367–391.

Lemon, B., Bengston, V., & Peterson, J. (1972). An exploration of the activity theory of aging: activity types and life satisfaction among inmates to a retirement community. *Journal of Gerontology, 27*, 511–523.

Lindzey, G., & Byrne, D. (1969). Measurement of social choice and interpersonal attractiveness. In G. Lindsey & E. Aronson (Eds.), *The handbook of social psychology.* Reading, MA: Addison-Wesley.

Litwak, E. (1965). Extended kin relations in an industrial democratic society. In E. Shanas & G. Streib (Eds.), *Social structure and the family: Generational relations.* Englewood Cliffs, NJ: Prentice-Hall.

Litwak, E. (1970). *Toward the multifactor theory and practice of linkages between formal organizations.* Washington, DC: Final report, Grant number CRD-4 25-C 1-9 USDHA.

Litwak, E., & Figueira, J. (1968). Technological innovation and theoretical functions of primary groups and bureaucratic structures. *American Journal of Sociology, 73,* 468–481.

Litwak, E., & Meyer, H. J. (1974). *School, family and neighborhood: The theory and practice of school-community relations.* New York: Columbia University Press.

Litwak, E., & Szelenyi, I. (1969). Primary group structures and their functions; Kin, neighbors, and friends. *American Sociological Review, 34,* 465–481.

Lopata, H. Z. (1975). Support systems of elderly urbanites: Chicago of the 1970's. *The Gerontologist, 15,* 35–41.

Lowenthal, M. F., & Boler, D. (1965). Voluntary versus involuntary social withdrawal. *Journal of Gerontology, 20,* 363–371.

Lowenthal, M. F., & Haven, C. (1968). Interaction and adaptation: Intimacy as a critical variable. *American Sociological Review, 33,* 20–30.

Lowenthal, M. R., & Robinson, B. (1976). Social networks and isolation. In R. Binstock & E. Shanas (Eds.), Handbook of aging and the social sciences. New York: Van Nostrand Reinhold.

Lowenthal, M. F., Thurner, M., & Chiriboga, D. (1975). *Four stages of life.* San Francisco: Jossey-Bass.

Martel, M. U., & Morris, W. W. (1960). *Life after sixty in Iowa: A report on the 1960 survey.* Ames: Iowa Commission for Senior Citizens.

Messer, M. (1965). *Engagement with disengagement: The effects of age concentration.* Unpublished.

Moriwaki, S. Y. (1973). Self-disclosure, significant others and psychological well-being in old age. *Journal of Health and Social Behavior, 14,* 226–232.

Moss, M. S., Gottesman, L. I., & Kleban, M. H. (1976). *Informal social relationships among community aged.* Presented at the Gerontological Society, New York.

Muir, D. E., & Weinstein, E. A. (1962). The social debt: An investigation of lower-class and middle-class norms of social obligation. *American Sociological Review, 27,* 537.

O'Brien, J., & Wagner, D. (1980). Help seeking by the frail elderly: Problems in network analysis. *The Gerontologist, 20,* 78–83.

Paine, R. (1969). In search of friendship: An exploratory analysis in middle-class culture. *MAN, 4,* 505–524.

Philblad, C., & Adams, D. L. (1972). Widowhood, social participation and life satisfaction. *Aging and Human Development, 4,* 323–330.

Philblad, C. T., Hessler, R., & Freshley, H. (1975). *The rural elderly eight years later: Changes in life satisfaction, living arrangements, and health status.* Columbia, MO: University of Missouri.

Powers, E., & Bultena, G. (1974). Correspondence between anticipated and actual use of services by the aged. *Social Services Review, 48,* 245-254.

Powers, E. A., & Bultena, G. L. (1976). Sex differences in intimate friendships of old age. *Journal of Marriage and the Family, 38*(4), 739-747.

Richardson, H. M. (1940). Community of values as a factor in friendship of college and adult women. *Journal of Social Psychology, 11,* 303-312.

Riley, M. W., & Foner, A. (1968). Friends and neighbors. In M. W. Riley & A. Foner (Eds.), *Aging and society* (Vol. 1). New York: Russell Sage Foundation.

Riley, M. W., Foner, A., Hess, B., & Toby, M. L. (1969). Socialization for the middle and later years. In D. A. Goslin (Ed.), *Handbook of socialization theory and research.* Chicago: Rand McNally.

Rosenberg, G. S. (1967). *Poverty, aging and social isolation.* Washington, DC: Bureau of Social Science Research, Inc.

Rosenberg, G. S. (1970). *The worker grows old.* San Francisco: Jossey-Bass.

Rosenkaimer, D., Saperstent, A., Ishizaki, B., & MacBride, S. M. (Oct. 1968). *Coping with age-sex differences.* Presented at the Gerontological Society, New York.

Rosenmayr, L., & Kockeis, E. (1962). Family relations and social contacts of the aged in Vienna. In C. Tibbetts & W. Donahue (Eds.), *Social and psychological aspects of aging.* New York: Columbia University Press.

Rosow, I. (1967). *Social integration of the aged.* New York: The Free Press.

Rutzen, R. (March 1977). *Varieties of social disengagement among the aged: A research report on correlates of primary socialization.* Presented at the Eastern Sociological Society, New York.

Shames, C. (1981). The scientific humanism of Lucien Seve. *Science & Society, 45,* 1-23.

Shanas, E. (1962). *The health of older people: A social survey.* Cambridge, MA: Harvard University Press.

Shanas, E. (1979). The family as a social support system in old age. *The Gerontologist, 19,* 169-174.

Schulman, N. (1975). Life-cycle variations in patterns of close relationships. *Journal of Marriage and the Family, 37,* 813-821.

Smith, J. (1966). The narrowing social world of the aged. In Simpson, I. & J. C. McKinney (Eds.), *Social aspects of aging.* Durham, NC: Duke University Press.

Smith, K., & Lipman, A. (1972). Constraint and life satisfaction. *Journal of Gerontology, 27,* 77-82.

Stephens, M. A. P., & Bernstein, M. D. (1984). Social support and well-being among residents of planned housing. *The Gerontologist, 24,* 144-148.

Sterne, R., Phillips, J. E., & Rabushka, A. (1974). *The urban elderly poor.* Lexington, MA: D. C. Heath.

Stoller, E. P., & Earl, L. L. (1983). Help with activities of everyday life: Sources of support for the institutionalized elderly. *The Gerontologist, 23,* 64–70.

Strain, L. A., & Chappell, N. L. (1982). Confidants: Do they make a difference in quality of life? *Research on Aging, 4,* 479–502.

Sussman, M. B. (1953). The help pattern in the middle class family. *American Sociological Review, 18,* 22–28.

Sussman, M. B. (1965). Relationships of adult children with their parents in the United States. In E. Shanas & G. Streib (Eds.), *Social structure and the family: Generational relations.* Englewood Cliffs, NJ: Prentice-Hall.

Sussman, M. (1977). The family bureaucracy, and the elderly individual: An organizational linkage perspective. In E. Shanas & M. Sussman (Eds.), *Family, bureaucracy and the elderly.* Durham, NC: Duke University Press.

Sussman, M. B., & White, C. (1959). *Hough, Cleveland, Ohio: A study of social life and change.* Cleveland, OH: Westin Reserve University Press.

Suttles, G. (1968). *The social order of the slum.* Chicago: University of Chicago Press.

Tallmar, M., & Kutner, B. (1969). Disengagement and the stresses of aging. *Journal of Gerontology, 24,* 70–75.

Tigges, L., Cowgill, O., & Habenstein, R. (Nov. 1980). *Confidant relations of the aged.* Presented at Gerontological Society, San Diego.

Townsend, Peter. (1957). *The family life of old people.* London: Routledge and Kegan Paul.

Trela, J. E., & Jackson, D. (Oct. 1976). *Family life and substitutes in old age.* Presented at the Gerontological Society, New York.

Verbrugge, L. M. (1977). The structure of adult friendship choices. *Social Forces, 56,* 576–597.

Verbrugge, L. M. (1979). Multiplexity in adult friendships. *Social Forces, 57,* 1286–1309.

Wagner, D., & Keast, F. (1981). Informal groups and the elderly: A preliminary examination of the mediation function. *Research on Aging, 3,* 325–332.

Ward, R. A., Sherman, S. R., & LaGory, M. (1984). Informal networks and knowledge of services for older persons. *Journal of Gerontology, 39,* 216–223.

Wood, V., & Robertson, J. F. (1978). Friendship and kinship interaction: Differential effect on the morale of the elderly. *Journal of Marriage and the Family, 40,* 367–375.

Youmans, E. G. (1962). *Leisure time activities of older persons in selected rural and urban areas of Kentucky.* Lexington, KY: Progress Report 115, Kentucky Agricultural Experiment Station.

Zander, A., & Havelin, A. (1960). Social comparison and interpersonal attraction. *Human Relations, 13,* 21–32.

Zborowski, M., & Eyde, L. D. (1962). Aging and social participation. *Journal of Gerontology, 17,* 424–430.

8

Social Support for Elders Through Community Ties: The Role of Voluntary Associations

Nicholas L. Danigelis

Americans of all ages, all conditions and all dispositions, constantly form associations. They have not only commercial and manufacturing companies, in which all take part, but associations of a thousand other kinds—religious, moral, serious, futile, extensive or restrictive, enormous or diminutive. . . .

Feelings and opinions are recruited, the heart is enlarged, and the human mind is developed by no other means than by the reciprocal influence of men upon each other . . . these influences are almost null in democratic countries; they must therefore be artificially created, and this can only be accomplished by associations. (de Tocqueville, 1841, pp. 114–117)

Well over a hundred years after de Tocqueville made these observations about the early 19th-century United States, the belief persists more strongly than ever that Americans are joiners and that joining voluntary associations—no matter what kinds—makes us better people in terms of both our hearts and our minds and improves our society (see, e.g., Babchuk, Peters, Hoyt, & Kaiser, 1979; Rose, 1967).

The idea that voluntary association membership and participation is especially beneficial to older Americans has been accepted to such a degree that it appears pointless to step back and ask fundamental questions about the real meaning of association ties for older people.

Nevertheless, that is exactly what this chapter attempts to do by reviewing the available evidence on three questions: (1) What is the

extent of participation in voluntary associations among the elderly?
(2) What facilitates and what inhibits elderly involvement in voluntary
associations? (3) What do the elderly gain from such participation?
After the research relevant to these issues has been assessed, the remainder of the chapter will discuss research priorities with respect to
the elderly and their voluntary association ties.

Distinguishing Voluntary Associations

Defining "voluntary association" in terms of the freedom of the individual to join or withdraw is tautological. Thus, the meaning of the
term may be more easily specified by considering and defining "involuntary association" and treating voluntary association as a residual
concept, or, more practically, to define voluntary association in terms
of those organizations we tend to list and treat as "voluntary" (Rose,
1967, p. 216). Several practical classification schemes have been offered and are worth mentioning to indicate the range of associations
this chapter will consider.

Gordon and Babchuk (1959) made an early effort to classify
voluntary associations. Two of their criteria are particularly useful:
"degree of accessibility" and "function." To these means of classifying
associations we can add "type of association," a distinction most recently used in several empirical studies (e.g., Babchuk et al., 1979;
Cutler, 1976a; Knoke & Thomson, 1977). There are two different
interpretations of function. Rose (1967), for example, distinguishes six
kinds of functions bearing on the individual's relationship to the social
structure: distributing power, orienting through information, providing a mechanism for social change, increasing social cohesion, providing personal identification, and promoting social and economic advancement. A simpler and probably more useful distinction is Gordon
and Babchuk's (1959) classification of instrumental, expressive, and
instrumental-expressive functions. Instrumental reflects organizational
purpose centered on achieving some set of goals outside of the group
(e.g., League of Women Voters), expressive relates to organizations
whose purpose is to provide "immediate and continuing gratification"
to its members (e.g., YMCA), and instrumental-expressive refers to
"those groups that incorporate both functions self-consciously" (e.g.,
Alcoholics Anonymous) (Gordon & Babchuk, 1959, pp. 27–28).

A second way of classifying voluntary associations is to look at the
specific activities toward which they are oriented and distinguish

"types." Babchuk and Booth (1969) used the following categories to distinguish types: church related, job related, recreational, fraternal-service, adult leadership of youth, and other (a more recent study using a comparable set of categories is by Knoke and Thomson, 1977). Quite recently Babchuk et al. (1979) put fraternal and service in different categories and added new categories like aged, women's, and political associations for a total of 12 different categories, including the residual "other." Cutler (1976a, 1976b, 1976c), meanwhile, has distinguished 16 different types of associations.

Finally, in those cases dealing with the voluntary association membership of the aged, a simple distinction between age-heterogeneous and age-homogeneous groups may be useful (Trela, 1976; Ward, 1979a, 1979b). A further breakdown between national (e.g., American Association of Retired Persons) and local (e.g., any number of town or city "senior citizen" organizations) may also be helpful in distinguishing whether the group is "organized by older people, rather than just for them" (Ward, 1979b, p. 442)—national associations tending to be the former kind and local ones the latter.

At this stage, it is premature to choose a "best" means for distinguishing voluntary associations from among the above typologies, but a couple of observations are in order. First, as originally suggested by Gordon and Babchuk (1959), a number of distinguishing characteristics may be combined into a single, complex classification scheme (e.g., function, type, and age-heterogeneous versus age-homogeneous). Second, the particular typology of associations used in any empirical research focusing on the elderly will have profound implications for the type of conclusions that can be drawn.

The Extent of Elderly Involvement in Voluntary Associations

The Arguments

Unfortunately the application of coherent, testable theory to the study of voluntary association involvement among the elderly has been largely lacking. The disengagement theory arguments by Cumming and Henry (1961) predict a decrease of social activity as individuals get older, so one would expect voluntary association membership and participation rates to be lower among the elderly than among the rest of the population. In contrast, what has been called the activity

(Lemon, Bengston, & Peterson, 1972) or interactionist (Rosow, 1967) perspective postulates that the loss of certain roles is compensated by the acquisition of new roles or the extension of presently held roles. Therefore, one would expect, on the basis of these assumptions, that the elderly would not show appreciable changes in voluntary association commitments overall and, in fact, might increase ties to voluntary associations to compensate for role losses in other areas.

Excellent criticisms and attempts to integrate or extend these two perspectives have recently surfaced (Gubrium, 1973; Hochschild, 1975; Rosow, 1967), and the implications of the disengagement and activity/interactionist perspectives for understanding the meaning of voluntary associations for the aged are still being unraveled. Some of those implications are briefly sketched below, but it is important to note here that there is a relative paucity of theoretical arguments specifically tailored to, and tested by, evidence bearing on the involvement of elders in voluntary associations.

The Evidence

While many studies have touched upon the relationship between age and voluntary association membership (see Babchuk et al., 1979, for a listing), only a handful in the last few years have provided, on the basis of their conceptual and methodological orientations, useful information about the dynamics and magnitude of the association between age and organizational membership. Early research, utilizing relatively primitive data analytic techniques (see, e.g., Hausknecht, 1962; Wilensky, 1961), demonstrated that membership levels first increase until middle age and then begin to decrease. More recent studies, utilizing advanced data analytic techniques, have tended to produce evidence to contradict this presumably curvilinear association between age and association membership.

On the one hand, Knoke and Thompson (1977) examined cross-sectional data from two national surveys and reported that age and voluntary association membership were indeed curvilinearly related so that organizational ties increased as an individual progressed through stages of the life cycle only until a certain point (generally middle age) and then decreased. Further, this relationship holds with sex, race, and education held constant.

On the other hand, Babchuk and Booth (1969) and Cutler (1977), using longitudinal data, and Cutler (1976c) and Babchuk et al. (1979), on the basis of cross-sectional data, found that membership in voluntary associations generally remained stable or increased as age increased, and when membership did decrease, it usually was attributable to socioeconomic differences between the elderly and other age-groups.

Membership in Different Types of Organizations

The discussion presented earlier regarding different classification schemes for distinguishing among voluntary associations highlighted conceptual issues which have not been empirically tested. Therefore, the only differences among organizations noted in research on elders' involvement in voluntary associations are those based on type of organization. As with the general age–membership relationship discussed above, the findings are not completely consistent, but the overall conclusion seems to be that type of organization does make a difference.

Knoke and Thomson (1977) have argued that "whether aggregated—or disaggregated by general type, voluntary association membership patterns display a pronounced curvilinear pattern over the family life cycle" (p. 61). At the same time, if one looks at the figures upon which Knoke and Thomson base their conclusion (1977, Table 3), the "pronounced curvilinear pattern" appears not to apply to "fraternal-service" and "other" (e.g., veterans; nationality) organizations in both the 1967 and 1974 studies they examined. While older single individuals had lower membership rates than older couples, the latter group had the highest membership rates in "fraternal-service" and "other" organizations for both studies among the seven different life-cycle stages.

Further evidence that type of organization makes a difference in participatory rates comes from Knoke and Thomson's (1977) recalculation of data from the Babchuk and Booth (1969) study, Cutler's (1976b) analysis of 16 types of voluntary associations, and the Babchuk et al. (1979) study distinguishing a dozen different organizations. Although some of the results are mixed, the data from these sources suggest that, while membership in youth and civic-political organizations reflect likely curvilinear patterns between age and voluntary association involvement, church and fraternal memberships appear to increase with age (see especially Cutler, 1976b, Table 3).

In the only empirically based research distinguishing associations in terms of function, Babchuk et al. (1979) reported that fewer than one in 10 of the memberships in their study of elders were instrumental in nature; fully one-half were a combination of instrumental and expressive and over 40% were expressive. Unfortunately, the data needed

for comparing this group to younger individuals are not available. If
the different types of organizations examined in the Babchuk and
Booth (1969), Cutler (1976b), Knoke and Thompson (1977), and Babchuk et al. (1979) studies are categorized on the basis of their functions, it would appear that the proportion of memberships in exclusively or primarily instrumental associations probably is lower among
older people (e.g., labor unions, professional or academic societies,
youth, civic, sports).

Membership Versus Participation

Clearly organizational involvement extends beyond mere membership. What happens to those elderly who do belong to voluntary
associations? How much do they participate? Does participation depend on the particular type of organization? on the number of other
organizational affiliations the person has? if so, how? Finally, does
participation change with age? Unfortunately, very little comparative
data bearing on these questions are available. The two studies which
can shed some light, however, do give interesting insights into likely
answers to these questions.

Babchuk et al. (1979, Tables 5 and 6) reported information on the
ratio of association meetings attended by the individual to meetings
held, and they distinguished by type of association and number of
different association memberships held. Half of the different types of
associations had a ratio of meetings attended to meetings held at .62 or
better, indicating a fairly active group of elders. The ratios ranged
from lows of .38 for fraternal-sororal, .40 for political, and .42 for
patriotic-veteran to highs of .80 for hobby and .97 for women's organizations.

In addition to the type of association, the actual number of memberships an elder had was investigated. Data indicated that the more
organizations elders belonged to, the more frequently they attended
meetings. The distinction was particularly noticeable between those
who had one or two memberships versus those who had three or more
memberships: the proportion of meetings attended was less than 50%
for the former group and over 70% for the latter.

Cutler's (1977) longitudinal analysis of two separate data sources
both is consistent with Babchuk et al.'s (1979) evidence regarding the
substantial amount of participation in voluntary associations by elders
and provides information relative to the questions of how age and
actual participation are related. In terms of comparing different age
cohorts at the same point in time, there does seem to be a slightly

lower attendance rate among those in their late 50s and 60s compared to those in their 40s and early 50s. Whether these differences stem from real involvement distinctions or from the different kinds of associations to which each age-group belongs cannot be determined from the data reported. At the same time, comparisons of both panel groups (Cutler, 1977, Tables 1 and 2) evidenced no loss of interest over time in the organizations to which the individuals belonged. In fact, in both panels, the oldest cohorts reflected slightly increased monthly attendance scores between the first and last interview.

Thus, the fragmentary evidence that exists supports the following conclusions: (1) elders who are members of voluntary associations tend to be active; (2) certain associations attract better attendance than others; (3) the more associations elders join, the more likely they are to participate; and (4) stability of commitment over time seems to characterize elders' association attendance.

Facilitators and Inhibitors of Elderly Involvement in Voluntary Associations: The Importance of Status Characteristics

On the basis of the evidence examined above, it appears reasonable to conclude that older Americans join and participate in voluntary associations at levels similar to the rest of the population. Why do elders get involved and continue their commitment to these organizations? In this section, selected characteristics (like sex, race, and socioeconomic status) will be examined to determine their relationship to involvement in voluntary associations.

Sex

Comparisons of male–female association memberships have produced mixed results, but the most recent evidence based on systematic comparisons between males and females for different age-groups suggests a pattern. While males tend to join significantly more often than females in the 45–64 year age range (Booth, 1972), there does not appear to be any appreciable difference in membership rates between the sexes among those 65 and over (Babchuk et al., 1979; Booth, 1972; Cutler, 1976b).

When organizations are examined by type, however, certain regularities emerge. Babchuk et al. (1979) commented that "women were significantly more likely to belong to church-related and to social-expressive voluntary groups than men. Men, on the other hand, were significantly more likely to belong to service and to professional-work-related associations" (p. 583). If organizations are distinguished by function, males are more likely to belong to instrumental and instrumental-expressive associations but less likely to belong to expressive associations than women (Booth, 1972), but it's not clear whether the relationship holds among the elderly.

Finally, when one measures participation, there is evidence to suggest that women attend meetings more often than men, in part perhaps because the instrumental organizations which men tend to join meet less often and because those organizations that meet less often have lower attendance rates (see the data in Cutler, 1977, and the arguments in Babchuk et al., 1979). Other data have revealed that the average attendance for elderly females is somewhat higher but that the difference is reduced over time (Cutler, 1977).

Race

While a rich literature examining black involvement in voluntary associations has demonstrated that blacks historically have participated at or above the levels of their white counterparts (see, e.g., Myrdal, 1964; Olsen, 1970; Orum, 1966; Williams, Babchuk, & Johnson, 1973), age has been seen as something which needed to be statistically controlled. Therefore, from such work it has been difficult to extract conclusions regarding the amount and nature of association involvement among older blacks compared to older whites. Clemente, Rexroad, and Hirsch (1975) have noted that there are major distinctions in terms of the types of organizations each race is more likely to join—church-related and social-recreational clubs among blacks and ethnic organizations and senior citizen clubs among whites.

Compared to what is known about the effect of sex on organizational involvement among the elderly, our accumulated wisdom regarding race effects among the elderly is quite small. Systematic comparisons including other major racial or ethnic groups (e.g., Hispanic-Americans) have surfaced but do not provide detailed comparisons for the elderly.

Socioeconomic Status

Information on the positive relationship between socioeconomic status (SES) and voluntary association involvement has been substantial and rather consistent (see, e.g., Hyman & Wright, 1971; Wright & Hyman, 1958). At the same time, recent efforts to understand the organizational ties of the elderly have tended to consider socioeconomic status as one explanation for lower organizational involvement among the elderly in comparisons between the young and the old. Therefore, investigators have statistically "controlled" for SES but have not examined its specific effect on involvement among the elderly (e.g., Cutler, 1976a; Knoke & Thomson, 1977).

Fortunately, two studies provide suggestive evidence regarding the relative importance of socioeconomic status in predicting how involved the elderly become in voluntary associations. Babchuk et al. (1979) found that SES substantially facilitated organizational involvement among the elderly, in distinguishing not only members from nonmembers but also attendees from nonattendees. In contrast, Trela's (1976) analysis of SES effects on organizational involvement among the elderly tends to refute Babchuk et al.'s (1979) findings. While social class was positively associated with organizational membership in "age-graded" asssociations (exclusively older individual memberships), Trela found no statistically significant difference between low- and high-SES elderly with respect to predicting membership in associations generally. Furthermore, he asserted that, on the basis of his data, "once they join, lower-class persons participate as actively as their middle-class age peers and . . . are at least as likely to continue their associational memberships over the years following their initial recruitment" (Trela, 1976, p. 202).

The evidence on the relevance of socioeconomic status for the voluntary association ties of the elderly, therefore, may not be as obvious as its importance for the general population. What data we have regarding this issue is instructive but by no means conclusive.

Age and Health

The elderly are obviously not a homogeneous group with respect to age, so that we can distinguish between young-old and old-old. There is empirical support for the commonly held assumption that association involvement is dramatically reduced as elders become very old and very frail (e.g., Riley & Foner, 1968). Nevertheless, this inference has been called into question by recent findings. For example, an examination of Cutler's (1976b, Table 2) distinction between 65–74-year-olds and those 75 and over finds no appreciable difference in association membership between the two groups. In addition, Babchuk et al. (1979, Table 1) found the 80+ group more likely to be members than the 75-79 group, although both were less likely to be association members than those 65-69 and 70-74 years old.

Altogether, therefore, the evidence regarding the importance of age and health in predicting organizational ties among the elderly is far from clear-cut, suggesting that other factors may be at work which have not yet been specified.

Benefits to the Elderly from Involvement in Voluntary Associations

The Arguments

A major underlying assumption of most of the research on voluntary associations, sometimes explicitly stated and sometimes merely implied, is that belonging is good—good for the individual, good for the group, and good for society. The intellectual roots of this assumption are Emile Durkheim's (1964) theory of social integration as well as de Tocqueville's (1841) arguments about the benefits voluntary associations produce for the society as well as the individual. A significant number of meaningful ties to fellow human beings in a variety of institutional contexts should enhance feelings about self and, by strenthening ties among individuals, make the society healthier as well.

In practical terms, the presumed benefits of association membership to the individual are the concern in this chapter and are best expressed in the language used earlier to describe the functions of organizations: expressive and instrumental. The expressive function of voluntary associations should give us psychic rewards, that is, "make us feel good." In contrast, there are organizations whose main purpose is to achieve some set of goals, either in a limited time span (e.g., certain lobbying groups) or on a continuing basis (e.g., League of Women Voters). As was mentioned previously, there are associations which presumably give the best of both worlds and make one feel good for a variety of non-task-related reasons and strive toward particular task-oriented goals. What evidence is there that voluntary associations are able to "deliver" these benefits in fact as well as in the abstract? The results available tend to focus exclusively on the presumed psychic rewards of association ties, so the discussion will focus on this function. In a postscript, the instrumental nature of certain association involvements will be considered.

The Evidence

The literature on individual sense of well-being is both large and becoming increasingly sophisticated theoretically and methodologically (Larson, 1978, is an excellent review). Unfortunately, much of the recent work has included voluntary association ties along with a host of other indicators as components of "objective social integration" indices (Liang, Dvorkin, Kahana, & Mazian, 1980, is an example). Therefore, potential information about the particular importance of organizational involvement in predicting sense of well-being is lost.

There are a few studies which do separate out the effects of voluntary association membership and participation in efforts to understand the causes of life satisfaction. Unfortunately, they suggest that assumptions about the psychic benefits of organizational involvement need serious rethinking. Three studies (Bull & Aucoin, 1975; Cutler, 1973; Edwards & Klemmack, 1973) indicate that voluntary association membership positively correlates with general life satisfaction but that this association is due in large measure to socioeconomic status and health.

When organizations are distinguished by type, the evidence suggests that church-related association membership alone tends to have a positive effect on sense of well-being, even when SES and health are controlled (Cutler, 1976a; Edwards & Klemmack, 1973). Cutler (1976a) has suggested that the explanation of this finding might lie not so much in the benefits of membership in church activities as in other factors which correlate with both church-related association membership and life satisfaction, like religiosity.

Other studies have distinguished type of organizational involvement, going beyond using only membership as an indicator of involvement. On the positive side, Graney's (1975) longitudinal study of 60 women showed that both membership and participation correlated positively with happiness in old age and over time. Knapp (1976) found participation correlated strongly and positively with one dimension of life satisfaction, even when relevant statistical controls were imposed.

At the same time, two other studies have produced evidence that certain kinds of organizational involvement may actually be negatively associated with a sense of well-being. Ward (1979a), for example, found that while active participation positively correlated with life satisfaction, card-playing association ties were negatively associated with satisfaction. Using a general measure of formal activity based on "the number of day segments in which the respondent attended or engaged in group meetings with set goals or agenda" (p. 715), Longino and Kart (1982) discovered that participation has a negative effect on life satisfaction for three different samples of elders.

In addition to distinguishing types of organizations and degree of involvement, recent research has also characterized different kinds of sense of well-being. When this is done, association membership (Hoyt, Kaiser, Peters, & Babchuk, 1980) and participation (Knapp, 1976) are found to correlate positively with one or more dimensions of life satisfaction, but not with all; no significant negative associations are reported. In a related vein, Ward (1979a) has argued that the global concept of well-being or life satisfaction can be conceptually distinguished from satisfaction specific to the organization under consideration. This evidence (Ward, 1979a) demonstrates that the relationship between reasons for enjoying group participation and general life satisfaction does not exist for some groups and is negative for others.

Finally, sex, race, socioeconomic status, and other characteristics generally have been taken into account by the studies described above in one of two ways: either they have been important focal points of the study and their direct impact on life satisfaction has been the central concern, or they have been considered possible important predictors of life satisfaction and statistically controlled. In either case, these characteristics have been treated primarily as predictors of life satisfaction.

Based on research to this point, we know very little about how organizational ties affect the well-being of different subgroups of the elderly. For example, although Graney's (1975) study focused exclusively on women, no research appears to be available which correlates voluntary association involvement and life satisfaction separately for men and women. Separate correlations for blacks and whites (Sauer, 1977) indicate that, while the number of organizational memberships positively correlates with sense of well-being among blacks, there is no association among whites and the association for blacks disappears when relevant statistical controls are imposed. In one sense, Longino and Kart's (1982) work represents an example of correlating association ties with life satisfaction for different socioeconomic groups because two of their samples are composed of middle-class and upper-middle-class respondents and the third of working-class individuals. The negative correlation between participation and satisfaction which the investigators have reported for each sample suggests that the relationship between participation and satisfaction is the same for different SES groups. It should be clear, however, that at present the evidence regarding the effect of association involvement on life satisfaction for different gender, race, and SES groups is still quite meager.

A Postscript on Age-Homogeneous Groups and Volunteerism

Two recent foci of research on voluntary association involvement among the elderly are relevant to this discussion. First, distinctions between age-homogeneous and age-heterogeneous organizations indicate that the former have many potential benefits for the elderly, but a seemingly necessary requirement is that the organizations be "run by older people, rather than for them and that they allow for active participation" (Ward, 1979a, p. 251). Simultaneously, membership in such associations appears not to be significantly related to a general sense of well-being, although "we know virtually nothing about the consequences of this participation for older persons" (Ward, 1979a, p. 252).

A second potentially useful distinction is between those situations in which the elderly individual does service work in a volunteer role, that is, without pay, and those in which such service is not done. Ward (1979a) has argued: "Few other activities can rival volunteer work as a source of 'good feelings' about oneself. For older people, the volunteer role is a potential source of meaningful activity and status which can counteract the marginality and demoralization of old age" (p. 258). Various Retired Senior Volunteeer Program activities like Foster Grandparents and Senior Companion appear to serve both expressive and instrumental functions and thus might provide substantial benefits to their participants (see Ward, 1979b, for a discussion of these issues).

While the rhetoric promoting volunteerism has been substantial, the empirical evidence has been fragmentary and somewhat contradictory. For example, Carp (1968) argued that older workers were better off physically than either volunteers or persons who neither work for pay nor volunteer. Alternatively, Hunter and Linn (1980–81) found higher life satisfaction among volunteers than among nonvolunteers, and Friedman (1975) and Fengler and Goodrich (1980) report positive experiences from volunteering among the institutionalized and disabled elderly, respectively. While there is reason for optimism regarding the potential benefits of such voluntary association involvement, much more systematic study is necessary.

Research Priorities for the Future

The above overview discussion on voluntary association involvement among the elderly has attempted to answer three important questions concerning how much the elderly participate in such organizations, why they participate, and what benefits they receive from their participation. This section briefly summarizes our present state of knowledge, then suggests a research agenda for the future with respect to each of these three areas.

The Extent of Elderly Involvement in Voluntary Associations

Although a fair amount of research has indicated that the elderly do not join and participate as much as younger people in voluntary associations, there is more to suggest that they do—especially when change over time is examined through longitudinal studies and when socioeconomic status and health are taken into account. Furthermore, it is clear that the elderly are more likely to belong to certain types of associations, especially those affiliated with churches or of a fraternal nature and containing a large expressive function. It also appears confirmed that the elderly don't just belong but actually participate quite a bit in their organizations and that participation does not appear to decline with advancing age.

The methodologically sophisticated longitudinal and cross-sectional studies trying to answer the question of how much the elderly are involved in voluntary associations have stemmed in most cases from efforts to test disengagement or activity theory. Given the recent substantial critiques of these two sets of arguments (in particular, Gubrium, 1973), we might well wonder whether these "theories," disengagement especially, are no more than convenient models upon which to hang some research findings. Lemon et al. (1972) and Hochschild (1975) are to be applauded for their recent efforts to provide testable propositions based on these models, but much more needs to be done in the way of theory construction.

It is time also to move beyond merely enumerating memberships, meetings attended, and hours spent participating and begin measuring the *quality* of participation. Cutler's (1976a) distinction between religious versus other organizations, Babchuk et al.'s (1979) discovery of the preponderance of expressive organizations, and recent findings on age-homogeneous groups and volunteerism suggest the need to reexamine our present inventory of classification schemes regarding volun-

tary associations. Perhaps a place to start is Dumazedier's (1974) classification of time use in which he distinguishes work, sociospiritual,
sociopolitical, and family obligations from leisure. Are voluntary association memberships to be considered exclusively leisure, or, as Dumazedier suggests, is there something obligatory about religious and
political organizations? Do individuals tend to participate in certain
clusters of organizations only or do they tend to spread themselves
out? What are the ramifications of either profile in terms of commitment? Factor analytic techniques could be utilized to test the simple
(and probably incorrect) proposition that organizational membership
and participation are unidimensional concepts.

Facilitators and Inhibitors of Elderly
Involvement in Voluntary Associations

Our previous discussion on the explanations for elderly involvement in
organizations focused exclusively on status characteristics in hopes of
inferring specific reasons why people join, participate in, and continue
to belong to voluntary associations. Comparisons between males and
females, between blacks and whites, and among various socioeconomic groups suggest that differences in type of membership exist
with respect to sex and race and differences in both membership and
participation exist with respect to socioeconomic status. Age and
health do not appear to affect involvement in any simple way, but
much more information is necessary before conclusions can be drawn
with any confidence.

Booth's (1972) attempt to tie gender and organization function together and Olsen's (1970) test of competing models of race-voluntary
association ties are suggestive of the type of work needed to extend
our thinking beyond consideration merely of status characteristics as
we try to pinpoint why the elderly join organizations. Conceptually,
we have to start making connections among status characteristics,
social psychological attributes which may distinguish individuals having different statuses, and association involvement. Do the elderly join
to compensate for role losses in other spheres? Do they join because it
is part of their gregarious nature? Are they forced? Is membership
merely a continuation of pleasurable activity they have been doing for
many years? Which of these reasons are important for different subgroups of the elderly? At present, we can be fairly confident that many
elderly are continuing activity in which they had been engaged for a
long time or are substituting for similar activities. But we still lack the
information necessary to tell us how important these various reasons

are among particular subgroups of the elderly, for example, the poor, the frail, the very old. Longitudinal data bearing on the social and psychological characteristics of the respondents and the kinds of detail about organizational ties described in the previous section will be necessary to sort out the answers to these questions.

Benefits from Involvement in Voluntary Associations

Put in the contexts of what little we still know about the different types of organizations to which different subgroups of the elderly belong for whatever reasons, it is not surprising that the evidence on benefits from organizational involvement is mixed. For many elderly, high organizational involvement is accompanied by low life satisfaction. For elders, high organizational involvement may be positively associated with a limited number of positive feelings but not with others and not with general life satisfaction. Why? Earlier, the preponderance of expressive organizational memberships among the elderly was noted. Maybe such associations perform a negative expressive function because of whom they attract and what the dynamics of interaction in the group are like. Longino and Kart (1982) offer two arguments in this vein. First, it may be that people with low life satisfaction are prompted by themselves or by others to join such organizations. Cross-sectional data are therefore inappropriate since the causal ordering is reversed from what one normally assumes—satisfaction may affect joining, rather than the reverse. Second, "the social activation of the bored may have the unintended consequence of reducing life satisfaction further" (Longino & Kart, 1982, p. 718). People dissatisfied with themselves and with life may become convenient symbols for the problems of life by other members (the "poor dear" syndrome).

Whatever the reason for these disturbing findings, the kinds of longitudinal data necessary to separate out the reasons for both organizational involvement and life satisfaction remain to be generated. When such research is undertaken, it should be done not only with detailed measures of all the concepts discussed until this point—kind of organization and kind of involvement, relationship between status and psychological characteristics—but also with an open mind as to what the unit of analysis should be. Longino and Kart (1982) have noted that "It is the relationships rather than the activities themselves that are important to self-concept" (p. 719). If relationships are the key, then data analytic techniques focusing on those relationships should be used.

One obvious procedure is structural or network analysis. Such an approach has been laid out conceptually with respect to interaction strategies among the elderly (Snow & Gordon, 1980) and could be adapted to a study of the meaning of voluntary association involvement, if problems in sampling could be overcome (see, e.g., Erikson, Nosanchuk, & Lee, 1981; Morgan & Rytina, 1977). There are two major advantages to employing networking techniques, especially in conjunction with panel studies. First, relationships become a focal point for analysis, so that the quality of organizational ties can be more clearly specified than has been the case until now. Second, and just as important, other interpersonal ties (e.g., family, friends, neighbors) also become an explicit focus of the analysis, so that organizational involvement is examined in context and the degree to which different networks overlap, support, and contradict each other can be determined.

The Scientific Investigator's Utopia

These suggestions for more longitudinal or panel studies in conjunction with structural or network analysis are offered in the spirit of challenging researchers to strive to gather and analyze meaningful data about which informed and confident conclusions can be made. It is clear that present budgeting constraints make such research designs very difficult to execute. At the same time, we must not continue to attempt to replicate studies which contain critical methodological deficiencies and which do not carry our knowledge sufficiently forward. Practitioners and service personnel await concrete results in which they can have confidence. With respect to understanding the meaning which voluntary association ties have for the elderly, quite a bit more needs to be done in order to ensure that such confidence is forthcoming.

References

Babchuk, N., & Booth, A. (1969). Voluntary association membership: A longitudinal analysis. *American Sociological Review, 34*, 31–45.

Babchuk, N., Peters, G. R., Hoyt, D. R., & Kaiser, M. A. (1979). The voluntary association of the aged. *Journal of Gerontology, 34*, 579–587.

Booth, A. (1972). Sex and social participation. *American Sociological Review, 37*, 183–193.

Bull, C. N., & Aucoin, J. B. (1975). Voluntary association participation and life satisfaction: A replication note. *Journal of Gerontology, 30*, 73–76.

Carp, F. (1968). Differences among older workers, volunteers and persons who are neither. *Journal of Gerontology, 23*, 497–501.

Clemente, F., Rexroad, P., & Hirsch, C. (1975). The participation of the black aged in voluntary associations. *Journal of Gerontology, 30,* 469–472.

Cumming, E., & Henry, W. H. (1961). *Growing old: The process of disengagement.* New York: Basic Books.

Cutler, S. J. (1973). Voluntary association participation and life satisfaction: A cautionary research note. *Journal of Gerontology, 28,* 96–100.

Cutler, S. J. (1976a). Membership in different types of voluntary associations and psychological well-being. *Gerontologist, 16,* 335–339.

Cutler, S. J. (1976b). Age profiles of membership in sixteen types of voluntary associations. *Journal of Gerontology, 31,* 462–470.

Cutler, S. J. (1976c). Age differences in voluntary association membership. *Social Forces, 55,* 43–58.

Cutler, S. J. (1977). Aging and voluntary association participation. *Journal of Gerontology, 32,* 470–479.

de Toqueville, A. (1841). *Democracy in America* (Vol. 2, trans. M. Reeve). New York: J. and H. G. Langley.

Dumazedier, J. (1974). *Sociology of leisure* (trans. M. A. McKenzie). Amsterdam: Elsevier.

Durkheim, E. (1964). *The division of labor in society* (trans. G. Simpson). New York: The Free Press.

Edwards, J., & Klemmack, D. (1973). Correlates of life satisfaction: A reexamination. *Journal of Gerontology, 28,* 497–502.

Erickson, B., Nosanchuk, T., & Lee, E. (1981). Network sampling in practice: Some second steps. *Social Networks, 3,* 129–136.

Fengler, A. P., & Goodrich, N. (1980). Money isn't everything: Opportunities for elderly handicapped men in a sheltered workshop. *Gerontologist, 20,* 636–641.

Friedman, S. (1975). The resident welcoming committee: Institutionalized elderly in volunteer services to their peers. *Gerontologist, 15,* 362–367.

Gordon, C. W., & Babchuk, N. A. (1959). A typology of voluntary associations. *American Sociological Review, 24,* 22–29.

Graney, M. J. (1975). Happiness and social participation in aging. *Journal of Gerontology, 30,* 701–706.

Gubrium, J. F. (1973). *The myth of the golden years: A socio-environmental theory of aging.* Springfield, IL: Charles C. Thomas.

Hausknecht, M. (1962). *The joiners.* New York: Bedminster Press.

Hochschild, A. R. (1975). Disengagement theory: A critique and proposal. *American Sociological Review, 40,* 553–569.

Hoyt, D. R., Kaiser, M. A., Peters, G. R., & Babchuk, N. (1980). Life satisfaction and activity theory: A multidimensional approach. *Journal of Gerontology, 35,* 935–941.

Hunter, K. I., & Linn, M. W. (1980–81). Psychological differences between elderly volunteers and nonvolunteers. *International Journal of Aging and Human Development, 12,* 205–213.

Hyman, H. H., & Wright, C. R. (1971). Trends in voluntary association memberships of American adults: Replication based on secondary analysis of national sample surveys. *American Sociological Review, 36,* 191–206.

Knapp, M. R. J. (1976). Predicting the dimensions of life satisfaction. *Journal of Gerontology, 31*, 595–604.

Knoke, D., & Thompson, R. (1977). Voluntary association membership trends and the family life cycle. *Social Forces, 56*, 48–65.

Larson, R. (1978). Thirty years of research on the subjective well-being of older Americans. *Journal of Gerontology, 33*, 109–125.

Lemon, B. W., Bengston, V. L., & Peterson, J. A. (1972). An exploration of the activity theory of aging: Activity types and life satisfaction among in-movers to a retirement community. *Journal of Gerontology, 27*, 511–523.

Liang, J., Dvorkin, L., Kahana, E., & Mazian, F. (1980). Social integration and morale: A reexamination. *Journal of Gerontology, 35*, 746–757.

Longino, C. F., Jr., & Kart, C. S. (1982). Explicating activity theory: A formal replication. *Journal of Gerontology, 37*, 713–722.

Morgan, D., & Rytina, S. (1977). Comment on "Network sampling: Some first steps," by M. Granovetter. *American Journal of Sociology, 83*, 722–727.

Myrdal, G. (1964). *An American dilemma* (Vol. 2). New York: McGraw-Hill.

Olsen, M. E. (1970). Social and political participation of blacks. *American Sociological Review, 35*, 682–697.

Orum, A. M. (1966). A reappraisal of the social and political participation of Negroes. *American Journal of Sociology, 72*, 32–46.

Riley, M., & Foner, A. (1968). *Aging and society, Vol. 1: An inventory of research findings.* New York: Russell Sage.

Rose, A. M. (1967). *The power structure.* London: Oxford.

Rosow, I. (1967). *Social integration of the aged.* New York: The Free Press.

Sauer, W. (1977). Morale of the urban aged: A regression analysis by race. *Journal of Gerontology, 32*, 600–608.

Snow, D. L., & Gordon, J. B. (1980). Social network analysis and intervention with the elderly. *Gerontologist, 20*, 463–467.

Trela, J. E. (1976). Social class and association membership: An analysis of age-graded and non-age-graded voluntary association participation. *Journal of Gerontology, 31*, 198–203.

Ward, R. A. (1979a). *The aging experience: An introduction to social gerontology.* New York: J. B. Lippincott.

Ward, R. A. (1979b). The meaning of voluntary association participation to older people. *Journal of Gerontology, 34*, 438–445.

Wilensky, H. L. (1961). Life cycle, work situation, and participation in formal associations. In R. W. Kleemeier (Ed.), *Aging and leisure.* New York: Oxford.

Williams, J., Jr., Babchuk, N., & Johnson, D. R. (1973). Voluntary associations and minority status: A comparative analysis of Anglo, Black, and Mexican Americans. *American Sociological Review, 38*, 637–646.

Wright, C. R., & Hyman, H. (1958). Voluntary association memberships of American adults: Evidence from national sample surveys. *American Sociological Review, 23*, 284–294.

9

Relationships Between Informal and Formal Organizational Networks

John A. Krout

The gerontological literature abounds with descriptions and analyses of the problems facing the elderly and of the limited personal resources that many elderly have to meet these needs (Butler, 1975; Harris, 1978; Soldo, 1980). As the preceding chapters have so ably documented, many of these elderly receive substantial assistance from informal networks in resolving unmet needs. Indeed, it has been estimated that 75% of the supportive care received by older persons is provided by older children (Brody, 1978, 1981).

Nevertheless, the ability of informal networks to care for elderly parents, siblings, or friends is limited by caregivers' skills, resources, and the financial and emotional stress associated with the giving of support (Blau, 1973; Calkins, 1972). The resources of many informal support systems would be quickly depleted were it not for a large array of formal, publicly funded services that provide substantial assistance to the elderly.

The purpose of this chapter is to identify and critically examine the nature of these public services or formal support networks. Formal support refers to "government mandated or sponsored professional services whether state administered or provided through chartered intermediaries such as private nonprofit organizations" (Froland et al., 1981, p. 262). Special attention will be given to outlining the types of services provided by such formal organizations and examining the degree to which the elderly know of, utilize, and benefit from them. The degree to which such programs help sustain or possibly inhibit the ability of informal networks to provide care and assistance to the elderly will also be examined. Finally, the nature of informal and formal support linkages, and their consequences for the well-being of the elderly, will be discussed.

The Nature and Scope of Formal Supports

Recent public debates concerning the solvency and future of the Social Security system as presently structured have heightened the average American's awareness of the huge public financial commitment that has been made to this nation's elderly. Fewer citizens realize, however, that fully one-quarter of the 1980 federal budget ($155 billion) was earmarked for the elderly (Soldo, 1980). Although all of these monies do not necessarily translate into direct benefits for the elderly (Lee & Estes, 1980), such a financial outlay obviously could and does support a massive organizational network of services and programs.

In fact, almost every layer of government, as well as many facets of the private sector, are in the business of funding, administering, or directly providing service programs to the elderly. While the exact number of governmental units involved in what Estes (1980) has labeled the "aging enterprise" is not easily determined, Soldo (1980) has argued that some 135 to 200 federal government programs affect the elderly in some way—either through providing services directly or by making available cash assistance or in-kind transfers. In addition, there is large private sector involvement in providing health and social support to the elderly (e.g., there are over 13,000 proprietary nursing homes in the United States). The massive size and complexity of the formal organizational network becomes evident to even the casual observer (Kart, 1981). The tendency of government to structure such programs to fit within the existing bureaucratic lines of authority leads to the fragmentation, duplication, and lack of coordination of services for the elderly. Soldo (1980) observed that 50 Congressional committees and subcommittees debate and formulate programs for the elderly that are administered by 7 executive departments and 5 individual agencies. As a consequence, for example, federal level transportation services that affect the elderly are connected with 31 separately funded programs and 8 of 12 executive departments.

The authorization for this bewildering and often incomprehensible array of formal support programs comes mainly from two pieces of legislation: the Social Security Act and the Older Americans Act. Both of these acts have been amended repeatedly. The Social Security

program provides retirement benefits to the elderly (or their benefi-
ciaries), disability payments, and cash grants to low-income elders
(Soldo, 1980). Over 90% of the elderly in this country receive some
income support through the retirement benefit portion of this legislation (which most people equate with the term *social security*). Such
payments account for approximately 70% of the total federal expenditures for the elderly each year (Kart, 1981).

A second major program administered by the federal government
under a 1965 amendment to the Social Security Act is Medicare—a
national system of financing health services of the elderly regardless of
their financial status (in contrast, Medicaid, also established in 1965,
was designed to take care of medical expenses not covered by Medicare as well as to pay for the medical expenses of the needy regardless
of age). Health care for the elderly under these two programs accounts
for slightly over 20% of the total federal outlay for the elderly (Kart,
1981). In addition to retirement and health care coverage, the Social
Security Act, under Title 20, established federal cost sharing for the
delivery of social services to the elderly.

The Older Americans Act of 1965 sought to articulate a national
policy on the aging and established an agency, the Administration on
Aging, to coordinate federal efforts aimed at assisting the elderly
(Estes, 1980). A major focus of this act was the development of
programs to meet the social needs of the elderly. The 1973 amendments to this act directed that services to the elderly be coordinated
and delivered at the local level via a system of state and local Area
Agencies on Aging (Beattie, 1976). These agencies generally do not
provide services directly but are charged with ensuring their availability. The services include health, continuing education, welfare, information, recreation, homemaking, counseling, and referral (Lowy,
1980a).

No attempt will be made here to engage in an in-depth analysis of
programs such as Medicare or Social Security. Many insightful and
thorough examinations of these topics have been completed already
(Butler, 1975; Estes, 1980; Graebner, 1981; Schulz, 1980). The purpose
of the following sections is to focus on the types of formal services
actually made available to the elderly through these programs. Two
broad categories of services are identified: (1) health (including mental and physical); and (2) social services. The emphasis in the following sections will be on what Lowy (1980a) defined as "open" care.
These are programs and services available in the community and
designed to support the independent living status of elders. "Closed"
care, in contrast, refers to services received in institutional settings.

Health Services for the Elderly

As was mentioned earlier, the major programs designed to meet the health care needs of the elderly are Medicare and Medicaid. These programs do not provide health services to the elderly directly but serve as a form of public insurance that reimburses the private health care system for services rendered. Kart (1981) has estimated that government sources pay 65% of the health care costs incurred by the elderly. This still leaves substantial amounts of medical expenses that must be paid by private insurance or the individual. Medicare and Medicaid cover some types of services very well but others almost not at all. For example, they cover almost 90% of the elderly's expenditures for hospital care, 60% of physician's services, and 50% of both nursing home care and other professional services. In contrast, only 13% or less of the elderly's dentist services, drugs, eyeglasses, or hearing aids expenses are paid for by either Medicare or Medicaid (Kart, 1981).

Numerous authors have criticized these programs citing critical gaps in coverage and increasing costs to the elderly and society. For example, Ward (1979) argued that the goal of Medicare was to increase access to and use of health services while encouraging greater coordination and comprehensiveness of health care for the elderly. While short-stay hospital visits and outpatient use for the elderly have increased with the passage of Medicare and Medicaid, there has been little increase in the use of physician services (Lee & Estes, 1980), a minimal impact on the organization and delivery of health services, and a recognizable lack of access to medical care for *all* older Americans—especially among the poor and minorities (Ward, 1979). In addition, there has been little in the way of a recognizable increase in the emphasis on alternatives to institutionalized health care—for example, preventive health care services and home health care.

Food Stamps—the principal federal program designed to ameliorate the nutrition problems of all needy Americans (Lee & Estes, 1980)—is another major program that could have a significant impact on the basic health of the elderly. The 1973 amendments to the Older Americans Act also established funding for nutrition services. Ninety percent of this funding was allocated for the delivery of congregate meals. The remaining 10% supports the Meals-on-Wheels program which provides food directly to the elderly in their homes. The goal of both these programs is to ensure that the elderly have nutritionally sound diets (Beattie, 1976). However, funds for such programs account for only one half of one percent of the federal monies spent on the elderly (Soldo, 1980). Local governments also sometimes run programs to provide health services to the elderly in their homes (home health care and home medical services are examples), but these are not very widespread (Lowy, 1980b).

A significant effort has been made by the government to help meet the physical health care needs of the elderly. While Medicare and other programs are far from perfect, they at least indicate a recognition that the elderly and/or their informal supports should not, and cannot, be expected to carry all the burden of health care. Unfortunately, comparable efforts to make formal services available in the area of mental health have not been implemented.

It has been estimated that as many as 20% of the elderly living in the community have either severe or moderate psychiatric problems; yet the vast majority are not receiving mental health services (Lee & Estes, 1980; Lowy, 1980a). Too often the elderly with mental problems receive no special care or only custodial care in public mental hospitals or nursing homes (Lowy, 1980a). With the emphasis on deinstitutionalization within mental health, or reducing the number of patients in mental hospitals, many formerly institutionalized elderly have been released into the community (Lee & Estes, 1980). Thus, elderly persons with a history of mental health problems may find themselves in a community where few after-care services are available. Medicare pays for only a small fraction of psychiatric fees and private health insurance also provides little coverage, so most elderly cannot afford to pay for private extended care (Lowy, 1980a).

The above is not meant to suggest that there are no community mental health services for the elderly. In fact there is a wide range of services. Lowy (1980a), using a very inclusive definition, identified such services as group work, crisis intervention, and suicide prevention but cautioned that only a very small amount of local mental health monies were allocated to the elderly. Furthermore, he asserted that staff members of community mental health centers are not trained to diagnose or treat older persons nor have the administrators of such facilities encouraged contact with the elderly. Thus, it appears that little in the way of mental health services is available to the elderly outside of institutional settings.

Social Services

This is a category under which almost any and all kinds of services are often included. The Older Americans Act identified the following as social services:

- Health, continuing education, welfare, informational, recreational, homemaker, counseling, or referral.
- Transportation services where necessary to facilitate access to social services.
- Services designed to encourage and assist older persons to use the facilities and services available to them.
- Services designed to assist older persons to obtain adequate housing.
- Services designed to assist older persons in avoiding institutionalization, including preinstitutionalization evaluation and screening, and home health services, or any other services, if such services are necessary for the general welfare of older persons (Beattie, 1976).

This Act also established that such services should be coordinated and delivered at the local level through a network of Area Agencies on Aging with funding from federal and other governmental sources. Over time, increased emphasis has been placed on providing such services in open versus closed settings and on fulfilling the needs of the elderly in their homes (Beattie, 1976).

The funding and extent of coverage of social services is extremely limited and woefully inadequate when compared to the number of elderly needing and wanting them (Lowy, 1980b). Funding for social services accounts for only 1% of the Federal monies spent on the elderly (Soldo, 1980). It also appears that the United States lags far behind many other Western nations in providing such services to the elderly in their own homes (Gibson, 1981).

One of the most visible symbols of service to the elderly is the community senior center. It has been estimated that the number of senior centers in this country has grown from 340 in 1966 to over 5,000 in 1975 (National Council on Aging, 1975). Such centers vary considerably in terms of size, funding, administration, and programming, but essentially they serve as places where older adults can gather to participate in a wide range of social activities. Senior centers also serve as "focal points" for the delivery of other more basic services such as hot meals, legal assistance, transportation, and information and referral. Of these services, transportation and information and referral are often seen as being most important.

Information and referral programs are designed to facilitate the elderly's access to existing services by giving them the necessary information about these programs (Lowy, 1980b). Transportation service programs aim to ensure that the elderly who have need of services can physically get to them. The lack of personal transportation and the paucity, dangers, and cost of public transportation often leave the elderly isolated. Community services are of no help to the elderly if they are not accessible because of inadequate transportation. Many community agencies operate vans and mini-buses that provide the elderly with transportation for necessary trips.

While any number of other programs do exist and could be examined, space does not permit such a description here. Further accounts of the wide variety of social programs and their services for the elderly have been developed by Lowy (1980a, 1980b), Beattie (1976), and Estes (1980).

Utilization of Services

Social gerontologists have spent a considerable effort in determining the degree to which the services available in a community are used by the elderly. The consensus conclusion of this research is that usage rates for the elderly are extremely low. For example, Soldo (1980) cited a government study which estimates that only 3% of the eligible elderly benefit from community services, 1% from Meals-on-Wheels, and less than 50% from Supplemental Security Income (the major income maintenance program for the very poor). Lee and Estes (1980) reported that only one of six eligible, low-income elderly persons participated in the federal Food Stamp program, and Atchley (1980) noted that the elderly represent only 2% of the psychiatric clinic patients and 4% of community mental health center patients. Usage rates of social programs are not much more encouraging; a recent review of the literature found that senior centers were restricted to between 10 and 20% of the aged (Krout, 1981).

The most obvious explanation for such low utilization of formal services is that the elderly know little about the programs that can provide them with formal support. Research findings on the degree of knowledge of medical and social services vary considerably from study to study and from service to service. Whereas between one-half and two-thirds of the elderly have heard of services such as senior centers, hot lunch sites, and transportation, much lower rates (less than 30%) of awareness are found for programs such as information and referral and home health and help services (Krout, 1981).

Whatever the true amount of service awareness among the elderly, it is clear that a large proportion of the elderly who know of services do not use them. A considerable amount of attention has been directed at determining why services are not utilized by either the general population or the elderly. In an excellent review of the literature, McKinlay (1972) identified six approaches to the study of utilization behavior: economic, sociodemographic, geographic, social-psychological, sociocultural, and organizational or service delivery. For the most part, social gerontologists have restricted their analyses to an examination of sociodemographic factors—an approach which McKinlay has argued has limited explanatory power. As a result, the literature on correlates of use is largely descriptive and provides little more than a catalogue of the socioeconomic characteristics that differentiate users from nonusers. Moreover, few attempts have been made to account for the often inconsistent results found by various researchers (McKinlay, 1972). General statements are difficult to make because of the different focuses of various researchers.

Some studies report that variables such as marital status, income, occupation, education, sex, race, and living arrangements do not distinguish between members versus nonmembers, users versus nonusers, or low usage versus high usage, whereas other researchers report that the same sociodemographic variables do indeed differentiate users from nonusers (Krout, 1981).

An improvement over the restrictive sociodemographic approach can be found in the work of Andersen, Kravits, and Anderson (1975). They identified three sets of variables (predisposing, enabling, and need) that were presumed to account for health service utilization among the elderly. Predisposing variables (e.g., age, race, sex, education, marital status, health beliefs, and attitudes) are seen as affecting the propensity of an individual or family to use health services. Enabling factors (e.g., income, insurance coverage, and transportation) facilitate or inhibit the utilization of services for those predisposed to use them. Finally, need variables indicate the level of problem and response by the individual. These three sets of factors combine variables included in several of the approaches identified by McKinlay (1972). Research applying the Andersen model has produced conflicting findings concerning the relative importance of the three classes of variables as predictors of service use among the elderly (Krout, 1981).

Other observers have argued that the values and beliefs held by many elderly reduce their service utilization even though they may be in need and such services may be available and accessible. Downing (1957) has proposed that the elderly are ambivalent toward service, while Moen (1978) noted a "non-acceptor" syndrome among the elderly where a striving for independence is associated with a reluctance to admit needs or accept help and even a denial of use. Moen (1978) further argued that the nonacceptor syndrome may be partly explained by a lack of knowledge of services, confusion over eligibility status, or program benefits being seen as not outweighing the costs of application (such as time and travel). In one of the few examples of longitudinal research on service utilization, Powers and Bultena (1974) found little relationship between statements of intent to use and subsequent actual use. These researchers hypothesized that the underlying reasons for nonuse lie in the self perceptions of the aged. Using services defines oneself as old and as accepting a form of charity. Lack of use (even when need is present) reaffirms a definition of self as *not* old and able to take care of oneself.

Another plausible explanation for low utilization rates lies not in the elderly themselves but in the service delivery system. McKinlay (1972) noted that the system's bureaucratic orientation toward potential clients may serve as a barrier to use (e.g., eligibility tests, application forms and procedures, and impersonal treatment). In addition, the attitudes and behaviors of professionals in the elderly service network may also account for the low usage rates (Lowy, 1980a). Butler (1975) has argued that the medical profession and other health personnel unfortunately share many of society's negative attitudes toward the aged. The consequence in a medical context may be active avoidance and dislike, paternalism, and a lack of aggressive, positive forms of treatment.

Beattie (1976), Lowy (1980a), and Soldo (1980) have all argued that a primary impediment to effective service provision is the lack of any real organization, coordination, or integration within and between agencies in the business of bringing health and social services to the elderly. Too often the older person assumes the burden of making independent requests at different service sites and through different procedures to receive various federal and local formal support. These multiple requests consume the time, energy, and resources of the elderly and frequently create confusion and frustration.

Butler (1975) has charged that many formal programs fail to reach the elderly because of "ageism" or discrimination against the elderly. He argued that this ageism manifests itself in numerous ways such as negative stereotypes, disdain or dislike of the elderly, avoidance of contact, and discriminatory practices in housing and employment. Levin and Levin (1980) have developed this line of reasoning in some detail and argue that elderly Americans constitute a minority group who suffer prejudice and discrimination as do other groups more traditionally labeled minorities. In addition, these authors note that gerontological theories and research generally emphasize decline and "blame the victim." That is, reductions in income and social status are explained by declines in the aptitude, productivity, and interests of the individual, not as a result of social policies regarding employment and health or societal attitudes that assign the elderly a secondary status.

Some researchers have reported empirical support for the idea that the elderly are discriminated against in public programs. Patterson (1976), for example, noted that his study of eight federally funded community mental health centers revealed that elderly patients often received less adequate care than others. Ehrlich and Ehrlich (1974) have argued that the predominant service model applied to the elderly (i.e., meeting needs through age-segregated services) results in a reinforcement of negative stereotypes about the aged.

An additional problem is that too often services are delivered to those who are not in the greatest need (Lowy, 1980b). Many observers agree that the very frail elderly are often the most inaccessible and thus least likely to receive needed services (Soldo, 1980). Krout and Larson (1981) reported that the elderly in their sample with the lowest education and income levels were less likely to use a wide range of social services than their more well-off counterparts.

Formal Support of Informal Care Networks

To this point, the discussion of formal services has focused on the direct support of the elderly by formal organizations, either through service provision, in-kind services, or cash grants. However, formal programs can also affect the well-being of the elderly through their support of the kinds of informal networks examined in other chapters of this volume. It is important to determine what kinds of linkages presently exist between formal agencies and informal support networks and to investigate the limitations and effectiveness of such arrangements for the care of the elderly. Such linkages and their impacts need to be understood not only because they currently exist, but also because much attention of late has been focused on the idea of reducing governmental support for formal programs and relying more heavily on informal sources of support.

Before examining the degree and nature of the formal support of informal networks, several basic assumptions need to be established. First, informal supports of the elderly do not, and cannot, exist *completely* independent of all formal agencies. The social organization and technology levels of modern urbanized and industrialized societies virtually ensure that individuals become dependent on an array of massive bureaucracies. Programs and services for the elderly are part of this bureaucratic tendency. Some functions previously carried out by family units have been taken over, for better or worse, by government or private industry. Thus, even should a family desperately want to provide for an elder, it is highly likely that the family will have contact with the formal agency network. All the essential services necessary for noninstitutionalized living in the community are managed by formal organizations—e.g., police, fire, medical care, and sanitation. Thus, the most pertinent question becomes not *whether* informal supports have contact with formal organizations, but rather do formal service agencies *complement* or *complicate* (even negate) the efforts of the informal networks.

Second, we must remember that formal and informal organizations are inherently different and, therefore, approach questions of how to best care for an elderly person from sometimes disparate perspectives. Informal networks are characterized by primary group ties that are based largely on feelings of emotion and obligation. A family's concern for an elderly parent or sibling is generally not based on utilitarian motives or on an objective view of the situation. Agencies and programs, in contrast, usually operate under systems of explicit categories for assessing need or eligibility, formal rules of procedures, and objective standards for treating clients. In publicly funded organizations the interaction of the staff with the elderly is typically characterized as a client/consumer relationship (Froland et al., 1981). It is likely, therefore, that some tension and conflict will exist between such different kinds of networks.

A final important point is that the capacities and capabilities of formal and informal networks differ significantly and that it is unrealistic, even ill-advised, to expect informal networks to assume responsibility for some of the functions of programs and agencies. For example, Bolles (1979) has suggested that much of the literature on this topic indicates that families should meet the emotional and environmental needs of older relatives and rely on formal organizations for economic assistance and health care. Many authors (Cantor, 1975; Shanas & Sussman, 1977) suggest that the proper role of the formal system is to provide "supportive services" to families (e.g., transportation, home medical, and respite care) and that professionals in the formal system can assist informal network members in identifying the important factors that affect the older person's quality of life (Johnson, 1978). Litwak (1965) introduced the concept of "shared functioning" and noted that the availability of *both* formal and informal support networks significantly improves the well-being of the elderly. These observations suggest that the formal–informal support debate is not, and should not, be put in either/or terms. Some kinds of support are more appropriately provided by formal or informal networks (Coward, 1982).

With these observations as a foundation, we can now review the types of assistance actually provided by formal organizations to the informal support networks of the elderly. One of the more comprehensive reviews of the policies and programs designed to facilitate informal support of the elderly living in noninstitutional settings is provided by Gibson (1981). She asserted that such policies in the United States lag far behind those found in Europe and Great Britain in their number, scope, and public funding. For example, housing assistance in the form of low-interest loans or allowances are given to families in Japan and Sweden who refurbish their homes to accommodate an elderly relative on a permanent basis. Pinker (1980) reported that 80% of the local authorities he surveyed in England and Wales "made provisions" for the elderly to live near relatives. Many of the industrialized nations (not the U.S.) provide financial assistance in the form of a cash benefit to families that care for disabled (often elderly) persons in the home (Tracy, 1974).

Research by Sussman (1979) has indicated that continual financial support, like tax deductions, is most popular with families providing care. However, Gibson (1981) cautioned that few evaluative research investigations have been completed on the actual impact of such financial aid programs or on their effectiveness as incentives to greater family care vis-à-vis other types of programs. Indeed, several studies (Arling & McAuley, 1983; Cantor, 1980; Cicirelli, 1980) have reported that financial considerations are not the primary motivating factors for family caregiving (at least of dependent elderly) nor are financial problems identified by caregivers as precipitating decisions to institutionalize their elderly charges. Emotional or physical exhaustion, worry about the aged person's health, and insufficient help from others are much more likely to be cited as problems associated with caregiving (Cantor, 1980).

Gibson (1981) also discussed a number of community-based services that aim to help ill older people remain in their own or a family member's home. Such services include home help and home health assistance (discussed earlier) and day care or day hospitals. Such services can free adult family members for other activities during the day and, thus, encourage them to care for older relatives with some degree of mental or physical incapacity. These services can help prevent the premature institutionalization of some older people and reduce the burden placed on the informal network. Other formal services are not directed at the elderly person but at the informal caregivers. Perhaps the best known example of such a formal support program is respite care. Although much less common in the United States than in Europe, this service is increasingly being offered at geriatric care facilities (Beattie, 1976).

The basic objective of respite care is to allow the caregiver of an ill older relative some time away from their caregiving responsibilities. Family members seem more willing and better able to continue long-term care in the home when assured of such support. Whitfield and Krompholz (1981), for example, found that families providing care for dependent elderly parents frequently expressed a need for counseling and respite care. Respite care often takes the form of the temporary placement of the ill elder in a nursing home or hospital. Respite care can also take place in the caregiver's home through the use of volunteers to relieve family caregivers during the day or night or through placing the elderly person in other private residences for short periods (Gibson, 1981).

An even newer approach among the formal networks is group support and training programs for families of the elderly. These programs are designed to reduce the isolation of family caregivers by bringing them together with others in the same situation in order to exchange information and skills related to taking care of older adults (Gibson, 1981). One of the few examples of this kind of program found in the United States is the natural Support Program of the Community Services Society of New York City. This program offers several kinds of group support to families, including educational groups, peer support, and self-help groups. Mental and physical health care professionals participate in such programs to increase the knowledge and understanding of the lay person (Hudis & Buchman, 1978).

While there are formal programs in the United States that support the informal caregivers of the elderly, there are also other formal programs and policies that serve as disincentives to informal, especially family, care of the elderly. For example, Supplemental Security Income benefits are reduced if an elderly person lives with children. Similarly, the income of family members who live with low-income elderly is considered when determining the eligibility of the latter for Food Stamps. Medicare and Medicaid reimbursement policies may also discourage family support of the indigent elderly in that they provide full support for the long-term institutional care of such persons but no financial compensation for in-home care (Gibson, 1981).

Such disincentives, when combined with the very limited scope of incentives for informal support, have created an unfortunate situation. Shanas and Sussman (1977) have argued that informal supports could offer more services to aged relatives if even a small portion of the huge resources available to the formal service bureaucracy were allocated to them.

At the same time, several authors have noted the dangers in a wholesale shifting of responsibility for elderly care from formal to informal networks without first carefully investigating the consequences such an action might have for the elderly as well as the informal network (Biegel & Maguire, 1982; Coward, 1982). These authors note that the current state of knowledge about formal and informal collaborative efforts is not sufficient to allow an accurate determination of the likely outcomes of a large change in the existing balance of caregiving. They caution against "jumping on the bandwagon" too quickly and stress that informal support is not without problems. Biegel and Maguire (1982) have argued that informal care of the elderly is not a cure-all, may duplicate services available from formal agencies, and can even undo the positive aspects of professional help. Coward (1982) also has identified a number of potential negative effects on elder care recipients including perpetuation of misinformation (especially in regard to health) and the avoidance of seeking needed professional assistance. He also noted the following potential harmful effects for the caregiver: physical, financial, and emotional strain, and the upsetting of informal network dynamics due to the intrusion of formal organization representatives.

In summary, informal helping networks are not without their limitations, and caution must be taken in moving too quickly to link them more closely with formal programs or to shift formal service responsibilities to their shoulders. Formal supports do play an important role in the care of the elderly, and it is naive, and possibly dangerous, to suggest uncritically that this care would be better or more efficiently handled by informal support networks.

Concluding Comments

Recent developments in U.S. public policy have led to the growth of a massive formal support network for the elderly. While suffering from numerous weaknesses, the programs and services that make up this network do offer considerable assistance to the elderly. Unfortunately, as presently structured, public aging policies generally encourage institutionalization and provide little in the way of support that might keep the vulnerable elderly living in the community even if dependent on some combination of formal and informal support. In addition, many existing formal agencies appear to be oblivious to the existence and needs of the informal caregivers who provide so much support for their elderly loved ones. Few programs exist that attempt to integrate the strengths, and overcome the weaknesses, of both through the comprehensive provision and planning of services.

There is a crying need for more and improved research on a number of basic questions concerning the structure and function of formal services. The following issues are seen as particularly deserving of attention: coordination and integration of formal service delivery systems; availability, acceptability, and accessibility of programs with particular emphasis on "needy" populations; alternative service delivery strategies—especially in rural areas; effectiveness of service organizations and training of their staff; impact of funding and reimbursement policies on the coverage and utilization of services; correlates of service knowledge and utilization; cost-effectiveness of various service modes; and the provision of supportive services in the home. There is a crucial lack of understanding of the dynamics of the interplay between formal and informal support systems of the elderly. It is clear that researchers and practitioners must move forward to a better definition and understanding of what constitutes an appropriate balance between the two systems of support. A multifaceted and multidisciplinary effort will be required to determine the impact of existing policies and programs on informal caregivers, or caregivers to be, with the knowledge and practical skills necessary for successful caregiving.

One of the central questions that gerontological researchers need to address in this area is that of the appropriateness and effectiveness of alternative mechanisms of formal service support of informal caregivers. Few of these alternatives (e.g., respite care, counseling, financial incentives) have been systematically designed, implemented, or evaluated. Thus, their utility in informal network care is unknown. In addition, many unanswered, and to some degree unasked, policy and programmatic issues exist concerning these alternatives. Take, for example, public financial payment to family caregivers of ill elderly. Arling and McAuley (1983) have identified a number of concerns that should be investigated before such a support mechanism is put into place. These include questions of eligibility requirements, determination of actual costs, appropriateness of financial payments as an incentive or motivation to informal caregiving vis-à-vis other types of support, and the impact on family dynamics and the nature of caregiving itself.

The question of how to best meet the needs of the elderly in our society is complex. In many ways, society is just beginning to realize that complexity and has only recently begun to investigate how informal and formal networks can be most efficiently and effectively integrated. As this chapter has sought to demonstrate, even the most basic questions concerning the delivery of comprehensive supports for the elderly have hardly been formulated let alone adequately examined. Equally important are the challenges that such questions create for public policy. The key to improving the quality of life of the nation's elderly and those who will eventually reach old age lies as much in the will or ability of policymakers to respond to new ideas and information as in the quality of those ideas. In this sense, academics, practitioners, and government officials are faced with a common challenge of utmost urgency and seriousness.

References

Andersen, R. J., Kravits, J., & Anderson, O. W. (1975). *Equity in health services: Empirical analyses in social policy.* Cambridge, MA: Ballinger.

Atchley, R. C. (1980). *The social forces in later life: An introduction to social gerontology.* Belmont, CA: Wadsworth.

Arling. G., & McAuley, W. J. (1983). The feasibility of public payments for family caregiving. *The Gerontologist, 23,* 300–306.

Beattie, W. M. (1976). Aging and the social services. In R. H. Binstock & E. Shanas (Eds.), *Handbook of aging and the social sciences.* New York: Van Nostrand Reinhold.

Biegel, D. E., & Maguire, L. (1982). *Developing linkages with community support systems: Limitations and dangers.* Paper presented at the meeting of Community Mental Health Centers, New York.

Bolles, M. (1979). *The impact of informal social support systems upon the needs, resources, and daily coping behaviors of elderly persons: An empirical evaluation.* Unpublished manuscript.

Blau, Z. (1973). *Old age in a changing society.* New York: Viewpoint Press.

Brody, E. M. (1978). *Long-term care of older people: A practical guide.* New York: Human Sciences Press.

Brody, E. M. (1981). "Women in the middle" and family help to older people. *The Gerontologist, 21*(5), 471–480.

Butler, R. N. (1975). *Why survive? Being old in America.* New York: Harper and Row.

Calkins, E. (1972). Shouldering a burden. *Omega, 3,* 23–36.

Cantor, M. (1975). Life space and the social support system of the inner city elderly of New York. *The Gerontologist, 15,* 23-27.

Cantor, M. (1980). Caring for the frail elderly: Impact on family, friends, and neighbors. Presented at the Annual Meeting of the Gerontological Society of America, San Diego.

Cicirelli, V. G. (1980). Personal strains and negative feelings in adult children's relationships with elderly parents. Presented at the Annual Meeting of the Gerontological Society of America, San Diego, CA.

Coward, R. T. (1982). Cautions about the role of natural helping networks in programs for the rural elderly. In N. Stinnett, J. DeFrain, K. King, H. Lingren, G. Rowe, S. Van Zandt, & R. Williams (Eds.), *Family strengths 4: Positive support systems* (pp. 291-306). Lincoln: The University of Nebraska Press.

Downing, J. (1957). Factors affecting the selective use of a social club for the aged. *Journal of Gerontology, 12,* 81-84.

Ehrlich, I., & Ehrlich, P. (1974). A service delivery model for the aged at the community level. *The Gerontologist, 14.*

Estes, C. L. (1980). *The aging enterprise: A critical examination of social policies and services for the aged.* San Francisco: Jossey-Bass.

Froland, C., Pancoast, D., Chapman, N., & Kimboko, P. (1981). Linking formal and informal support systems. In B. Gottlieb (Ed.), *Social networks and support.* Beverly Hills, CA: Sage.

Gibson, M. J. (1981). *Family support patterns, policies, and programs in developed nations.* Paper presented at the Annual Meeting of the Gerontological Society of America, Toronto, Ontario, Canada.

Graebner, W. (1981). *A history of retirement.* New Haven, CT: Yale University Press.

Harris, C. (1978). *Factbook on aging: A profile of America's older population.* Washington, DC: The National Council on the Aging.

Hudis, I., & Buchbaum, M. (1978). *Components of community-based group programs for family caregivers of the aging.* Paper presented at the Annual Meeting of the Gerontological Society of America, New York.

Johnson, E. (1978). Good relations between older mothers and their daughters: A causal model. *The Gerontologist, 18,* 301-306.

Kart, G. S. (1981). *The realities of aging.* New York: Allyn and Bacon.

Krout, J. A. (1981). Service utilization by the elderly: A critical review of the literature. Presented at the Annual Meeting of the Gerontological Society of America, Toronto, Ontario, Canada.

Krout, J. A., & Larson, D. L. (1981). *Service utilization patterns of the rural elderly.* Final Report, Washington, DC: Administration on Aging.

Lee, G. R., & Estes, C. L. (1980). Eighty federal programs for the elderly. In C. Estes (Ed.), *The aging enterprise: A critical examination of social policies and services.* San Francisco: Jossey-Bass.

Levin, J., & Levin, W. C. (1980). *Ageism: Prejudice and discrimination against the elderly.* Belmont, CA: Wadsworth.

Litwak, E. (1965). Extended kin relations in an industrial democratic society. In E. Shanas & G. Streib (Eds.), *Social structures and the family: Generational relations*. Englewood Cliffs, NJ: Prentice-Hall.

Lowy, L. (1980a). Mental health services in the community. In L. Birrien & R. Sloane (Eds.), *Mental health and aging*. NJ: Prentice-Hall.

Lowy, L. (1980b). *Social policies and programs on aging: What is and what should be in later years*. Lexington, MA: Lexington Books.

McKinlay, J. (1972). Some approaches and problems in the study of the use of services: An overview. *Journal of Health and Social Behavior, 13*, 115–152.

Moen, E. (1978). The reluctance of the elderly to accept help. *Social Problems, 25*, 293–303.

National Council on the Aging. (1975). *Directory of senior centers and clubs*. Washington, DC: Author.

Patterson, R. D. (1976). Services for the aged in community mental health centers. *American Journal of Psychiatry, 133*, 271–273.

Pinker, R. A. (1980). Facing up to the eighties: Health and welfare needs of British elderly. *The Gerontologist, 20*, 273–283.

Powers, E. A., & Bultena, G. L. (1974). Correspondence between anticipated and actual uses of public services by the aged. *Social Service Review, 48*, 245–254.

Shanas, E., & Sussman, M. (1977). *Family, bureaucracy, and the elderly*. Durham, NC: Duke University Press.

Soldo, B. J. (1980). America's elderly in the 1980s. *Population Bulletin, 35*.

Sussman, M. B. (1979). *Social and economic supports and family environments for the elderly: Final report*. Washington, DC: Administration on Aging.

Tracy, M. D. (Nov. 1974). Constant attendance allowances for non-work related disability. *Social Security Bulletin*.

Ward, R. A. (1979). *The aging experience: An introduction to social gerontology*. New York: J. B. Lippincott.

Whitfield, S., & Krompholz, B. (1981). *Report to the general assembly on the family support system demonstration program*. Maryland Office on the Aging.

Part IV
Social Networks Under Special Circumstances

10

The Social Networks of Ethnic Minorities

David Guttmann

The informal supports of family, friends, and neighbors assume greater significance in the well-being of elderly persons as the impact of inflation and impending threats to Social Security cause them to rely more on themselves and on those who are truly significant in their lives. Aside from relatives, the "significant others" regularly consist of people belonging to social networks organized along ethnic lines and constitute a safety net which keeps many elderly from sinking into destitution and despair.

Despite hard-won social and economic benefits, Medicare and Medicaid, Food Stamps and other "benefits of old age" (Kutza, 1982), the likelihood of elderly in minority groups being poor is twice as great as for the white elderly population. Poverty is widespread, and traditional kinship support of the family diminishes when the family as a whole is impoverished or when the needs of its elderly member outstrip the family's ability to help.

This chapter examines the concept of social networks that affect the elderly in different ethnic groups and the impact of these networks on social policy on aging. Social networks, ethnicity, and minority are defined, and the relationship between ethnicity and minority is discussed. Theoretical issues related to kinship and social networks are highlighted with research illustrations drawn from recent studies, including ongoing research on stress management, which provides an additional perspective. Finally, suggestions for further research in social gerontology are presented.

Conceptual Definitions of Social Networks, Ethnicity, and Minority

The 1981 White House Conference on Aging focused some of its spotlight on social networks as one means of achieving two major goals in the emerging national policy on aging: (1) the enhancement of the lives of older persons through their full participation in the life of the nation; and (2) the facilitation of positive changes in social institutions to accommodate the growing numbers of elderly individuals. The discovery, or rather rediscovery, of social networks as a potential asset in achieving the above national goals, while significant, is not in itself a major breakthrough in policymaking. Rather, it may be seen as an admission of an obvious yet surprisingly often overlooked fact. Social networks, after all, have been around for a long time.

More fascinating, however, is that the terms *social networks*, *networking*, and *informal supports* have quickly gained approval and increasingly greater use by members of the helping professions. This change of heart by the social-behavioral disciplines concerning social networks is a relatively recent phenomenon. Only 15 years ago the prestigious *International Encyclopedia of the Social Sciences* (Sills, 1968) did not include "social networks" among the many sociologically worthy subjects it treated so distinctively. Rather, it was subsumed, or implied, under the broad category of social systems. Similarly, the *Dictionary of Behavioral Science*, published less than a decade ago (Wolman, 1973), did not devote a separate explanation to this term, nor did the *Encyclopedia of Social Work* (NASW, 1971), or recent texts on social gerontology (Kimmel, 1974) or on the sociology of aging (Harris & Cole, 1980).

The omission of social networks from some of the major publications of the social sciences is even more surprising in light of the growing numbers of studies dealing with support systems for the aged and the renewed calls for greater attention to the role social networks can, should, or may play in the welfare of the nation's elderly. *Social networks*, for lack of a better definition and as used in this chapter, refer to those *common elements* that bind together various people under specific circumstances. For example, the social networks of widows, known as widow-to-widow programs, imply an interconnected or interrelated chain, a system of lines, channels, or other organizational elements that hold together a network in some fashion around a central nucleus, in this case the common emotional social problems of widows, and their common need for ways to deal with their specific circumstances in society.

Ethnic minorities are even more complex both as a concept and as a term in need of definition. To combine "ethnic" and "minority" into a single unit inevitably invites some risk of confrontation with scholars of both disciplines. Ethnicity, in particular, is not open to the ups and downs or the ins and outs of political designations as is the term *minority*. As Gelfand and Kutzik (1979) point out, every American is an ethnic to some extent. He or she shares values in his or her ethnic group which are distinct from the common values of American society in general. Or as Greeley (1978) states: "When I use the word [*ethnic*] I normally refer simply to the variety of American subcultures; whether that variety be based on race, religion, nationality, language, or even region" (p. 28).

In this chapter, ethnicity is defined as cultural uniqueness, historically derived. In the United States distinct ethnic groups are the result of cultural traditions transplanted by immigrants from their countries of origin. Their cultural traditions consist of a shared symbolic system of meanings that chiefly concern values and attitudes but that also include distinct relational and communicational patterns of verbal and nonverbal behaviors. On the social level, the maintenance of cultural distinctiveness by groups in a larger society leads to the concept of cultural or ethnic pluralism which, if fully developed, may result in cultural enrichment of the general society, heightened sensitivity to coping with relational problems, and strengthening unity (of the whole) through diversity (of its parts) (Kolm, 1980). In this respect, each cultural group has developed over the centuries its unique patterns of aging, along with coping and caring behaviors associated with being an ethnic elderly.

Wirth (1965) defines minority as "a group of people who, because of their physical or cultural characteristics, are singled out from others in the society in which they live for differential and unequal treatment, and who, therefore, regard themselves as objects of collective discrimination" (p. 309). The existence of a minority group in society implies the existence of a corresponding dominant group enjoying higher social status and greater privileges. One aspect of full participation in the life of a society is the degree to which persons receive those public benefits to which they are entitled as members of that society. In this sense, the plight of the "minority elderly," those close to 3 million people who belong to one of the four commonly accepted minorities by race (blacks, Hispanics of any race, Asian-American, and Native American Indians) has been characterized as one of "double jeopardy," "triple jeopardy" or "multiple jeopardy" (Butler, 1975; Dowd & Bengston, 1978; Jackson, 1970).

The common bond among these minority groups is that they encompass people whose basic needs have not been sufficiently understood by those involved in the planning and development of services. Thus the President's Commission on Mental Health (1978), for example, found that appropriate services are not available to many minority elderly, even though social, economic, and environmental factors render them particularly vulnerable to acute and prolonged psychological and emotional distress.

Viewed from the perspective of relative deprivation, the term *minority elderly* has commonly been used to describe the situation of large numbers of elderly who were either poor prior to or became poor after entering the official age (65 years) at which one is regarded as elderly. According to the *Chartbook on Aging in America* (1981), which is based on 1979 population, the following percentages represent some of the minority elderly in the United States who are poor: blacks, 42% females and 27% males; Hispanics (may be of any race), 28% females and 23% males. These figures compare with 16% females and 9% males in the white population.

"Ethnic Minorities": A Misnomer

As a nation of immigrants, the United States of America has absorbed well over 50 million newcomers from all corners of the world, comprising over 100 ethnic groups, about 50 of them major groups. This statement by the President's Commission on Mental Health (1978) illustrates an often overlooked fact in the discussions of minorities, namely, that in one respect every American is an ethnic person, whether or not he or she belongs to any of the officially recognized groups of minority elderly, by virtue of membership in a culturally diverse group. This definition of ethnicity implies that in addition to minorities by race, such as black, Hispanic, Asian, Native-American, white, or European-American elderly, native born and immigrant citizens have legitimate claims on the lofty status of ethnic minority.

Before the 1981 White House Conference on Aging, the often forgotten and overlooked block of population 65 years of age and older had not been counted. Yet for this ethnically diverse group (numbering close to seven million or one-quarter of the total population) with Italian, Polish, Greek, Jewish, Hungarian, Estonian, Lithuanian, Latvian, Ukrainian, Irish, German, French, Swedish, or other backgrounds, the maintenance of ethnic culture is a central factor in their well-being.

Lack of previous political assertiveness by the elderly, however, does not correspond to a lack of interest in matters related to their welfare nor to a lack of needs, wishes, and expectations concerning improvements deemed necessary to bring about wholesome and meaningful lives for all older Americans. Rather, it is a result of instinctive shying away from the limelight, from activism, and from self-assertion that characterizes this generation of elderly Euro-Americans. After all, two centuries of assimilationist and melting pot indoctrination has intimidated them and undermined their belief in the legitimacy and value of their ethnic patterns to society (Kolm, 1980).

While it is true that older people in some industrial societies experience the devaluation of old age, which in turn designates them a minority, the real minority elderly, those usually so classified by the government, face not only problems associated with aging (i.e., a disproportionate share of poverty), but also the accumulated problems of a lifetime of membership in a minority group and living in a society where racial equality remains more an ideal than public policy. Much of the impact of the aging process hits especially hard those who are unable to afford quality goods or services or who, by virtue of their minority status, have always occupied a disadvantaged position in American society. It is important to recognize that, in addition to the many distinctions between the minority and nonminority elderly, there also exist innumerable situational variants among minority groups of elderly people. Each group has its own history, subculture, and means of coping with the different meanings of its own symbols and values within the larger society.

Dependence on Social Networks for Survival

At present, some two million elderly Americans 65 and older speak a language other than English in their daily communications. For example, some speak only Spanish, many Asian-American elderly do not speak English, and large numbers of elderly from various parts of Europe, despite many years of living in the United States, do not speak English well. In addition, while lack of education is seen as the most frequently mentioned barrier to a sense of fulfillment in life, the majority of the elderly in these many minority groups have not completed grade school, are functionally illiterate, and lack the skills and knowledge to successfully cope with life in our modern society.

In every major city in the United States, thousands of limited-English-speaking elderly live in large ethnic enclaves. They are generally deprived of opportunities to benefit fully from available public (government) services by their cultural values, which often prevent them from admitting a need and seeking assistance. For example, Spanish-speaking populations vary considerably from coast to coast in their perceptions of self and of society. Differences between U.S.-born and immigrant Spanish-speaking elderly imply differential use and reliance on social networks that may be available to them. Similarly, social class differences, sometimes confused with either "ethnicity" or "minority" (Kalish, 1971, p. 80), constitute a factor in differential use of public benefits by older black people. Bell and Zellman (1975) found that among the elderly of simliar socioeconomic status, whites are more likely to consult and visit private doctors, whereas blacks tend to use clinics and hospital emergency rooms more for routine health care.

There are, however, elderly who could and would use public services if they knew how to obtain them. These people are usually new to the community (e.g., refugees, migrant or transitory workers, or those who gradually lose their resources with aging and are left behind in changing neighborhoods), and they become dependent on social networks in their ethnic minority communities and neighborhoods. Surprisingly, as Kalish (1971) notes, little has been written about the ways in which ethnic communities may ease life for these aging persons (or make it more difficult). In recent years, research on the ethnic elderly not only concentrated on deprived racial minorities, but lumped together and treated as homogeneous the culturally dissimilar ethnic groups within the larger blocks of Asian, Hispanic, and Native-American Indian elderly. Ignoring the cultural dimension results in misunderstandings about differences not only in lifestyles, but, more important, in the ways people make sense of their realities while undergoing the aging process.

The heterogeneity noted within each ethnic group is expressed by a differential use of social and cultural resources by members of the supposedly "same" culture (Guttmann, 1973). For example, Eastern-European and American born and raised Jewish elderly differ significantly in their leisure-time activity interests because of different backgrounds and culturally conditioned preferences for meaningful and enjoyable activities. While they certainly share a common sense of peoplehood, ancient history, and positive attitudes toward Jewish values, they may differ rather sharply in the social networks they utilize. They also differ in use of language (Yiddish vs. English), and especially in their participation in social club and voluntary associations.

Lumping together culturally diverse groups of elderly under a common label such as "Asians" or "whites," and further labeling them as "minorities," demonstrates insensitivity to cultural distinctiveness. More dangerous, however, is the possibility that such labeling may be used for the sake of expediency by planners or policymakers.

Theoretical Considerations: Traditional Kinship Approach in the Study of Social Networks

Social network research has traditionally centered on kinship observations, organization, and options regarding the supports extended (or withheld) to the elderly family member. Because kinship theory is set in social and cultural anthropology, and specifically in social systems, a few words about these systems are in order. Parsons (1978) has stated that, "A social system, like all living systems, is inherently an open system engaged in processes of interchange (or 'input-output relations') with its environment, as well as consisting of interchanges among its internal units" (p. 460). The processes of interchange are sometimes the main objectives of research within the broad area of "support systems" in social gerontology. Thus, for example, Cantor's (1979) study of the helping networks operating among the elderly living in the inner city of New York is an illustration of how one system, the patterns of assistance between children and parents, functions within itself and along ethnically differentiated lines.

The functioning of the kinship system may be perceived as aimed toward self-sufficiency or autonomy in implementing its normative culture (i.e., values, norms, and collective goals), and toward solidarity. The latter is defined as the degree to which its collective interest can be expected to prevail over the unit interests of its members wherever the two conflict.

Returning now to the concept of kinship as the most commonly thought of form of social network (from a theoretical perspective), Eggan (1968) has noted that kinship is one of the universals in human society and therefore plays an important role in both the regulation of behavior and the formation of social groups. He further states that:

> all societies distinguish various categories of relationship by descent or consanguinity, and most societies distinguish relationships by marriage or affinity as well. The resulting *network of social relations* may constitute almost the whole social structure in some of the simpler societies or be a relatively small part of a highly complex structure, as in modern industrial societies. (p. 390)

This differentiation between simple and complex societies is a useful one, not only for theoretical clarity, but also for properly delineating the subject and its boundaries. Following Eggan's differentiation, this chapter will therefore deal almost exclusively with the social networks operating among ethnic minorities within urban industrialized society in the United States.

While the scientific study of kinship systems dates back well over a hundred years, the bulk of these studies more often asks "what" than "why." Controversies among theories and theorists abound in the studies conducted in the past four decades and center around descriptive versus classificatory system, methodological versus theoretical distinctions, and cross-cultural versus linguistic analysis. Among these studies some of the more conceptually outstanding work was done by Sussman and Burchinal (1962). These authors focused on the importance of the extended family (as a social network) in disaster situations. Their study has been followed by a host of other empirical research efforts which, in general, have demonstrated the existence of such networks and their relevance for noting how this support system is utilized by individual members in furthering their personal goals and ambitions within or outside of the network.

However, in speaking of the aged and their normal dependencies, it is not enough to cite well-known functions of the family as an emotional system or primary group best suited to care for the elderly dependent (functionally impaired) member. The quality and quantity of reciprocal behavior in helping among family members in kinship networks have been explained along the lines of linkage theory by Litwak (1960) and others. According to this theory, families are most competent to handle unusual events such as crises or disasters. They also differ from formal institutions by their structure and functioning. Emotional support is given regardless of the value of the individual's contribution to the overall welfare of the unit. The extended family thus functions as a social support network which complements more institutionalized forms of care that modern society makes available to people in need. Utilization of resources provided by the social network of the extended family is particularly evident in cases of serious illness and events related to role transitions, such as retirement, forced unemployment, and death. These events, along with specific celebrations of major holidays, wedding anniversaries, and graduations, serve to reunite scattered members of the family.

This perception of the social network concept as related to the kinship system is a useful one in explaining both family functioning and the "give and take" operations that characterize exchanges among its members. In recent years, social network functions of the family have taken an increasingly larger role in professional interventions on behalf of elderly clients. In Miami, for example, attempts were made to develop both the concept and the corresponding methodology of the "neighborhood family," which operates on the principle of shared responsibility in obtaining and using resources (Ross, 1978). Staff members serve as "regular family members"; volunteers provide free labor, and the elderly—including those with various degrees of functional impairment—are able to maintain themselves in the "family" for long periods. Similar attempts were developed in Michigan (Silverman, 1978) and elsewhere. Rueveni (1979), on the other hand, used social network as a theoretical frame of reference in therapy, while Sussman (1978) investigated the feasibility, circumstances, and conditions under which the family network may be used as an alternative to institutionalization by providing care and a home environment for its aged members.

Social Networks as Resistance Resources to Stress

In dealing with social networks from the family or kinship system perspective, attention was called to this system's ability to function as a buffer or barrier to stress, illness, and crises that at times affect its members, especially the aged. Network utilization can teach us about the aged person's ability to cope with stress, and of the availability and responsiveness of network (family) members, whose emotional attachment and filial obligations lead to the provision of care. In this light, it is surprising that very little research has been done on the differences among various ethnic minorities in dealing with stress experienced by their aged members, for despite progress made during the past 20 years in developing and implementing a wide range of services and benefits for older Americans, old age is still considered a period of hardship and stress, especially by minority elderly.

Perhaps the most common source of stress is decreased economic resources. Among all races, elderly women are the heaviest hit by poverty, while of all poor persons, 7 in 10 men aged 65 years and older live in poverty (Rowan, 1981). For Hispanic elderly the facts are even more discouraging—3 out of 7 elderly Hispanics were poor or "near poor" in 1980 (Lacayo, 1982).

Rather than focusing on the "what," as does linkage theory in explaining the role of social networks in the general schema of well-being of its members, new theories and new research on stress focus on issues of "why" and examine people's ability to deal with the inevitable stresses of everyday life. Here the emphasis is on the differences of coping styles, social and psychological resources, motivation, and outlook on life that people exhibit in their attempts to maintain health while coping with stress. Antonovsky (1979), a leading theorist in this field, brings together knowledge from behavioral medical and psychiatric research conducted in recent years to support his theory that even when aging is perceived positively, coping with stressful life events, such as death of a spouse or friends, requires mobilization of resources.

Stressful life events are viewed by researchers and by some health care practitioners as processes in which the individual or group has a major role and a major stake in the outcome. Therefore, by increasing individual and group awareness of available resources and knowledge of procedures necessary to obtain them, and by bolstering their decision-making capabilities, some can be mitigated or even eliminated, thus helping to sustain mental health.

What causes the differences between pathological and nonpathological response to stress? Why do substantial numbers of subjects living under similar conditions (e.g., poverty, ignorance) not become ill? The answer to both questions is *resistance resources*, which are defined by Antonovsky as, "the power which can be applied to resolve a tension expressive of a state of disturbed homeostasis." The rapidity and the completeness with which problems are resolved and tension dissipated are central elements of tension management that can be applied to the social-emotional functioning of individuals and groups.

There are three major social-psychological resources available in varying degrees to the individual dealing with stress. The first is *homeostatic flexibility*, or the ability to accept alternatives relative to (1) social roles (e.g., accepting alternatives to employment); (2) values (e.g., accepting values other than your own as legitimate); and (3) personal behavior (e.g., overcoming personality conflicts in a work situation).

The second major resistance resource to stress is *ties to others*, which focuses on connections people have outside their families, such as close friends.

Finally, the third major resistance resource to stress, called *ties to the community*, involves the nature of people's relationships within their communities, including the frequency of their interaction and involvement with community members and functions as well as their perceptions of the status and power available to them.

Recent research illustrates the latter two concepts. Lopata (1976), in an excellent presentation entitled *Polish American* (subtitled *Status in an Ethnic Community*) shows the differences in the availability of social networks between numbers of the old and new emigrants of Polish Americans. She cites the classification of several types of societies that are involved in the life of the ethnic community:

1. The *tribal society*, designated by a distinct name, united by a belief in common ancestors from which culture was originally derived, and possessing some degree of social integration.
2. The *political society*, which has a common legal system and an organized, independent government controlling all the people who inhabit a definite territory.
3. The *ecclesiastical society*, which has a common and distinct literary, religious culture and an independent, organized church.
4. The *national culture society*, which has a common and distinct secular, literary culture and an independent organization functioning for the preservation, growth, and expansion of this culture.

Each of these societies may be perceived as consisting of a social network or organizations and informal social relations of varying degrees of institutional completeness, so that members can, but do not necessarily need to, limit their significant and important interactions to its confines (pp. 4–6).

Members of the old emigration have village and regional idealities in common. New emigration Poles share common experiences of displacement. Each group identifies differently with Poland, America, and Polonia. Other important variables distinguishing one Polish American from another include generation in America, occupation, age, sex, marital and parental status, education, and presence or absence of an extended kinship group. These traits affect a Polish American's (1) social class life style; (2) involvement in Polish, Polonia, and American variations of this life style; and (3) content of life. (p. 96)

Social Networks as Social Worlds

The three major resistance resources to stress may be broadened to include the concept of social works, a new area of research in social gerontology. Lopata's presentation of the social networks that dominate the lives of Polish-Americans is illustrative of the many different social worlds that exist within the broad framework of an ethnic community. However, the individual's own social world consists first and foremost of the meanings assigned to it. A social world can be envisioned as an enlarging circle, the center of which consists of the person for whom this world has specific meaning. Within the social world are people who occupy specific positions and are frequently referred to as "significant others" (Kulys & Tobin, 1980).

As we age, our circle of significant others changes. For most elderly people, there is a narrowing of the number of friends and confidants available as resistance resources to stress. Issues in social network research concerning ethnic minority elderly are complex. How do they engage and involve themselves in acquiring new people to serve as significant others within their social context? How do they go about enlarging their social worlds or life spaces? How do older people differ in utilizing to the fullest their life spaces, which include the areas of social interaction around which people organize their behavior, the physical environment of home and familiar possessions, and the psychological environment of roles and status within the community? Life space makes up the assumptive world. Changes in any of its areas—whether positive (achievement or gain) or negative (loss)—signify transition. Since life space is part of us, these changes raise anxiety and lead to stress, which, in turn, necessitates activation of resistance resources, restructuring of our thoughts, feelings, values, and action, and coping with new situations.

Recent research illustrates the social world concept. According to Cuellar (1978), a subculture of older Chicanos exists within the Chicano community of East Los Angeles. This subculture developed because older Chicanos were not respected and obeyed as in the past. When traditional arenas of engagement (i.e., their social worlds) no longer completely respond to their needs, Cuellar wrote, elderly Chicanos increasingly form their own senior citizens' organizations to offset their loss of status.

> These ethnic-based senior citizens' organizations are more than simply neighborhood associations of elderly people because the members share much in common with one another, such as pride in common origin, group history, language, food preferences, and ability to function in terms of previous identities. (p. 208)

In other words, these elderly Chicanos have constructed a social network to fill their social worlds with meaning and purpose. While obviously interested in restoring as much as possible some of the lost territory of respect and care enjoyed under the old system of values, they created barriers to feelings of loneliness on one hand, and to sources of support on the other.

The importance of the social world as a living and functioning web of social networks that sustain ethnic minority elderly is further supported by the study of support system utilization among Euro-American elderly (Guttmann et al., 1979). Elderly immigrants from Eastern, Central, and Southern European countries preferred to use informal and formal support systems to sustain their stay in their ethnic communities—their familiar social worlds—rather than opt for nursing or old-age homes. Furthermore, in cases of need for institutionalization, all eight ethnic groups in the study (Estonian, Latvian, Lithuanian, Greek, Italian, Jewish, Hungarian, and Polish) preferred to have their own ethnic staffs in nursing homes by a ratio of two to one.

Social worlds, through the interacting chain of social networks, provide individuals with a sense of coherence or way of perceiving the world. Antonovsky (1979) explains sense of coherence as a "global orientation that expresses the extent to which one has a pervasive, enduring though dynamic feeling of confidence that one's internal and external environments are predictable and that there is a high probability that things will work out as well as can reasonably be expected" (p. 10).

Social Networks and Ethnic Minority Elderly: Some Less Common Illustrations from Research

Because people of different cultural backgrounds put their social worlds together differently, their needs and resources as well as the ways in which they use available services vary (Woehrer, 1978, p. 335).

Informal social networks of kith and kin have been described at considerable length by various researchers in aging and ethnicity. Reciprocity in caregiving, or exchanges of help between elderly parents and their children, has been noted in several of these studies (Gelfand & Kutzik, 1979; Guttman et al., 1980). Cantor and Johnson (1978), in their study of families as social networks, found them to be the main providers of care during prolonged illness (lasting two months or more).

In particular, it was noted that length of the illness was directly related to variation in caring for sick elderly between formal (i.e., government) and informal support networks. In cases of prolonged

illness, spouses or "functional children" accounted for 72% of the total
assistance and care given to sick elderly parents. The negligible role
formal organizations had in caring for the sick elderly was virtually the
same for those elderly using nuclear support networks and those using
distant support networks: 2.0% for the former and 0.0% for the latter.
Elderly without families tended to manage themselves during the
shorter periods of illness, but became increasingly dependent upon
formal support networks of various institutions in cases of prolonged
illness.

Aside from the major role the family plays in care for the elderly,
a less commonly explored social network consists of religious organizations. Along with the ethnic voluntary associations of clubs, fraterni-
ties, and "societies," these constitute the bulk of social networks that
have critical relevance of meaningful existence in old age. In its broad-
est sense religion encompasses spiritual well-being and is one of the
most significant, and, surprisingly, one of the least explored factors
that affects ethnic elderly. Churches, synagogues, temples, and
mosques comprise centers for socioreligious networks of the highest
importance for large segments of the elderly population, not only with
regard to the religious calendar of holidays and observances but also
with regard to the center's own traditions and rituals. The religious
foundation permeates actions and provides strength, while the concomitant social attitude maintained by the ethnic community as a
social network regulates the behavior of its members.

In some ethnic minorities, there is a unity of religious, national,
and family life. Native American Indians, for example, feel as one with
their universe, and this feeling affects behavior in most aspects of their
lives. Yet the existence of hundreds of tribes, along with over 300
distinct languages, cultures, and lifestyles, implies great variation in
religious outlooks on life. In particular, the close connection between
religion and medicine practiced by Native American Indians means
that specific customs and practices of each tribe need to be understood and respected in the provision of services to this population.

The importance of religion in the general welfare of people has
been documented by numerous studies on demographics, such as the
various Gallup polls (1978) and the President's Commission on Mental
Health (1978). Baum and Baum (1982) found that religion has the
strongest influence on psychomoral health of those aged 68–72 who
have already undergone the scrutiny of their past lives, but that this
influence can lead to integrity or despair depending on which mechanisms are operating. They also found that social class and ethnicity are
generally more benign but less influential. (This finding was perhaps
due to the fact that the research sample contained an insufficient

number of subjects to allow for the examination of particular sub-group differences.)

Among racial ethnic minorities, the church has been a vital social network in the black communities, from its early roots in slavery when it provided social and emotional cohesion necessary to survive the hardships of slavery to its most recent, sophisticated, and institutionalized influence as a "substitute society" (Comer & Hamilton-Lee, 1982). As these authors note, today's black churches continue to serve as important support systems and sanctuaries from tension, as well as bases of economic cooperation and networks of social and cultural life. At the same time, the black church is experiencing decreased power and a reduction in the intensity of the emotional ties of blacks because of increasing reliance on science and technology in dealing with human problems (p. 126).

The central place religion plays in the lives of the elderly is supported by other findings as well. In a study of Euro-American elderly, membership in religious congregations ranged from a high of 97% for Poles to a low of 55% for Jewish subjects. However, all ethnic elderly in the eight groups studied were quite actively involved in the religious life of their neighborhoods and frequently attended services (Guttmann et al., 1980).

Turning now to ethnic organizations as social networks, in the study cited above significant differences were found among the eight ethnic groups in terms of belonging to such organizations: about 90% for Jewish, Estonian, and Polish elderly to 35% for Italians ($F = 50.838$, $df = 8$; $p = \leq .001$). These differences in belonging and participation in ethnic voluntary associations were compensated in all groups by strong feelings of closeness to the ethnic group. There was no evidence, however, that these strong ethnic reference orientations automatically indicated aloofness from the larger society. On the contrary, Euro-American respondents were considerably involved in the broader context. While only a small percentage claimed intense involvement in national political activities, voting levels averaged 75%, thus exceeding the national average of 62% for all elderly.

One of the most important informal social networks for elderly in ethnic minorities consists of friends and neighbors. These groups are most heavily relied upon by the elderly characterized as living in distant (nonnuclear) family networks, as well as by those without any functional kin (Cantor & Johnson, 1978). Social networks of friends consist of individuals who have special meaning for an older person. The ties of friendship may be weak or strong in intensity of feelings, but they enable members of the friendship network to experience a sense of security. The security stems from the realization and inner assurance that in case of need, there are friends to rely upon. Independence in functioning thus may be strengthened—a goal which all social networks try to foster. Availability of trusted friends is, therefore, not only a matter of necessity for mental health, as Lowenthal and Robinson (1976) pointed out, but a measure of one's emotional and social standing in the ethnic/minority neighborhood as well. For elderly Euro-Americans, blacks, Asian, Hispanic, Native-Americans, and so forth, ethnic friends provide the opportunity to communicate in the native language and are clearly preferred for association over nonethnic friends by a ratio of two to one. Second only to family, they are the "responsible others" (Kulys & Tobin, 1980) to whom the elderly confidently turn for assistance in case of need.

Social Networks: A Need Area for Research and Demonstration in Aging

Having presented some concepts and findings from research on social networks in general, and those operating among diverse ethnic minority communities in particular, we return now to the national policy goals in aging. An examination of the literature has shown the relative abundance of social networks in each ethnic community. These networks range from informal kinship systems, friends, and neighbors to formal organizations of voluntary associations and religious, cultural, and political networks. The goal of the 1981 White House Conference on Aging to involve these networks in its efforts to improve the general welfare of the aged is in itself a positive development. After all, there is ample documentation of the critical importance of family, friends, fraternal organizations, parishes, and ethnic neighborhoods to the well-being of the ethnic (and nonethnic) elderly population.

The problem, however, is that presently no factual knowledge exists regarding the capacity of social networks to serve as viable partners with the federal, state, and local governments in meeting the needs of the aged. For example, research on Native-American Indians has demonstrated that their elderly are four times more likely to live with extended families on reservations than are their non-Indian counterparts. Of course, other Indian elderly do not live on reservations, unless certain enclaves in many large metropolises may be regarded as such. But even in urban areas in general, they outnumber other elderly in extended family settings by a ratio of two to one. This is rather remarkable considering that 43% of Indian elderly live today in urban areas and not on reservations (Association of American Indian Physicians, Inc., 1978). If we then add to this finding another, that one-third of American Indian families are poor, and hence increasing numbers of younger Indian members of the kinship network leave the elderly behind when they migrate to cities to seek employment in the hope of improving their standards of living, we cannot help but question the ability of such social networks as extended Native-American Indian families to care for their functionally dependent elderly.

At present, we lack reliable information on the capacity of religious, cultural, and ethnic organizations to provide support to elderly members in their networks. Moreover, community spokespersons who represent ethnic minority elderly groups often lack specific and systematic knowledge of those in need (Guttmann et al., 1980). Sometimes there is reliance on volunteers with intimate knowledge of those ethnic community networks who can be marshalled to offer help in specific cases. In the majority of ethnic neighborhoods there is usually a particular person to whom people turn when a special, critical condition requires the intervention of the entire community. While such help is important in itself, it cannot replace collective responsibility by the social network of the ethnic community. The research question in need of investigation is therefore rather obvious: Why do certain ethnic communities, such as the Jewish community, accept responsibility for their own elderly in need, while others spend no concerted effort in the same direction?

Another relatively unexplored aspect of social networks involves the gamut of mutual expectations and sharing of responsibilities between networks and professional service providers working in nonsectarian agencies. The critical questions are: Do what? Under what conditions? How often? In which way? Complementarity in roles may lead to collaboration and/or conflict. Research can help demonstrate the limits in the undertakings of each entity.

Still another area for study concerns financial incentives needed to prompt social networks to assume nontraditional roles in caring for ethnic minority elderly, especially those without families. Research should help discover those nonmonetary incentives social networks need to engage in helping activities. For example, social networks are especially suited to develop buddy systems as nonprofessional services which may be operated by the elderly themselves. By taking the responsibility for daily or weekly phone calls to elderly who are homebound by incapacitating illness, members help reassure the elderly that assistance is available. In due time, the buddies may become real friends, thereby promoting the well-being and mental health of all involved. Such buddy systems can be relatively easily instituted in congregate housing projects for the elderly, nutrition sites, senior centers, and other settings. Research can assist in determining the extent to which these social networks might prevent premature institutionalization of sick elderly.

Finally, there is a need for the federal government to support research and demonstration projects aimed at improving living conditions of the elderly population. An essential element of this support is a clear explication of which areas and activities the government considers as belonging exclusively to social networks by function, tradition, and/or other designation, and which areas and activities need to be shared responsibilities. To look upon informal supports that are subsumed under the broad category of social networks as substitutes for governmental responsibility for the welfare of the aged can only result in the opposite of the goals so eloquently stated at the 1981 White House Conference on Aging.

References

Antonovsky, A. (1979). *Health, stress and coping.* San Francisco: Jossey-Bass.
Association of American Indian Physicians, Inc. (1978). *Physical and mental health of elderly American Indians.* Silver Springs, MD: Indian Health Services.
Baum, M., & Baum, R. C. (1982). Psycho-moral health in the later years: Some social network correlates. In D. E. Biegel & A. J. Naparstek (Eds.), *Community support systems and mental health* (pp. 54–72). New York: Springer Publishing Company.
Bell, D., & Zellman, G. L. (Oct. 1975). The significance of race for service delivery to the elderly. *The Gerontologist,* Part II.
Butler, R. N. (1975). *Why survive? being old in America.* New York: Harper and Row.
Cantor, M. H. (1979). The informal support system of New York's inner city elderly: Is ethnicity a factor? In D. E. Gelfand & A. J. Kutzik (Eds.), *Ethnicity and aging.* New York: Springer Publishing Company.
Cantor, M. H., & Johnson, J. L. (1978). The informal support system of "familyless" elderly—who takes over? *The elderly in the inner city.* Report from the New York City Department for the Aging, AOA Grant No. 4-70-82-02 (Mimeo).
Chartbook on Aging in America, compiled by C. Allen & H. Broman. (1981). The 1981 White House Conference on Aging.
Comer, J. P., & Hamilton-Lee, M. E. (1982). Support systems in the black community. *Community support systems and mental health* (pp. 121–136). New York: Springer Publishing Company.

Cuellar, E. (1978). El Senior Citizens Club: The older Mexican-American in the voluntary association. In B. Myerhoff & A. Simic (Eds.), *Life's career-aging: Cultural variations growing old*. Beverly Hills, CA: Sage Publications.

Dowd, J. J., & Bengston, V. L. (1978). Aging in minority populations: An examination of the double jeopardy hypothesis. *Journal of Gerontology*, 33, 427–436.

Eggan, F. (1968). Kinship. *International encyclopedia of the social sciences* (Vol. 15, pp. 390–401). New York: The Macmillan Company and The Free Press.

Gallup Opinion Index. (1978). *Religion in America*. Princeton, NJ: American Institute of Public Opinion.

Gelfand, D. E., & Kutzik, A. J. (Eds.). (1979). *Ethnicity and aging*. New York: Springer Publishing Company.

Greeley, A. M. (Nov. 1978). After Ellis Island. *Harpers*, pp. 27–30.

Guttmann, D. (1973). Leisure-time activity interest of Jewish elderly. *The Gerontologist*, 13, 219–223.

Guttmann, D. et al. (Mar. 1979). Informal and formal support systems and their effect on the lives of the elderly in selected ethnic groups. Washington, DC: The Catholic University of America, *Final Report*, AOA Grant No. 90-A-1671.

Harris, D. K., & Cole, W. E. (1980). *Sociology of aging*. Boston: Houghton Mifflin.

Jackson, J. (Summer 1970). Aged Negroes: Their cultural departures from statistical stereotypes and rural urban differences. *The Gerontologist*, Part 1, 140–145.

Kalish, R. A. (1971). A gerontological look at ethnicity, human capacities and individual adjustment. *The Gerontologist*, 11, 78–87.

Kimmel, D. C. (1974). *Adulthood and aging*. New York: John Wiley & Sons.

Kolm, R. (Nov. 10, 1980). *Issues of Euro-American elderly in the 80's*. Paper presented at the White House Mini-Conference for Euro-American elderly, in Baltimore, MD.

Kulys, R., & Tobin, S. S. (Mar. 1980). Older people and their "responsible others." *Social Work*, 25(2), 138–145.

Kutza, E. A. (1982). *The benefits of old age: Social-welfare policy for the elderly*. Chicago, IL: University of Chicago Press.

Lacayo, C. G. (Spring 1982). Triple jeopardy: Underserved Hispanic elderly. *Generations*, VI(3).

Litwak, E. (June 1960). Geographic mobility and extended family cohesion. *American Sociological Review*, XXV, 385–394.

Lopata, H. Z. (1976). *Polish Americans*. Englewood Cliffs, NJ: Prentice-Hall.

Lowenthal, M. F., & Robinson, B. (1976). Social networks and isolation. In R. H. Binstock & E. Shanas (Eds.), *Handbook of aging and the social sciences*. New York: Van Nostrand Reinhold.

Parsons, T. (1978). Social systems. In D. L. Sills (Ed.), *International encyclopedia of the social sciences* (Vol. 15, pp. 458–472). New York: The Macmillan Company and The Free Press.

President's Commission on Mental Health. (1978). Vol. III, 139–235.

Ross, H. R. (1978). *How to develop a neighborhood family: An action manual.* Miami, FL: Northside Neighborhood Family Services, Inc.

Rowan, C. (Aug. 26, 1981). New poverty figures mean new trouble. *Washington Post.*

Rueveni, U. (1979). *Networking families in crisis.* New York: Human Services Press.

Sills, D. L. (Ed.). (1968). *International encyclopedia of the social sciences.* New York: The Macmillan Company and The Free Press.

Silverman, A. G. (Nov. 16–20, 1978). *As parents grow older: An intervention model.* Paper presented at the 31st Annual Meeting of the Gerontological Society, Dallas, TX.

Sussman, M. B. (Nov. 17, 1978). *A reconstituted young-old family: Social and economic supports in family formation.* Paper presented at symposium: Informal Supports—Implications of Research for Practice and Policy. The Gerontological Society Annual Meeting, Dallas, TX.

Sussman, M. B., & Burchinal, L. (1962). Kin family network: Unheralded structure in current conceptualizations of family functioning. *Marriage and Family Living, 24,* 231–240.

The 1981 White House Conference on Aging. Report of the Mini-Conference on Euro-American Elderly. David Guttman and John Kromkowsky (Eds.).

Turner, J. B., Morris, R., Ozawa, M. N., Phillips, B., Schreiber, P., Simon, B. K., & Saunders, B. N. (1971). *Encyclopedia of Social Work.* Washington, DC: National Association of Social Workers.

Wirth, L. (1965). The problem of minority groups. In T. Parsons et al., (Eds.), *Theories of society.* New York: The Free Press.

Woehrer, C. E. (Oct. 1978). Cultural pluralism in American families: The influence of ethnicity on social aspects of aging. *The Family Coordinator, 27*(4), 328–339.

Wolman, B. B. (Ed.). (1973). *Dictionary of behavioral science.* U.S. Commission on Civil Rights. To know or not to know: Collection and use of racial and ethnic data in Federal Assistance Programs. New York: Van Nostrand Reinhold.

11

The Support Systems of Women

Charles F. Longino, Jr.
Aaron Lipman

The systematic support which all older persons receive from those who care about them is a gerontological issue. The support available to older women is, in addition, a feminist issue and one that will grow in importance as women increasingly dominate the over age 70 population in the United States during this decade.

Consider these facts presented by the Older Women's League Education Fund and the Western Gerontological Society: (1) Women form over half of the nation's 25 million elderly population. (2) There are twice as many women at age 75 as men. (3) Over twice as many women as men are in nursing homes. (4) About 85% of all surviving spouses are women. (5) The average age of widowhood is 56. (6) One third of all widows live in poverty—the median income for older women is half that for older men; about 50% of the 5 million older women who live alone have yearly incomes of less than $3,000. (7) Less than 10% of widows receive pensions. (8) About 4 million women aged 45 to 56 are without health insurance. (9) Of women over 65 years of age, 91% are white, 8% are black, and 2% are Hispanic (*Aspects*, 1981).

There are two primary approaches to conceptualizing support systems in general, depending upon whether one's interest centers on the provision or the individual's appropriation of support (Longino, 1979). From the first perspective, a person can utilize several support systems, meaning that he or she is the client of more than one such system. Researchers studying these clients can examine the structural relationships between systems, such as the family system versus the organized service system in the community.

When emphasis is placed upon the dynamics of support appropriation, however, the particular combination of resources that provide support to individuals is seen as constituting their own unique and dynamic systems of support. From this perspective, a support system is a network through which various types of support flow to the individual at its center. The term *informal support system* is often used in this way, and the extent of support from informal resources is well documented (Bott, 1957; Cantor, 1975; Litwak & Szelenyi, 1969). Following in the tradition of such studies, the term *resources* as used in this chapter means individuals.

At the heart of the informal support system is the principle of exchange, which postulates that voluntary social behavior is motivated by expectation of the returns this behavior will bring from others. People exchange not only instrumental services and material objects, but also intangibles such as love, admiration, respect, power, and influence. That is, they receive from persons (resources) in their support network not only instrumental support but social and emotional support as well.

The starting mechanism for social exchange is the norm of reciprocity, which implies that there are duties, rights, and obligations placed on all individuals in the exchange relationship. People invest in a relationship with the expectation of being rewarded, and there is a need to reciprocate for the benefits received in order to continue receiving them. Gouldner's (1960) norm of reciprocity, "in its universal form, makes two interrelated, minimal demands: (1) people should help those who have helped them, and (2) people should not injure those who have helped them" (p. 171). Social exchange entails diffuse, unspecified, and comparatively indeterminate obligations which are nonrevocable; it requires trusting others to discharge these nonspecific obligations in some manner at some future date.

Reciprocity is the foundation of social interaction and social relations. People in kinship patterns reward each other for their contributions, investments, continuity, and loyalty, thus maintaining a network of mutual rights and duties. There is a normative obligation on the part of kin to help, and a complementary normative expectation on the part of older persons to receive this help.

Reciprocity has its origins in the past, is anchored in the present, and makes claims on the future. People feel a sense of responsibility, duty, and obligation to reciprocate to others who have rendered support, be it material or emotional, during the course of a relationship.

Traditionally, men have been obligated to perform instrumental roles and to repress their expressive character. In fact, their central role was defined instrumentally as "economic provider." Women have been socialized to provide emotional and social support for the bread-winner and other family members. These gender roles were more clearly demarcated in the past and provided reliable guidelines for social conduct. The stability of these role conceptions provided a certain sense of security for most people; at the same time they strongly curtailed the entry of women into other meaningful life work, thus denying them supportive resources they could more easily control. Hence, gender roles reinforced social barriers which often prevented women from attaining economic and emotional independence (Andre, 1981).

When the entire system functioned smoothly, women had considerably less power than men. Nonetheless, some have argued women were protected from economic and emotional deprivation by the devotion of men to their duties and obligations and by the availability of other family members who would take their side in disputes over role obligations. Recent historical research, however, considers this position not only utopian but ideologically male-defensive. Women have had to be more adaptive than men, but the economic and emotional oppressiveness of the traditional system, even when smoothly functioning, stifled human potential in women and caused them to suffer a great deal (Brownlee & Brownlee, 1976; Oakley, 1981).

In traditional gender role conceptions, the family is clearly defined as the woman's world. The family is the starting point for life chances of children, and gives them various handicaps or advantages relative to others in many competitive situations. The family also is the central factor in the life chances of most women, given their denial by society of opportunities in other institutional areas. The family strongly affects women's economic situations, and continues to be the primary pool from which emotional and social sustenance is drawn. Given this social construction of reality, it makes sense to examine the supportive relationships of older women who are in different positions in the institutional structure of the family in the United States. Some of the most frequently occurring features of the support systems of married women are described below. Next, the major systematic features of support flowing to spouseless women (widowed, divorced, or never married) are discussed.

Married Women

Over 90% of the people in the United States of every birth cohort on record have eventually married (Cherlin, 1981). Marriage is still the norm in our society. For the married woman, the husband has the longest history of exchange relations with her, and in that sense is the key figure in her support system. Husbands and wives are completely dependent on one another for the continuation of their relationship; the dyadic group would cease to exist without mutual participation.

Throughout marriage both parties make exchange deposits to be withdrawn at some later unspecified time, although their supportive acts are not thought of in this way at the time of the exchange. Later, however, the equity of the exchange may be questioned if a husband or wife is viewed as unsupportive. The weight of compounded obligations and interdependency seems to keep the husband in the leading position in the support systems of married women, even though other relationships rise and fall in critical short-term dominance, especially those concerning children. Mutual support over long periods of time can generate high marital satisfaction among older couples. Cross-sectional studies have found that wives tend to describe their later years as one of the happiest times of their married lives (Rollins & Feldman, 1970; Spanier, Lewis, & Cole, 1975).

In a study of the support networks of residents in two life care communities (Longino & Lipman, 1981), married women were identified as having stronger and more fully developed support systems than spouseless women. In addition, they received more support from family members than did men, even if the men were also married. Of the four spouse-and-gender groups, married women had the largest number of primary relationships, and the largest number of persons providing emotional, social, and instrumental support, particularly among family members. Unmarried men had the least amount of support.

The principle of exchange can be used to explain the advantage of married women in comparing support networks. In contemporary society, and perhaps historically as well, women, particularly married women, take responsibility for family and friendship ties through correspondence. It is the woman who remembers birthdays and names of the ever-increasing tide of relatives' spouses and children. It is she who follows the ongoing saga, the marital and career ups and downs, the crises and successes of family members of friends. Among other things, she is the expressive leader of the family (Lipman, 1962, 1977; Zeldich, 1955). Many adult men find this kind of attention to detail tedious, if not downright distasteful. As a consequence, they usually invest less in maintaining ties and links in the support network. Thus in old age, it is women who reap the rewards of their investments.

Centrality of the spouse is substantiated by the Holmes-Rahe Stress Scale (Holmes & Rahe, 1967), where the loss of a spouse through death, divorce, or separation represents the three serially highest ranked stressors. Death of a close family member (other than spouse) ranked 5th, while the death of a close friend ranked 17th. Hoyt and Babchuk (1983) indicate that spouses are about 30 times more likely to be selected as a confidant than are young children or extended relatives. While other family members and close friends may also be supportive, they usually have not developed as strong a sense of obligation to reciprocate all that has taken place before as has the married woman's spouse. Normative obligation and sentiment on the part of spouses appear more binding than ties of sentiment with kin, friends, and neighbors (Troll & Smith, 1976).

In a study of family relationships of golden wedding couples, Parron (1978) found that respondents ranked their spouse first, their children next, their siblings third, and their friends last in order of importance. In times of distress, women tend to call first upon their husband and if he is unavailable, a child (typically a daughter) intervenes. If there are no children, a more distant relative may be called upon, and if there are no relatives, then friends or neighbors are approached (Cantor, 1979). Thus, as exchange theory predicts, a hierarchy of drawing rights emerges based on previous supportive relationships.

Spouseless Women

Next, some relationships which provide support to spouseless women in old age are examined and compared, where possible, with those of married women. Spouselessness is not a unidimensional category when it comes to the issue of supportive relationships. There are important differences between those of widowed, divorced, and never-married elderly women.

In the early 1970s, approximately 43% of families headed by women were headed by widows. This was twice the proportion of families headed by divorced women. By 1980, only a decade later, the percentages were almost reversed; divorced women accounted for 34% of female-headed households, while widows represented 29% of the total (Levitan & Belous, 1981). In addition, the relative rate of never-married women heading families doubled during the same period. The increased value placed on living alone rather than as a subunit in relatives' households has also increased for women.

The Widowed

Most materials written about informal support systems of women deal with widowed women, since in the past this group represented the largest proportion of female-headed families. There are about five times as many widowed women as men in the United States. Lopata (1979) has done extensive research in the area and characterizes widows as "targets of discrimination." "They are," she says, "women in a male-dominated society, and they are old in a society that values youth. Many are grieving and lonely in a country that would deny and ignore such unhappy emotions. They are without mates in a social network of couples . . ." (p. 92).

For women who have never married, one expects siblings, parents, and more distant relatives to be support contributors. But for married and formerly married, the issue becomes more complicated. Perhaps married women have the most viable support systems, not because of their husbands, but because they more often have living children. On the other hand, perhaps it is the husband, not the children, who provides the lion's share of support for the older woman, since it is he who is most likely to be in daily contact with her. There is a third alternative as well. Husbands may specialize in meeting a different set of needs than do the children. In this case, one would provide more support than the other depending upon the type of support.

Older women in two Midwestern life-care retirement communities were subdivided into three categories by Longino and Lipman (1982): married, formerly married, and never married. Not surprisingly, women who had never married received less emotional, social, and instrumental support from their families than did women who had been or were presently married. Lopata's (1978) earlier finding that children were of the greatest importance to widows was reaffirmed. For married women in the study, husbands were expected to provide the most support in all three support areas, and children were expected only to compensate for the husband's loss. The presence of a husband, however, seems only to assure the married woman of significantly more instrumental, task-oriented support in these kinds of communities. Rather than finding evidence for a pattern of compensation, as suggested by Cantor (1979), it suggests role specialization within supportive relationships. Perhaps the issue is not one of centrality of the relationship in the support system, since the husband has a considerable investment advantage over his children, but rather one of function and skill.

It seems likely that older men, after a lifetime of internalizing the traditional male gender role, have not been able to meet these emotional and social needs as well as do their children. This does not mean that older men do not love their wives; most probably do. Rather, it means that most women are, and traditionally have been, better at self-disclosure than are men (Pleck, 1976; Sattle, 1976). Children and female friends provide a reservoir of emotional support for women throughout their lives. Husbands, and men in general, tend to specialize instead in doing things *for* their families, such as providing financially and keeping the house in good repair. When their wives have problems, they are more likely to express concern by asking what they can *do* to help.

Children, of course, continue to be the chief providers of emotional and social support when their mothers become widowed, and also begin to pick up some of the slack in instrumental support provided earlier by their fathers. While Troll, Miller, and Atchley (1979) believe that more distant kin may serve as a reservoir of substitutes for nonexistent closer kin, Lopata (1979) found that the potentials for aid from relatives other than children have been highly exaggerated. It is past relationships that provide support; friends who later enter the support systems often do so on a superficial level, and they do not become confidants.

The important role of children for widows cannot be overstated. In their study of widowed women aged 60–75, Beckman and Houser (1982) found that elderly widows without children are more lonely and dissatisfied and are in lower states of general well-being than are widowed mothers.

The Divorced

Comparatively little information exists dealing specifically with divorced elderly women. However, with more marriages currently dissolving from divorce rather than death, we can expect that divorce will have great impact on the lives of elderly women in the future. It is estimated that about half of those married in 1970 will eventually be divorced (U.S. National Center of Health Statistics, 1979, 1980), and although the majority (75–80%) remarry, remarriage rates for women are much lower than remarriage rates for men. Even for those 65 years and over, marriage dissolution has become a widespread phenomenon. Between 1960 and 1980, for example, the divorce rate for those age 65 years and over increased by 85% (Levitan & Belous, 1981). The divorced female who will become elderly is therefore an important topic for future research.

Present research evidence places the aged divorcee in many of the same difficulties experienced by widows. Thus, in losing her husband through divorce, she also loses concomitant instrumental support which the husband traditionally supplies. A grim reality of divorce in this age-group, in addition to the disrupted family relationships, is that poverty is one of its major negative consequences for the elderly female. Not having a spouse also serves as a crude index of lack of affiliation and is reflected in higher rates of suicide and morbidity and a lower life satisfaction for people in this single state (Maddox, 1975).

Again, as in the case of widows, the presence of children appears to be important in generating social and emotional support. Most divorced people have children. Relatives (but not often in-laws), friends, and neighbors supply the remainder of a divorced woman's informal support resources.

There is a period of historical effect that should be noted in considering the economic deprivation experienced by many widowed and divorced women in their later years. The kinds of jobs women have held outside their homes have tended to be in the secondary tier of a dual-market economy (Blau, 1979). It is possible that when the current divorced cohort (which is very large) reaches old age, structural changes in the economic institution will increase the financial autonomy of older divorced women.

The Never-Married

Older women who never married comprise a small percentage of the elderly female population. Studies have demonstrated that people in this small category achieved self-sufficiency and lived independently from an early age, and they seem to maintain this successful instrumentalism in later life (Haan & Day, 1974; Peterson, 1981).

As we have seen in our discussion of supports for married women, husbands, as part of the male role, usually stressed instrumental tasks. Most women, then, when they lose a husband through death or divorce, find this instrumental deficit difficult to restore. The only group for whom this is not true is the never-married. For these women, the challenges and successes of day-to-day living provide inner resources which further increase their skills in coping with life. Single elderly women believe in their ability to accomplish tasks and feel that the successful or even unsuccessful accomplishment of these tasks results from their own efforts, rather than from luck or fate. As Ward (1979) indicates, highly educated women are most likely to remain single until old age; they possess an armamentarium of adaptive mechanisms that have grown through gradual accretion, thus reaffirming an internal locus of control.

In her study of single female academicians, Kieffer (1979) refers to the principle of psychogenic economy, which is a process of "building adaptive or substitute affiliative, affect-laden elements of personality structure while at the same time consolidating an achievement status through wrapping additional layers of protective armor around the core intellect" (pp. 191–192). These women, in order to gain a more instrumental orientation, may have downgraded the emotional component of their lives, but this has not been confirmed. They are active with friends and neighbors who "are a viable source of support in meeting the needs of sociability, but they are less likely to increase their support involvement . . . with the onset of impairment" (Johnson & Catalano, 1981).

Since never-married women have had no spouse and (usually) no children, expressive social and emotional support is received most often from brothers and sisters, followed by nieces, nephews, and friends (Johnson & Catalano, 1981). "Following the principle of female linkage observed in other kinship attachments, sister/sister ties have been observed to be stronger than sister/brother ties . . ." (Troll et al., 1979). Some evidence suggests that friends may compensate for fewer family resources in the support systems of never-married women, at least in age-segregated community settings (Longino & Lipman, 1982). Research findings are especially clear on one point: Of all elderly women, the never-married are the most likely to turn to formal resources when in need; use of public institutions and formal community support services is highest among the never-married (Gubrium, 1975; Kivett & Learner, 1980).

The Principle of Family Substitutions

Family members are the most prominent resources in the support systems of elderly women, who receive more instrumental, social, and emotional support from all family members together than from their friends or from others (Longino & Lipman, 1981, 1982). The only exception to this pattern is found among the never-married, who have many fewer family members in their support systems and thus tend to rely more upon friends for social and instrumental support. The kind and amount of support women receive from different types of famly members, however, varies with their position within the family constellation. Married women, widows, divorced women, and the never-married differ in their support configuration partly because of the differential availability of certain family roles and relationships. Shanas (1979) maintains that despite the prominence given to the isolated elderly by the news media, isolation of the elderly person in the United States is a rarity. Her research suggests that for elderly who have no children other relatives such as siblings, nephews, and nieces often fulfill the roles that would be assumed by children.

This principle can also be seen in Rosow's (1968) classic study, in which more friendships were reported in neighborhoods with high concentrations of older people. The increase in reported friendships was stronger among the widowed and single than among the married. Rosow reported that the number of friendships was extremely sensitive to density differences among these two spouseless groups. Powers and Bultena (1976) also demonstrated the principle of family substitutions in showing that the widowed had a higher intimacy rate with friends than did the married.

It would appear that this principle functions in a downward hierarchical direction, in accordance with the preferential list of support persons mentioned in Parron's (1978) study. Thus, women who have husbands and children tend to consider their husbands as the primary resource in their support systems, and then their children, siblings, other relatives, and friends, respectively. Children were mentioned most prominently as resources in the support systems of women who had lost their husbands through death or divorce. Unmarried women tended to consider siblings as their most important support resources.

The principle of family substitutions should not obscure the fact that there is usually one person in the family—most frequently a female—who is elected as "the caregiver" (Silverstone & Hyman, 1976).

Antecedent and Causal Factors

The traditional female role has required women to invest more time and energy into family and other caring relationships. Not all women have adopted these cultural expectations, but the pressure to be the expressive leader in the family is often there by default, and more often than not women do assume these caretaking duties. The older woman typically not only gave emotional and social support to her husband and children in the past but was responsible for maintaining social communications with the rest of the kinship group and with outside friends. She was expected to write letters, make phone calls, send birthday, anniversary, get well, and holiday greeting cards. She extended and accepted social invitations, as well as performing other functions which kept the family in touch with in-laws, aunts and uncles, cousins, and other relatives and friends. She also retained the role of primary communicator once her children were grown. Since this female role component has been fairly consistent throughout time, research has shown that it is mainly the daughters and daughters-in-law who enter this latter communication network, rather than their male counterparts (Silverstone & Hyman, 1976).

In addition, women maintain confidante relationships and intimate friendships much more frequently than do men (Lowenthal & Haven, 1968). Married men rely primarily upon their wives for emotional support; this has been postulated as a possible explanation for higher mortality rates among older men who remain unmarried after their wives die as opposed to the lower mortality rate for those who re-marry (Helsing, Szklo, & Comstock, 1981).

It appears reasonable to assume that investments women made throughout their younger years in the family social system would find their payoff in her relatively well developed social network in old age. The exchanges in which elderly women have participated throughout their adult lives lead to a return of reciprocal obligations in their times of need.

To put this picture in a more balanced perspective, it must also be added that men generally do not appreciate efforts women make in maintaining the network of family relationships. These activities are often considered trivial and nonproductive, and their value is per-ceived as depreciating relative to the more important world of work outside the home. As women gradually restore the gender balance in productive occupations men have tended to value most, the network maintenance work women once did so well will almost inevitably suffer. The implication for family cohesion and commitment in the adult years, as well as for the support systems of older women, is obvious.

Current Research Priorities

There has been an increasing gap in the life expectancy of males and females, resulting in a disproportionate sex ratio, especially among the elderly. Not only is there a large number of elderly women today, but this number will increase in the future. Current research on support systems of women is therefore of critical importance.

One of the most crucial needs is for longitudinal studies of the support systems of women. These systems are dynamic since they are negotiated by individuals. People build support systems over time, adding and dropping resources as their needs change. Additionally, there is a time dimension in the frequency, volume, and salience of support flowing from resources to the supported person. Some supports may lie dormant for a period of time and be reactivated later. Some may dispense support regularly and others sporadically, depending upon the perception of need, the viability of the self resource, and the ability of the supported person to reciprocate in a mutually meaningful manner.

The sharp increase in divorce at all age levels has brought to light a serious dearth of information regarding elderly divorces; most literature loses their individuality in a category called the "formerly married," which lumps together divorcees and widows (Hunt, 1966).

The dynamics of caregiving must also be investigated. Support providers (caregivers) are limited in their ability to provide because they are also centers of their *own* support systems. Thus, for example, when a 60-year-old child becomes burdened by the amount of support given to an 85-year-old parent, there are several ways to reduce the strain caused by the pull of obligation and the limits of the child's time, energy, and economic ability. First, he or she is likely to attempt to bolster other caregivers in the parent's present support system. Siblings may be asked to take turns caring for the parent. A second strategy, seeking additional caregivers from outside the family, may be tried. In this case one or more resources in the support system of the parent may reimburse yet another resource for services, such as a nurse-housekeeper. Another strategy is to locate resources for expanding the caregiver's capacity to provide more adequate support. Counseling, for example, aimed at preparing the child of a stroke patient to cope with new demands on self and on the home environment prior to the parent's release from the hospital would increase the child's capacity for support and perhaps postpone the parent's entry into a nursing home.

In the support systems of many older women, there is one primary caregiver, and the demands upon that one person for support are large. Methods of negotiating these demands over time should be better understood in order to deal logically with questions of social obligations in caring relationships. The relationships between network structure, psychological well-being, and social support are important research topics (McLanahan, Wedemeyer, & Adelberg, 1981).

A key policy research question, of course, concerns the availability and diffusion of formal resources that will make it easier for caregivers to continue to provide informal support (Maddox, 1975; Smyer, 1980). The most exciting applied research is likely to involve the interface between informal and formal resources in elderly persons' systems of support (Lipman & Longino, 1982).

References

Andre, R. (1981). *Homemakers: The forgotten workers.* Chicago: University of Chicago Press.

Aspects of the aging national population. Information on Aging, Institute of Gerontology at Wayne State University, No. 23 (Oct. 1981), pp. 5–7.

Beckman, L. J., & Houser, B. B. (1982). The consequences of childlessness on the social-psychological well-being of older women. *Journal of Gerontology, 37,* 243–250.

Blau, F. D. (1979). Women in the labor force: An overview. In J. Freeman (Ed.), *Women: A feminist perspective* (2nd ed.). La Jolla, CA: Mayfield.

Bott, E. (1957). *Family and social network.* London: Tavistock.

Brownlee, W. E., & Brownlee, M. M. (1976). *Women in the American economy: A documentary history 1675 to 1929.* New Haven: Yale University Press.

Cantor, M. H. (1975). Life space and the support systems of the inner city elderly. *The Gerontologist, 15,* 23–27.

Cherlin, A. J. (1981). *Marriage, divorce, remarriage.* Cambridge, MA: Harvard University Press.

Gouldner, A. W. (1960). The norm of reciprocity. *American Sociological Review, 25,* 161–178.

Gubrium, J. F. (1975). Being single in old age. *International Journal of Aging and Human Development, 6,* 29–41.

Haan, N., & Day, D. (1974). A longitudinal study of change and sameness in personality development: Adolescence to later adulthood. *International Journal of Aging and Human Development, 5.*

Helsing, K. J., Szklo, M., & Comstock, G. W. (1981). Factors associated with mortality after widowhood. *American Journal of Public Health, 71,* 802–809.

Holmes, T. H., & Rahe, R. H. (1967). The social adjustment rating scale. *Journal of Psychosomatic Research, 11,* 213–218.

Hoyt, D. R., & Babchuk, N. (1983). Adult kinship networks: The selective formation of intimate ties with kin. *Social Forces, 62,* 84–101.

Hunt, M. (1966). *The world of the formerly married.* New York: McGraw-Hill.

Johnson, C. L., & Catalano, D. J. (1981). Childless elderly and their family supports. *The Gerontologist, 21,* 610–618.

Kieffer, C. M. (1979). *The never-married mature academic women: A life history analysis.* Unpublished doctoral dissertation, University of Missouri-Columbia.

Kivett, V. R., & Learner, R. M. (1980). Perspectives on the childless rural elderly: A comparative analysis. *The Gerontologist, 20,* 709–716.

Levitan, S., & Belous, R. S. (1981). *What's happening to the American family.* Baltimore: The Johns Hopkins University Press.

Lipman, A. (1962). Role conceptions of couples in retirement. In C. Tibbits & W. Donahue (Eds.), *Social and psychological aspects of aging.* New York: Columbia University Press.

Lipman, A. (1977). Marriage and family roles of the aged. *Encyclopedia of Psychiatry, Psychology, Psychoanalysis and Neurology, 7,* 24–26.

Lipman, A., & Longino, Jr., C. F. (1982). Formal and informal support: A conceptual clarification. *Journal of Applied Gerontology, 1,* 141–146.

Litwak, E., & Szelenyi, I. (1969). Primary group structures and their functions: Kin, neighbors and friends. *American Sociological Review, 34,* 465–481.

Longino, Jr., C. F. (1979). *The unit of analysis problem and network measures of changing support.* Paper presented at the Annual Scientific Meeting of the Gerontological Society of America, Washington, DC.

Longino, Jr., C. F., & Lipman, A. (1981). Married and spouseless men and women in planned retirement communities: Support network differentials. *Journal of Marriage and the Family, 43,* 169–177.

Longino, Jr., C. F., & Lipman, A. (1982). The married, the formerly married and the never married: Support system differentials of older women in planned retirement communities. *International Journal of Aging and Human Development, 14,* 285–297.

Lopata, H. Z. (1978). Contributions of extended families to the support systems of metropolitan area widows: Limitations of the modified kin network. *Journal of Marriage and the Family, 40,* 355–364.

Lopata, H. Z. (1979). *Women as widows: Support systems.* New York: Elsevier-North Holland.

Lowenthal, M. F., & Haven, C. (1968). Interaction and adaptation: Intimacy as a critical variable. *American Sociological Review, 33,* 20–31.

Maddox, G. L. (1975). Families as context and resource in chronic illness. In S. Sherwood (Ed.), *Long-term care.* New York: Spectrum.

McLanahan, S. S., Wedemeyer, N. V., & Adelberg, T. (1981). Network structure, social support and psychological well-being in the single-parent family. *Journal of Marriage and the Family, 43,* 601–612.

Oakley, A. (1981). *Subject: Women.* New York: Pantheon.

Parron, E. (1978). *An exploratory study of intimacy in golden wedding couples.* Unpublished master's thesis, Rutgers University, Brunswick, New Jersey.

Peterson, N. L. (1981). *Our lives for ourselves: Women who have never married.* New York: Putnam's.

Pleck, J. H. (1976). The male sex role: Definitions, problems, and sources of change. *Journal of Social Issues, 32,* 155–164.

Powers, E. A., & Bultena, G. L. (1976). Sex differences in intimate friendships of old age. *Journal of Marriage and the Family, 38,* 739–747.

Rollins, B. C., & Feldman, H. (1970). Marital satisfaction over the family life cycle. *Journal of Marriage and the Family, 32,* 20–28.

Rosow, I. (1968). *Social integration of the aged.* New York: The Free Press.

Sattel, J. W. (1976). The inexpressive male: Tragedy or sexual politics? *Social Problems, 23,* 469–477.

Shanas, E. (1979). The family as a social support system in old age. *The Gerontologist, 19,* 169–174.

Silverstone, B., & Hyman, H. K. (1976). *You and your aging parent.* New York: Pantheon.

Smyer, M. A. (1980). The differential usage of service by impaired elderly. *Journal of Gerontology, 2,* 249–255.

Spanier, G. B., Lewis, R. A., & Cole, C. L. (1975). Marital adjustment over the family cycle: The issue of curvilinearity. *Journal of Marriage and the Family, 37,* 263–275.

Troll, L. E., & Smith, J. (1976). Attachment through the life span: Some questions about dyadic relationships in later life. *Human Development, 19,* 156–171.

Troll, L. E., Miller, S. J., & Atchley, R. C. (1979). *Families in later life.* Belmont, CA: Wadsworth.

U.S. National Center for Health Statistics. (1980). *National estimates of marital dissolution and survivorship.* Vital and Health Statistics, Series 3, No. 19. Washington, DC: U.S. Government Printing Office.

U.S. National Center for Health Statistics. (1979). *Divorces by marriage cohort.* Vital and Health Statistics, Series 21, No. 34. Washington, DC: U.S. Government Printing Office.

Ward, R. L. (1979). The never married in late life. *Journal of Gerontology, 34,* 861–869.

Zeldich, M. (1955). Role differences in the nuclear family. In T. Parsons & R. Bales (Eds.), *Family socialization and interaction process.* Glencoe, IL: Free Press.

12

Social Support for the Frail Elderly

Eloise E. Rathbone-McCuan
Nancy Hooyman
Anne E. Fortune

Since the 1970s gerontologists have argued that social advocacy for the elderly and a greater recognition of the family's role in providing care for the aged would be important issues for the 1980s (Brody & Brody, 1974). In each Congressional session since 1975, the issue of filial responsibility has been raised and some stance proposed on family responsibility. The specific legislation offered usually represents one of two divergent approaches: (1) requiring adult children to support their older parents or (2) supplementing family care to ensure support. These different viewpoints are also reflected in the thinking of respected gerontologists. Some professionals stress the limitations of family support systems and urge the expansion of governmental and private interventions in the care of the aged (Treas, 1977), whereas others argue that the endless expansion of nonfamily alternatives is doomed, and, therefore, they advocate policies and programs that coordinate formal organizational and family activities through improved mediating structures (Allison-Cooke, 1982; Sussman & Peter, 1981).

This chapter addresses some of the social policy dilemmas of providing long-term care of the aged. In particular, we focus on the frail elderly—those elderly persons who may be institutionalized (or are at risk of institutionalization) but who could, with some assistance, be maintained in the community.

In selecting to discuss the frail elderly, we recognize the multiple hazards inherent in the term. Gadow (1983) recently analyzed the conflicting images that exist within gerontology and broader social science circles with regard to frailty. Those elders to whom we refer are individuals with both the energy and the capacity for performing many important social functions and life management tasks; however, that ability is not sufficient to allow them to be totally autonomous in basic and essential activities. For the majority, they are not "dependent" in the stereotypic sense, but rather interdependent with their social network because they are engaged in a giving exchange with those who provide supportive assistance to ensure a greater personal safety and state of well-being.

This chapter explores the literature about social networks and the frail elderly and discusses critical policy considerations and intervention issues relevant to the individuals providing and receiving supportive care. We will emphasize conditions of mental and physical impairment that combine to make the elderly person's condition (1) unsafe without significant and regular assistance from others; (2) unstable with rapid and unpredictable functional setbacks; (3) not reversible to any significant extent because of chronic conditions; and (4) unmanageable in the community without some extensive support from informal, nonpaid, sources. Streib (1983) recently challenged researchers for excluding this segment of the aged population. The continuation of inadequate and insufficient data makes the task of policy formulation even more difficult and subject to change as more knowledge is developed.

While agreement generally exists that both formal organizations and the family are responsible for the care of frail and dependent members, disagreement persists about how to translate the concept of "shared responsibility" between family and state into specific policies and programs (Moroney, 1976). The functions appropriate to both the family and the state have been variously defined, with some policies supporting the family, others competing with the family. That the family is a major provider in the long-term care system is clear, as indicated by the continued documentation of the strength of intergenerational ties, the frequency of intergenerational contacts, and the percentage of service provided by family caregivers. While the myth of family abandonment of their elderly relatives appears to have been successfully challenged, a new counter-myth is emerging that the family can do it all and does. The diversity of views about the support for the frail elderly translates into a confused configuration of policies and unstable funding base for programs that are known to be of help to the frail aged. No single analysis can clarify all of the perspectives required for rational policy and program development; however, this chapter considers some alternatives.

Debate over Care Responsibilities

Public expenditures for long-term care are rapidly increasing, while simultaneously a vocal public is demanding limitations on the costs of government and its intrusion into the lives of individuals and families. Accordingly, policymakers are increasingly recognizing the importance of the family in the caregiving system, oftentimes as a means to reduce the rising costs of long-term care. As Brody (1981) has noted, the "natural" or informal support system, which has always been present, has been discovered and advocated as an alternative to institutionalization and the family is being "cheered on" in its caregiving role. Yet, little is known about the long-term ability of family members to provide care and about the impact of caregiving responsibilities both on family members and on the quality of care for the older relative (Tobin & Kulys, 1981).

It is unwise for societal pressures to force families into giving care to the elderly to the extent that it places the larger family unit at risk. The advantages and disadvantages of long-term high-demand family caregiving must be investigated before a national trend is blindly advocated. Gerontologists are beginning to study systematically the costs and benefits of family caregiving (Rosenmayr, 1977). In his exploration of the family as a context and resource in chronic illness, Maddox (1975) stated that the family is not always a benign environment for chronically ill or disabled members. In fact, studies of elderly abuse suggest that the family can be the cause of some problems experienced by the elderly. While the family may be able to respond to crises, such as hospitalization and short-term tasks, their capacity to provide care over time can be eroded without supplemental services from social agencies (Eggert, Granger, Morris, & Pendleton, 1977). The reality that family members are often ill-prepared to perform the role of care provider as their relatives become increasingly dependent, the negative impact of unrelieved caregiving on families, and the limitations on the family to provide quality long-term care suggest that a balance of "shared responsibility" between the family and the state has not yet been achieved and remains a critical policy issue for the 1980s. There is a serious program implication that emerges from confused policy. Resources available at the community level may either leave the family to care for a frail elder without any meaningful support or defer the support to older family members with major care needs. Finding the appropriate balance is a major challenge to practitioners, policymakers, and families.

Variables Shifting the Sources and Forms of Caregiving

Several social and demographic trends limit the family's caregiving ability: the increasing number of employed women, especially middle-aged married women; the multiple responsibilities faced by this group of women; the aging of the older population itself and, accordingly, of the adult caregivers; the fact that there are fewer adult children—and fewer "maiden aunts"—upon which the elderly can rely; the increasing divorce rate; and the emergence of new and diverse family structures. The consequences of these trends is not merely that existing tasks have to be redistributed, but that a larger package of responsibilities has to be assumed by fewer people (Brody, 1981). The complexity of this situation increases as more elderly people with chronic physical and mental conditions survive many years at a marginal to minimal functional level. An increasing number of families are now facing multiple elder care responsibilities within a single multigenerational family unit.

Despite data on the negative effects of unrelieved caregiving and the above trends which have limited the long-term supportive capacity of the family, the family is being expected to assume greater responsibility for caregiving. When the focus of that care is the frail elderly, the family's contribution emerges as the unsupported source of community care. Families are often silent to the external world about the demands of psychological, physical, and financial supports. That silence can easily be misinterpreted as "no stress" to the support network, but practitioners working in community care programs for the aged offer another interpretation. They note that stress accumulates in isolation until a major breakdown occurs.

Social policies in the field of aging have focused on the aging individual, with little recognition of the family as a viable unit in its own right and with its own needs (Nelson, 1982). Nevertheless, policies directed toward the impaired elderly are not neutral in terms of their impact on the family system and community-based care does not equate with family support. It is spurious to argue that if older individuals living with the family receive support, the entire family is supported. Yet such arguments have been advanced as justification primarily for the provision of services to frail elderly. Often those services totally ignore the family context, giving no recognition to the personal preferences of younger generations. Agency providers pronounce what is available in the form of supplemental services and the family and the frail aged person are in a take-it-or-leave-it bind. Under such conditions it is not hard to understand why families reject services even though there is great need for help.

Institutionalization is one outcome of a family exhausting their care capacities (Brody, Poulshock, & Masciocchi, 1978). Institutionalization of the frail can be conceptualized as the result of a lack of congruence between the resources of the family and the needs of the elderly (Montgomery, 1982). This lack of congruence has been created, in part, by the absence of a comprehensive continuum of community- and home-based services that both increases the family's resources for caregiving and decreases the elderly's need for care from family members.

Responsibility for the Frail: An Undecided Issue

The conditions of the frail aged are not usually stable and, therefore, their care demands vary. New symptoms of a chronic disease may manifest themselves as new limitations of the elderly persons. For example, mobility within the house may be reduced to a bed-to-chair transfer. Reduced capacity demands a change in the supportive environment. Family members may have to quickly increase care; may have to move into the elder's residence or do swing shifts. Many families are able to adapt to these changing needs and demands, but *not* without cost.

In contrast, formal organizations more effectively perform predictable tasks requiring extensive, specialized knowledge. Litwak and Figueira (1968) imply that to achieve the "optimal sharing of functions" between bureaucratic and familial sources of aid to the elderly, routine or uniform support tasks (such as cleaning) should be delegated to formal service agencies. Such an arrangement could free the family to handle the tasks at which they are best suited, for example, responding to the social and emotional needs of the individual. Flexibility seems to be a very important feature of supportive services to the frail elderly; however, few long-term care policies take individual need into account.

According to Bell (1974), two contrasting models of responsibility for the elderly vie for dominance—the supplantal model and the supplemental model. In the supplantal model, families have increasingly relinquished responsibility for the care of the aged to formal organizations, presumably further weakening family bonds. This relinquishing is often difficult when the vulnerability of the frail elder is great. Family and friends must weigh these considerations in decision making about care. Bell (1974) argued, however, that the supplantal model ignores the realities that some elders are without family, that some families lack the resources to provide care, and that most older persons prefer not to live with their adult children. Bell (1974) proposed the supplemental mode in which the family does not relinquish fundamental charge for elderly members, but increasingly shares these caregiving functions with other formal organizations. This approach is valuable with the frail elderly because it can encourage families to be realistic about their care roles and not assume more than they can handle.

Moroney (1976) conceptualized the relationship between family and state as a function of two factors—whether the transfer of responsibility from family to the state was (1) complete or partial and (2) permanent or temporary. For example, institutional care represents a complete, permanent transfer of care; respite care a complete, temporary transfer; chore services a partial, permanent transfer; and homemaker services a partial, temporary transfer of care. A third dimension identified by Moroney (1976) was whether the policy or program supported the family or substituted for it in the family's function as a source of service.

Nelson (1982) has provided a particularly useful framework for analyzing the impacts of policies on the family system. Adopting Litwak's concept of "optimal fit," Nelson proposed that policies and programs can assume three basic roles in relation to the family: competitive, complementary, or substitutive. Competitive policies are destructive to the family's mutual support network and may serve to discourage the caregiving efforts of the family over extended periods for the frail elderly. For example, the Supplemental Security Income program (SSI) can be competitive with the efforts of the family to support their elder. Under SSI, formal recognition is not given to the family caregiver nor to the reality that this care generally involves additional financial stress; indeed, the SSI policies penalize some families. For example, the Supplemental Security Income regulations work against cash and in-kind contributions and, therefore, probably lead to gifts in kind rather than cash, to giving that is irregular where it might have been regular, and to neglecting to report the contributions. In turn, the principle of this regulation achieves an estimated government savings of $30 million a year—a relatively small savings in a multimillion dollar program (Schoor, 1980). Parents whose children assist them are, in effect, penalized by reductions in SSI benefits and, in some cases, lose their eligibility for needed health care benefits through Medicare (Estes, 1979). The regulations that reduce SSI recipients' benefits for room and board by one-third, if the aged person resides with relatives, may not necessarily deter living together. It may, however, strain family relationships. For an older person living with kin, this regulation minimizes the opportunity for them to feel that they are contributing to household expenses (Schorr, 1980). Substitute policies and complementary programmatic supports can offer more desirable outcomes that do not cancel out supports from family nor pay for services the family wants to give to the frail person.

Some Directions for Policy Reform

Research has consistently shown that home health and personal care services are extremely important to families caring for older frail relatives, and yet these services are the least well-financed. Less than 2% of the budgets of Medicare and Medicaid, the major insurers of the elderly, are spent on in-home services (Doherty, Segal, & Hicks, 1978). This operates against the expansion of noninstitutional care for the frail elderly. Federal regulations on the provision of in-home supportive services to people in need can have disruptive and contradictory impacts on families. Examples of such negative impacts are the Title XIX funds that prohibit in-home supportive services to an "able and available spouse," in practice, the caregiver wife (Newman, 1980). Given the widespread desire of families to help their frail members, such regulations work against having that support so important to the elders' functions. Proposals to make relatives responsible for Medicaid patients continue to be advocated despite the fact that caring cannot be legislated and that 25% of those in nursing homes reside there because of the lack of support services in the home and community (Schoor, 1980).

A two-tier entitlement policy has been proposed, for example, whereby one tier provides comprehensive services for older people without family supports, and the second tier provides modest benefits to complement family assistance (Frankfather, Smith, & Caro, 1981). Yet both to avoid penalizing caregiving families and to meet the economic and health care needs of the elderly, the presence of family members should not be used as a reason for withholding services to elderly relatives (Horowitz & Dobrof, 1982). While some elderly do lack viable family networks, an array of supportive services should be available to all older people, regardless of the existence of family supports.

Clearly, policies complementary to the family are needed which coordinate the formal and informal systems (see Chapter 11), minimize the economic and service stressors of caregiving, and maximize the use of available support options. Government policies and programs should complement the helping role of the family and recognize the dependency of the aged upon the public sector and the importance and persistence of the natural family helping network. Such a perspective makes explicit the limitations of the family as a support system for the impaired elderly and acknowledges that the economic, social, and emotional costs of caregiving are too great for the family to bear alone.

Numerous proposals have been made regarding methods whereby the government can encourage informal supports for the frail elderly. One incentive consists of tax credits, tax-free stipends, and tax deductions designed to offset the costs of family-provided care, especially in situations when major expenses are involved or the caregivers seek to remain part of the labor force while providing these services. For example, expenses may be involved in modifying the household or adding special technical devices to help with difficult management of the frail elder. Also, the pattern of care may be so regular and demanding that work outside the house is impossible. Such subsidies to help cover cost or handle job opportunities might further intergenerational solidarity for families that have agreed that family care is best, but have been prevented from doing so because of inadequate finances. Another approach, initially put forth by Callahan, Diamond, Giele, & Monis (1980), is the public recognition that families who care for their elders need periodic respite services, supplemental day care, and home health services.

Impact of In-Home Services
Cuts in Washington State

The current cutback climate, indeed, appears to support not the passage of complementary legislation, but rather the elimination of programs that were intended to complement the family. This has been the case, for example, in the state of Washington, where revisions in the income eligibility for chore services reduced the budget by one-third and terminated approximately 2,000 chore clients. Chore services are intended to complement the family by diminishing the frail elderly's needs to a level that the family can meet. By providing routine services (such as meal preparation, transportation, and house cleaning), the state has partial long-term responsibility for the support needed by older persons to remain in their homes. Accordingly, cuts in programs such as chore services may increase the elder's needs without any accompanying policies or programs to increase the resources of the family to meet these needs. In the state of Washington, indeed, the underlying assumption was that families would, and could, step in to fill any gaps in services. If families are expected to assume a caregiver role, without state-provided supports, a complete and permanent transfer of responsibility through institutionalization may be an outcome.

The Washington legislature, concerned about possible increases in institutionalization, mandated that the Department of Social and Health Services (DSHS) undertake a study of the effects on older clients of terminating chore services. Although the study found that over 50% of former clients were receiving some chore service assistance from their families three months after termination, it did not attempt to assess the impact of the increased caregiving responsibilities upon the families who were providing assistance.

Recognizing the need to know more about the impacts of program reductions upon the family members who assume increased caregiving responsibilities, the University of Washington School of Social Work and the Pacific Northwest Long Term Care Center aimed to assess the impact of the chore service policy change upon family members—in effect, the secondary client system affected by budget reductions (Gonyea, Montgomery, & Hooyman, 1982). The presence or absence of chore services did not appear to be related to time spent in caregiving, types of tasks, perception of burden, affective relationships, or stress. The findings that are of significance to the development of family policy are the strong correlations among assisting the older relative with personal care of body contact tasks, perceived burden, negative affect, and reported stress.

Perceived burden was a key factor affecting the quality of the relationship between the elderly and their family caregivers and the stress level of the caregiver. This relationship suggests the importance of increased understanding about what contributes to the family members' perception of burden. It appears that the amount of caregiving (e.g., hours taken to provide care and length of time providing care) is less important than the type of caregiving (e.g., performing personal care of body-contact tasks, such as assisting with bathing, toileting, and dressing, as compared to the more impersonal tasks of helping the older person to manage their environment through providing transportation, shopping, and housework). The strong relationship between performance of personal-care tasks and perceptions of burden suggests the importance of the caregivers' expectations and norms regarding appropriate caregiving behavior. Family members may expect to perform tasks that assist their elderly relatives with managing their household and community affairs, or that provide psychosocial support (such as telephone checkups and companionship); however, when the family member, especially the adult child, is placed in the situation of assisting their relative with intimate, bodily tasks, the distribution of power and resources within the family system is significantly altered.

In the latter situations, the exchange relationship between the family caregiver and the older person becomes very unequal, with the caregiver required to assist with the kinds of body tasks that one performs typically with a dependent child. Accordingly, the family member is being asked to respond to the older relative in ways that may run counter to their conception of reciprocal relationships and may be experienced as a role reversal (Gonyea et al., 1982).

The relationship between perceived burden and the affective quality of the caregiving relationship also has implications for family-centered policy. It may well be that a consequence of expecting families to perform a wider range of tasks, especially those that involve personal care and intimate body contact, is that families may become less effective in performing the social-emotional exchanges for which they are best suited.

Future Research Issues to Be Explored

More research is needed to determine whether interventions can minimize the risk to specific family groups caring for the frail elderly. A priority area to study is how clinical counseling can be combined with supportive services in the external environment. Some promising new approaches have recently been reported, for example, a family-behavioral approach for management of the cognitively impaired aged (Haley, 1983), the development of day-care services for Alzheimer's patients and their families (Sands & Suzuki, 1983), and support groups for relatives of dependent older adults (Hartford & Parsons, 1982). The challenge for society is to reform policies and programs to strengthen family involvement. The challenge for clinical researchers is to determine what approaches enable families to increase their own effectiveness in managing caregiving functions of the frail elderly. Better assessment approaches are in need of development that would enable families and aged persons to make an anticipatory appraisal of their needs and determine their capacity to respond.

In addition, we need to develop mechanisms for introducing professionally guided situational evaluations at critical points, for example, when an elderly person is being discharged from an acute hospital and in need of rehabilitation to regain self-maintenance capacity. More attention needs to be directed toward evaluating which particular family counseling approaches might be most effective. Circumstances facing the frail elderly and their families often escalate into crisis situations. Practitioners can be of greatest value if they can apply short-term approaches that respond to the problems immediately at hand. It would also be valuable to study family members' perceptions of frailness and compare these with self-perceptions of the aged who are impaired. Counseling or the availability of a practitioner to help complete an assessment of the conditions confronting families could lead to a greater perceptual match based on preferences. Additional research and demonstration projects that focus on intergenerational family systems could provide much needed information about family exchanges with the highly dependent elder.

The social policy barriers that prevent or preclude extensive attention to the needs of families must be corrected. The authors believe that families and the elderly should have a voice in setting policy and contributing to the evaluation of policy impact. Researchers who are in a position to evaluate outcomes would be well-directed to collect more data on the consequences to the family of the enactment of particular policies or the withdrawing of certain programs. Many programs supportive to the physically and mentally impaired elderly have never been assessed in regard to the outcomes for families. This oversight has been perpetuated by both limited definitions of the client system and definitions of the frame that exclude connection to the eldest generations and/or family members with major functional limitations. If the objectives are to first understand family need in relationship to the care of frail elderly and second to provide intervention, more research is required that addresses both goals. When projects are conceptualized, they must account for the varied circumstances which confront caregiving families. Cohler's (1983) argument for more differentiated understanding of family members across adulthood directly applies to the need for clinical intervention and policy innovation for the multigenerational family supportive of impaired elders. Knowledge about different coping strategies among social networks confronted by the dynamics of impairment and dependency must be conducted to provide directions for future social policy and program development.

Conditions of frailness and disability are realities that a majority of aged persons face, but those same conditions are also faced by family networks. It appears that families are not retreating from caregiving needs, but they are struggling to find an acceptable and functional equilibrium. (For many years the emphasis has been on children and the aged without equal concern to encompass a family context in policy design.) Perhaps it is time to reverse directions and begin looking toward policies that address the family needs created by dependency among members in order to maximize appropriate and essential interdependence and independence. These conditions are universal and central to the family's experience to the frail elderly, but they have been ignored. A more evolved knowledge base about these dynamics through clinical research could significantly contribute to clarifications required for policy and programmatic investigations.

References

Allison-Cooke, S. (1982). Deinstitutionalizing nursing home patients: Potential versus impediments. *The Gerontologist, 22,* 404–408.

Bell, W. G. (1974). *Policy and practice in long-term care of elderly: A proposal for change.* Paper presented at the 27th Annual Scientific Meeting of the Gerontological Society, Portland, OR.

Brody, E. (1981). "Women in the middle" and family help to older people. *The Gerontologist, 21,* 471–480.

Brody, E. M., & Brody, S. J. (1974). Decade of decision for the elderly. *Social Work, 19,* 544–554.

Brody, S. J., Poulshock, S. W., & Masciocchi, C. F. (1978). The family caring unit: A major consideration in the long-term support system. *The Gerontologist, 18,* 556–561.

Callahan, J., Diamond, L., Giele, J., & Monis, R. (1980). Responsibility of the family for their severely disabled elders. *Home Care Financing Review, 1,* 24–48.

Cicirelli, V. G. (1981). *Helping elderly parents: The role of adult children.* Boston, MA: Auburn House.

Cohler, B. J. (1983). Autonomy and interdependence in the family of adulthood: A psychological perspective. *The Gerontologist, 22,* 33–39.

Doherty, N., Segal, J., & Hicks, B. (1978). Alternatives to institutionalization for the aged: Viability and cost-effectiveness. *Aged Care and Service Review*, *1*, 1–16.

Eggert, C., Granger, C. W., Morris, R., & Pendleton, S. F. (Oct. 1977). Caring for the patient with long-term disability. *Geriatrics*, 102–104.

Estes, C. L. (1979). The aging enterprise: A critical examination of social policies and service for the aged. San Francisco: Jossey-Bass.

Frankfather, D., Smith, M. J., & Caro, F. G. (1981). *Family care of the elderly: Public initiatives and public obligations.* Lexington, MA: Lexington Books.

Gadow, S. (1983). Frailty and strength: The dialectic in aging. *The Gerontologist*, *23*, 144–147.

Gonyea, J., Mongomery, R., & Hooyman, N. (1982). *The impact of chore service termination on family caregivers.* Paper presented at the 35th Annual Scientific Meeting of the Gerontological Society of America, Boston, MA.

Haley, W. E. (1983). A family-behavior approach to the treatment of the cognitively impaired elderly. *The Gerontologist*, *23*, 18–20.

Hartford, M. E., & Parsons, R. (1982). Groups with relatives of dependent older adults. *The Gerontologist*, *22*, 294–298.

Horowitz, A., & Dobrof, R. (1982). *The role of families in providing long-term care to the frail and chronically ill elderly living in the community.* New York: Hunter College, Brookdale Center on Aging.

Litwak, E., & Figueira, J. (Jan. 1968). Technological innovation and theoretical functions of primary groups and bureaucratic structures. *American Journal of Sociology*, 468–481.

Maddox, G. L. Families as a context and resource in chronic illness. In S. Sherwood (Ed.), *Long-term care: A handbook for researchers, planners and providers.* New York: Spectrum, 1975.

Montgomery, R. J. V. (1982). Impact of institutional care policies on family integration. *The Gerontologist*, *22*, 54–58.

Moroney, R. M. (1976). *The family and the state: Considerations for social policy.* New York: Longman.

Nelson, G. M. (1982). Support for the aged: Public and private responsibility. *Social Work*, *27*, 137–143.

Newman, S. J. (1980). *Government policy and the relationship between adult children and their aging parents: Filial support, Medicare and Medicaid.* Ann Arbor: University of Michigan, Institute for Social Research.

Rosenmayr, L. (1977). The family—A source for the elderly. In E. Shanas & M. Sussman (Eds.), *Family bureaucracy and the elderly.* Durham, NC: Duke University Press.

Sands, D., & Suzuki, T. (1983). Adult day care for Alzheimer's patients and their families. *The Gerontologist*, *33*, 21–23.

Schorr, A. (1980). *Thy father and thy mother . . . A second look at filial responsibility and family policy.* Washington, DC: U.S. Government Printing Office.

Streib, G.F. (1983). The frail elderly: Research dilemmas and research opportunities. *The Gerontologist, 23,* 40–44.

Sussman, M. D., & Peter, K. (1981). Support network for families: Some policy initiatives. Newark, DE: College of Human Resources, University of Delaware. Document control 35-14-001-81-04-02.

Tobin, S. S., & Kulys, R. (1981). The family and services. In C. Eisdorfer (Ed.), *Annual Review of Gerontology and Geriatrics.* New York: Springer Publishing Company.

Treas, J. (1977). Family support system for the aged: Some social and demographic considerations. *The Gerontologist, 16,* 486–491.

Part V

The Applications
of Theory
and Research

13

The Application of Network Theory and Research to the Field of Aging

David E. Biegel

There is tremendous interest today in the utilization of informal support systems to help address the growing social welfare needs in our country. In fact, informal systems have always provided a far greater amount of help to those in need that do professional services. In the last several years, an increasing number of aging network providers have developed interventions to strengthen or create informal support systems (family, friends, neighbors, peers, natural helpers, self-help groups, etc.) in the community.

The purpose of this chapter is to examine the nature of these interventions. The following issues will be addressed: (1) What do social network theory and research tell us about the strengths, weaknesses, and limitations of informal support systems for the elderly? (2) What models of social network intervention with the elderly have been developed? (3) What are the obstacles, limitations, and/or difficulties in developing these interventions?

Social Support and the Elderly: Research Highlights

There is a significant body of research concerning the role of social support and the elderly. Much of these data have been reviewed in detail in earlier chapters of this book. Here, we will briefly outline demographic trends and particular research findings especially relevant to an understanding of social network interventions.

Demographic trends and "at risk" groups

- The elderly are not one homogeneous group but rather are very heterogeneous. In fact, the elderly are more diverse than other population groups (Cantor, 1979; Kahn & Antonucci, 1981; Palmore, 1974).
- The population 60 years and over has been increasing steadily since 1900, with the population 75 years and over growing at an even faster rate than the elderly population as a whole. This faster rate of increase is expected to continue through the century.
- Those 75 years and older are more likely to have health problems, require assistance in meeting the needs of daily living, live alone, and be at greater risk for institutionalization. At the same time, this group with the most need for assistance is least likely to have an adequate social network and is often underserved by professional services.
- Women, as a subgroup of the elderly, are also at high risk. In fact, the "old-old" population contains far more women than men, and the women are more likely to be widowed or divorced, live alone, be poor, and be chronically ill (Nowak & Brice, 1983).
- Another subgroup of the elderly at high risk is minority elderly. They are said to suffer *triple jeopardy* (being old, poor, and minority), are more likely to live in poverty, and have more chronic health problems than white elderly. Minority elderly also face more barriers to the utilization of professional services (Hooyman, 1983).
- There are many stresses affecting both mental and physical health in old age. While these stresses are not unique to the elderly, they tend to be multiple and pervasive in that group. At the same time, the elderly make less use of professional services than other population groups (Antonucci & Bornstein, 1978; Biegel & Sherman, 1979; Kulka & Tamir, 1978) and are likely to have weaker social supports than non-elderly (Cassel, 1976; Dean & Lin, 1977; Eaton, 1978; Gore, 1978). This situation becomes compounded when one realizes that minorities, single persons, the poor, and those with little education are also at a disadvantage in terms of such support systems (Fischer et al., 1977).

Support system strengths

- As many researchers have shown, it is a myth that the elderly are abandoned by their families. Rather, family members provide extensive support and represent the elderly's most significant social resource (Brody, 1982; Cantor, 1975; Shanas, 1979; Sussman, 1976). Research shows that most basic and extended needs of the elderly are provided within the family network. Children of the elderly provide significant amounts of support, and children of frail elderly assume an even larger portion of the care needs (Sussman, 1976). The great majority of old persons live near at least one child and see their children frequently. These family members provide the great bulk (80%) of medically related and personal care services for the noninstitutionalized elderly (Brody, 1982; U.S.G.A.O., 1977).
- Friends and neighbors are also significant providers of social support for the elderly (Baum & Baum, 1980; Biegel, 1982; Guttmann, 1982). In fact, because of their physical proximity, neighbors may be the most valuable resource to the elderly in times of emergency (Hooyman, 1983).
- Although the elderly's rate of participation in organizations is lower than that of other population groups, community groups and associations are also very important to the well-being of the elderly (Lopata, 1973; Lowenthal & Haven, 1968; Rose & Peterson, 1965; Shanas et al., 1968; Townsend, 1975).

Support system limitations

- A small but disturbing number of elderly have no significant others they can turn to for any significant help and assistance (Biegel, 1982; Cantor, 1979; Guttmann, 1982).
- Social and demographic trends may portend lessened availability of family support in the future. These trends include increasing geographical distance between elderly and their children, smaller family sizes, increasing number of women in the work place, higher divorce rates, and growth in the number of elderly who outlive their children (Gelfand & Gelfand, 1982; Slater, 1970; Smyer, 1983).
- Family members providing support for an elderly relative may be burdened by their caregiving responsibilities. The most significant problems identified by researchers for caretakers include

coping with physical and mental illness and increased needs of the elderly; restrictions on social and leisure activities; disruption of household and work routines; conflicting multiple role demands (wife, mother, worker, and caretaker of parent or in-laws); lack of support and assistance from other family members; and lack of information and support from agency professionals on how to care for an aging parent (Brody, 1982; Butler, 1981; Nowak & Brice, 1983; Smyer, 1983).

- Friends and relatives may be unable to address long-term and specialized needs of the elderly (Litwak, 1979).
- Existing informal support systems are often fragmented, with few linkages between providers of informal support and even fewer linkages between informal and professional providers (Biegel & Sherman, 1979; Guttmann, 1979).

Interventions by professionals to strengthen support systems of the elderly should build on existing strengths as well as address the limitations that have been identified above. Specifically:

Implications of research findings for network interventions

- Professional interventions should recognize the heterogeneity of the elderly population and should be geared to those elderly most at risk (i.e., those 75 years and over, especially women and blacks) and those without families, confidants, or significant others (in practice, this latter group may be difficult to locate and serve).
- Interventions should strengthen the families' ability to provide support to their elderly members and in so doing should attempt to relieve or reduce the stress of "family burden." Such interventions should take into consideration the changing social and demographic circumstances of families and the expected new burdens of the future.
- Interventions should strengthen the ability of friends, neighbors, and other neighborhood-based caretakers to provide increased social support to the elderly, keeping in mind the realistic limitations of these providers. In this regard, new policy initiatives need to be developed, such as reimbursement of community members willing to provide ongoing and skilled care to elderly members.
- Finally, professionals need to strengthen existing networks and enhance the coordination of informal and formal service providers to help overcome fragmentation of services.

Social Network Interventions

A Framework for Examining Interventions

There have been a number of attempts at conceptualizing social network interventions in social welfare (Froland et al., 1979; Maguire & Biegel, 1982; Pancoast & Chapman, 1982; Trimble, 1980). This chapter utilizes an adaptation of the framework developed by Maguire and Biegel (1982). Social network interventions with the elderly are conceptualized along a multicontinuum grid. Seven types of network interventions are identified: Clinical Treatment, Family Caretaker Enhancement, Case Management, Neighborhood Helping, Volunteer Linking, Mutual Help/Self-Help, and Community Empowerment.[*]

The distinctions made here between the types of network interventions oversimplify reality. In actuality, they represent analytically separable rather than discrete categories. Interventions in practice often utilize multiple network strategies. The caretaker enhancement category is somewhat different from the other six in that its primary focus is upon a client group rather than a single intervention strategy. However, it is felt that the disadvantage to conceptual "neatness" by the inclusion of this category is far outweighed by the usefulness to practitioners of its inclusion in this manner.

For each of these seven types of network intervention strategies, four salient defining variables have been identified as follows (see Table 13.1):

1. *Client group.* An elderly individual, family caretakers, or at-large elderly in the neighborhood.
2. *Helper type.* Either informal helpers, which includes family, friends, neighbors, people with similar problems, volunteers, and so on, or formal or agency helpers.
3. *Locus of help.* Neighborhood or community based, or nongeographic.
4. *Level of help.* Prevention, treatment, or rehabilitation.

For each intervention strategy, illustrative examples will be given of current or recent programs utilizing the technique. These illustrations are representative, but are by no means comprehensive or inclusive.

[*]The author is indebted to Froland et al. (1981) at Portland State University for their pioneering work in the development of a typology of network-based interventions.

TABLE 13.1. Social Network Interventions with the Elderly

Type of Network Intervention	Client Group	Helper Type	Locus of Help	Level of Help*
1. Clinical treatment	An elderly individual	Professional helpers, family, neighbors, friends	Nongeographic	T,R
2. Family caretaker enhancement Education & training Direct services Indirect services	Family members of the elderly	Family, neighbors, friends, and professional helpers	Nongeographic	P,T
3. Case management	An elderly individual	Agency staff and personal network	Neighborhood, nongeographic	T
4. Neighborhood helping	An elderly individual or at-large elderly in the neighborhood	Natural helpers, role-related helpers (gatekeepers)	Neighborhood	P,T,R
5. Volunteer linking	An elderly individual	Volunteers	Neighborhood, community	P,T,R
6. Mutual aid/self-help	At-large elderly in the neighborhood	People with similar problems	Neighborhood, community, or nongeographic	P,T,R
7. Community empowerment	At-large elderly in the neighborhood	Lay and professional helpers	Neighborhood	P,T,R

*P = Prevention; T = Treatment; R = Rehabilitation.

Clinical Treatment

This approach involves direct clinical intervention with the elderly individual as the client in order to assess and strengthen the support systems of at-risk individuals. Garrison and Howe (1976) and Cohen and Sokolovsky (1981) have done significant work in this area.

Garrison's intervention technique relies on the direct involvement of all significant members of the subject's social network in the intervention process. The goals of this intervention are twofold: first, to modify the emotional influence (or affective content) of the social network on the client; and, second, to formulate the needed instrumental resources that are represented by professional caregivers, community agencies, and other significant supports. These goals are reached through a "network session" guided by the client's clinician. The clinician assesses problems through a social systems, rather than intrapsychic, viewpoint. The role of the professional is not that of traditional therapist, but rather one of facilitator and catalyst.

Cohen and Sokolovsky (1981) also propose therapeutic intervention with the elderly through a social networks strategy. However, their approach is somewhat different from that of Garrison and Howe. It is based upon research with elderly persons in single room occupancy (SRO) hotels. The tenants in these establishments have a range of mental, physical, and social pathologies. They typically have great needs, but they distrust and therefore underutilize professional services.

The authors have developed an instrument, the Network Analysis Profile, to analyze the social networks of these individuals. This instrument has both research and therapeutic applicability. The profile charts the interaction among various components of the resident's personal network, namely, tenant–tenant, tenant–nontenant, tenant–kin, tenant–hotel staff, tenant–agency staff, and tenant–social institution. Among variables examined for each interaction are content of the relationship and frequency, duration, intensity, and directional flow of the links.

The authors state that the instrument is very useful at both the agency and client levels. At the agency level it can sensitize agency personnel to the strengths of even the most deviate population groups; it can assist staff to understand human behavior within a systems framework; it can help the agency allocate staff resources to those individuals most at risk; and it can help agency personnel establish relationships with natural helpers identified by the instrument.

At the client level, the instrument can be completed as part of standard intake forms used by a service agency. The resultant information can help the agency identify individuals at high risk and can assess the strengths and weaknesses of an individual's social network.

In undertaking such assessments, workers must understand that individuals vary in their need for and styles of interaction. Thus the same amount of interaction will be experienced differently by particular individuals.

Once the worker has obtained this information, interventions can be planned through this network. Thus before the worker would intervene professionally to help a client solve a problem or meet a need, he or she would see whether help was available by a caregiver in that client's network. And very importantly, the worker would assess whether any professional services being planned would have a negative impact upon the positive assistance being provided through the informal network. For example, as Cohen and Sokolovsky point out, if an agency offers a loan to a client, it may harm the client's relationship with a neighbor who provides not only a loan but also social support and companionship. An additional role of the professional would be to assess the fragility of the network: Is the client relying on one particular person whose loss might be devastating? Of course, the analysis of social networks might well reveal individuals who have significant needs not being met by their present informal network. For these individuals, professionals need to create networks—either targeted to one individual or on a group level targeted to a number of at-risk individuals (i.e., a self-help group).

Family Caretaker Enhancement

This intervention modality involves intervening with family caretakers of the elderly to enhance family supports and to avoid undue family or parent burden. Depending on the specific strategy, it may be considered as either primary or secondary prevention. There are a number of ways in which professionals can provide assistance to family caretakers:

> *Education and training*—topics include the aging process, community resources, stress management, caretaking skills, peer support mechanisms, and so on.
>
> *Direct services*—respite care, counseling, financial assistance to caretakers, technical assistance, referrals.
>
> *Indirect services*—helping to strengthen informal networks of family caregivers through involvement of other family members, friends, neighbors, clergy, neighborhood groups, and the like.

Education and Training. A variety of educational interventions have been reported in the literature (Brice & Nowak, 1981; OAS, 1979; Smyer, 1983; Zimmer & Mellor, 1981). An interesting training program was developed in 1981 by the Center for the Study of Aging at the State University of New York at Buffalo. This project, entitled "Caregivers Assistance and Resources for the Elderly's Relatives Series" (CARERS), has the goal of reducing stress and improving competencies by geriatric family caregivers. The program consists of 13 two and one-half hour sessions held one morning per month. Training issues include basic processes of aging, practical care-giving skills, coping with inevitable stresses of caregiving, and consumer advocacy in contracting for professional services. The program costs $5.00 per session and is aimed at family members caring for an elderly relative, with particular interest given to situations where some form of dementia or physical disability is involved. An average of 30 persons per session have attended the program so far. A formal evaluation was recently conducted, but the results are not yet available (Brice & Nowak, 1981).

Smyer reports on an educational program for family caretakers and the general community called *The Family After Forty Project*; this is a joint venture of the Cooperative Extension Service and the Gerontology Center of Pennsylvania State University. The methodology of this program is printed materials rather than interactive training. Six pamphlets, prepared for high school level reading, have been developed on such topics as giving and receiving help, emotional well-being, physical well-being, living arrangements, financial concerns, and communication skills. The goal is to help individuals in the community anticipate the problems of aging they and/or their relatives will face, to prepare in advance for these crises, and to become more knowledgeable of community resources. The pamphlets have been utilized through a self-referred list of 86 persons in a rural Pennsylvania county. The author does not indicate whether any outcome evaluation of these materials has been conducted (Smyer, 1983).

Direct and Indirect Services. Other professional efforts to assist family caretakers have included the formation of support groups and other service delivery strategies. For example, the University of Michigan, Institute for Gerontology, has developed a program to provide social support and intervention skills to family caretakers in an effort at early intervention to prevent crises among caretakers before they occur (Smyer, 1983). The University of Southern California has developed a support program for demented elderly and their family members that includes individual counseling for the family caregivers and meetings of family members to strengthen the support systems of the family caretakers (Smyer, 1983). Until recently, the Community Service Society of New York offered a Natural Supports Program which included education, skills training, social support, advocacy, respite care, day care, and counseling for family service providers (Zimmer & Mellor, 1981).

Frankfather, Smith, and Caro (1981) and Smyer (1983) report the results of another Community Service Society program—the *Family Support Project*, which is an intervention program with disabled elderly. This research and demonstration project examined the range of informal and formal services needed by caretakers of functionally impaired elderly persons. Findings showed that informal support services had greater flexibility and diversity than formal services. The informal sector had more ability to respond to changing service needs and could offer services more appropriately, at more convenient times, and in smaller and more frequent service unit intervals. Importantly, families receiving professional services did not withdraw or reduce their own services. It is suggested that for elderly with family support systems, the appropriate role for professionals is one of providing limited benefits to complement these services, but that for persons without any family support a complete range of professional services is required.

The Department of Human Resources of the State of Maine has developed an interesting alternative approach to the needs of impaired elderly. This program implements a policy recommendation suggested by Sussman (1976), that is, providing financial support to encourage and enable family members and neighbors who would not otherwise be able to do so to provide care to the elderly. The program is structured such that funding to families or neighbors is provided only when all other resources are exhausted. In this way, previous maintenance of effort is assured. The Department gives the following case example, which illustrates this approach:

> Mr. E., 79 years old, a severe arthritic with Alzheimer's Disease, needs two people to help him out of bed. He is incontinent and requires assistance with all activities such as bathing, eating and dressing. His wife, 76 years old, is a diabetic, had a stroke resulting in partial paralysis and has oxygen periodically for respiratory distress. The granddaughter gave up her job and with assistance from her husband and other family members, has been the primary caretaker of both grandparents since last March, for which she is being paid $100 per week. They continue to do well at home, with Mr. E showing some improvement recently. (DHS, 1983, p. 2)

The Department of Human Services states that such an approach is a cost-effective alternative to the provision of nursing home care. The program has been evaluated through a family and client satisfaction questionnaire, the results of which have been very positive. However, additional research mechanisms are needed to evaluate the cost effectiveness of this effort.

Case Management

The third type of network intervention in our continuum is a treatment approach in which professionals have major involvement. Its aim is to help address the issues of fragmentation, lack of accessibility, and lack of accountability in the delivery of services to older persons. Case management is a micro-oriented approach in which the client is an individual or family, and professional helpers are defined primarily as the network members. The case manager attempts to coordinate a variety of public and private services for the maximum benefit of the client and in so doing makes the impact of the service more efficient as well as more effective.

Case management approaches have been criticized for concentrating on the coordination of professional services to the exclusion of informal support systems. Recently, there have been attempts in the aging field to include informal support systems in client assessment and treatment plans. For example, in 1982, the Department of Aging, Commonwealth of Pennsylvania, supported research to develop a guide for the utilization and support of informal resources to serve the aging. The Department was interested in assisting Area Agencies on Aging to become better informed about the existence and utilization of informal resources for their clients. Recommendations based on this research, which has now been completed, include the following: (1) Service agencies should restructure their philosophy of service to make support and utilization of informal support an important component in meeting the needs of their clients; (2) Utilization of informal supports should be incorporated into the Agency's service management systems; (3) Primary caregivers (usually family members) should be included in the assessment process from the beginning to affirm their role in client's care; and (4) case managers should assist primary caregivers by providing supportive services and helping to mobilize additional informal supports on the client's behalf (Worts & Melton, 1982).

A number of states have already integrated information about informal support systems into client assessment forms. For example, the client assessment form utilized by the State of Florida, Department of Health and Rehabilitative Services, contains a section on services and social support. The following questions are included: How much help per week is the client receiving from his or her informal network of family and friends? Who is primarily providing help? Is the client's informal network of family and friends able to continue giving this current level of help? Does the client's informal network of family and friends appear to be sufficiently resilient to respond to an increased demand for service in case of illness or accident?

Although the data which would be elicited by the above questions are useful, they are very brief and may not provide sufficient information on which to develop interventions to strengthen social networks. Additional information is needed to identify the members of the client's network, to assess the types of support provided and the client's satisfaction with that support, and to identify obstacles and/or limitations which may militate against the provision of additional support from the informal support system. Finally, information is needed concerning the client's participation in neighborhood, community, and other groups.

Neighborhood Helping

Neighborhood helping as an intervention modality involves strengthening the networks of elderly individuals through enhancing their ties with natural helpers and community gatekeepers. This is done in an identified target area, usually a neighborhood or larger community.

Natural helpers are ordinary individuals identified by others in the community as being good listeners and helpers. They provide social support to the elderly consisting of alleviation of social isolation; emotional support-encouragement, reassurance; communication activities such as being a confidant; and problem-centered services such as light housekeeping, errands, transportation, cooking (Smith, 1975). Advantages of help provided by natural helpers include its easy accessibility, lack of stigma, no cost, mutuality of helping, and its basis in proximity, friendship, or long-term acquaintanceship.

A number of researchers have developed guidelines for working with natural helpers (Collins & Pancoast, 1976; Crawford, Smith, & Taylor, 1978; Smith, 1975). Suggested intervention strategies include consultation and linkage models. The consultation model, developed by Collins and Pancoast (1976), states that one full-time professional can work with up to 15 natural helpers. The goal is to strengthen the natural helpers' ability to provide assistance to members of their networks as well as to reach out to other individuals. Professionals can provide natural helpers with information about new programs and services and can also reinforce the work of the natural helpers by assuring them that they are providing a valuable and helpful service. Such a strategy helps the professional as well as the natural helper. Professionals can develop a better understanding of the ways in which elderly in particular communities seek and receive help. Natural helpers can offer suggestions, based upon their extensive experience with the elderly in the community, as to how professional interventions could be organized and strengthened.

The linkage model encourages partnerships between natural helpers and professionals to help identify community strengths, unmet needs, and obstacles to effective service delivery. The premise is that neither natural helpers nor professionals alone have all the expertise and resources needed to solve problems and meet needs. By working together, however, new and innovative approaches to service delivery can be developed.

An example of such a partnership is the Clergy, Agency & Community Case Study/Brown Bag Luncheons developed through the University of Southern California, Washington Public Affairs Center's Neighborhood and Family Services Project (Biegel & Naparstek, 1982). In this project, natural helpers (many of whom were age 60 years and older), clergy, and agency professionals meet together monthly in small mixed groups of eight persons each to discuss a problem from a group member's caseload. After a brief presentation, a discussion ensues. The emphasis of the discussion is on seeking alternative ways to address needs indicated in the case studies, to utilize the varied expertise present in each group, and to explore the various resources in the community able to help with the problem. This process achieves a number of objectives. First, through the interaction of community and professional helpers, mutual respect develops for each group's areas of expertise. Second, knowledge of new or additional resources to meet community needs is identified by participants. Third, the feedback individual helpers receive from their helping peers leads to a renewed sense of competence. Finally, the sessions indicate areas of unmet need within the community and stimulate the development of new services to meet those needs.

Other helpers at the neighborhood level are community gatekeepers—clergy, nurses, pharmacists, physicians, bus drivers, letter carriers, and so on. These individuals are turned to naturally because they are available, trusted, or felt to have professional expertise. Numerous interventions have been developed that utilize these resources. In Philadelphia, community gatekeepers were provided training in crisis intervention (Snyder, 1971). In southern California, rapid transit bus drivers were trained to recognize sensory and motor losses of aging (Hooyman, 1983). A community mental health center in Spokane, Washington, trains a number of service providers (taxi drivers, fuel oil dealers, firefighters, letter carriers, and meter readers) to watch for situations and symptoms that may indicate a need for services by the frail elderly (Hooyman, in press).

Volunteer Linking

This intervention involves the creation of ties, usually targeted directly to individuals in need. Assistance is provided through a helper who is trained, supervised, and organized by a formal agency. Volunteer linking is very different from other forms of network intervention. Pancoast and Chapman (1982) studied 30 agencies that operated network intervention programs with various population groups. They state that volunteer linking is the network intervention modality that, ". . . is the most likely to involve inequality of status between the helper and recipient—both in terms of socioeconomic status and general coping ability. There is an unequal exchange relationship in which the volunteer is clearly defined as the helper. While a mutual relationship may develop and indeed is often encouraged by these agencies, it is not usually part of the standard volunteer role" (Pancoast & Chapman, 1982, p. 223). Volunteer linking demands significant and continued involvement from professionals, initially in the recruitment and training of volunteers, and then in ongoing efforts to sustain the created relationships.

In some intervention programs, the primary clients are elderly individuals in need of assistance. For example, through the Northwest Salem Community Association in Oregon, chronically mentally ill older persons without families receive assistance from volunteers from local churches. This linking seeks to create artificial families (Hooyman, 1983). In other programs, such as the Retired Senior Volunteer Program, the emphasis is upon meeting the needs of the older volunteers and matching their interests and skills with individuals in need of service. Recently, interest has grown in intergenerational programming—such as pairing an older volunteer with a young child. The Foster Grandparent Program matches elderly volunteers with children in need of support and assistance. A similar effort is the Generations Together Program at the University of Pittsburgh, which utilizes elderly volunteers in public school classrooms to help teachers with educational tasks and to positively alter children's views of older persons.

Mutual Aid/Self-Help

Interventions with the elderly of a mutual aid/self-help nature vary in type. First, there is the formalized mutual aid/self-help group, which for our purposes will be limited to those groups which meet for the goal of mutual support and guidance in response to a common problem. Second, there are formalized barter or service-exchange programs. Third, there are programs that create artificial networks among older persons in order to increase the exchange of helping resources.

Mutual Aid/Self-Help Groups.   There is abundant literature that documents the importance of self-help groups in community mental health (Caplan & Killilea, 1976; Maguire, 1983; President's Commission on Mental Health, 1978; Silverman, 1970). Among the reasons for the effectiveness of self-help groups according to Spiegel (1982) are commonality of experience, mutual support, receiving help through giving it, collective willpower, information sharing, and goal-directed problem solving. Self-help groups can often reach individuals who would never go to professionals for assistance.

Numerous self-help groups for elderly individuals have been organized throughout the country with the assistance of churches, community organizations, and mental health centers. These groups provide social support, acceptance, companionship, and a host of educational and recreational opportunities. One such program, What Are Friends For?, developed by the American Association for the Blind, is a self-help peer discussion group program for older persons with sensory loss. The program is designed to encourage older people to work together to identify their needs, to learn how to modify the physical and social environment to meet those needs, and to compensate for the loss of one sense through the better use of other senses. The American Foundation for the Blind (1982) states that no previous experience is necessary to lead an effective self-help discussion and offers a package of materials for implementing such groups.

Service Exchange.   Self-help interventions of this type seek to assist individuals to meet their needs through a formalized exchange of services. For example, Work Exchange, Inc., located in Milwaukee, Wisconsin, currently has over 1,000 members, of which 40% are 60 years and older. In order to join Work Exchange, an individual must be willing and able to perform at least one service for someone else, such as snow shoveling, sharing meals, cutting grass, doing laundry, minor appliance repair, lessons in knitting, and so on. By its very nature this program helps to enhance social support systems of the participants in addition to enabling the exchange of services.

Another such program is Project LINC (Living Independently through Neighborhood Cooperation) of the Andrus Gerontology Center of the University of Southern California. The project was designed to help meet the needs of the frail elderly on a neighborhood basis so as to prevent or delay unnecessary institutionalization. A key component of this project is an exchange bank of skills and services. This bank includes residents who volunteer use of their skills or who agree to offer a specific service to their neighbors. Residents are thus givers as well as receivers of services. A total of 220 individuals participated in Project LINC, and the authors report some interesting findings. First, program recipients were reluctant to request assistance for in-home helping services, preferring to do such things all by themselves despite great effort. Transportation to medical appointments, shopping, banks, and the like was the most frequently exchanged service. Second, program participants resisted asking others for help for fear of being seen as helpless. Because of this they seemed to prefer "repaying" the same persons who provided them with a service rather than providing a service to someone else in return (Kaplan & Fleisher, 1981).

Creation of Artificial Networks. Another variety of self-help intervention can be seen in The Elder Program of the University of Louisville Gerontology Center. This effort was funded through a three-year AOA Model Projects grant and was designed to strengthen neighborhood support systems for older persons through an educational program that emphasized information, resources, and skill development. Approximately 200 people in seven neighborhoods participated in this program of eight weekly, half-day educational meetings. Topics included outreach, helping methods, advocacy, problem solving, and group maintenance skills. Evaluation instruments were administered at the beginning of the educational program and at two- and six-month intervals after its conclusion. Findings indicate a significant increase in the amount of helping activities occurring between group members (Crowe et al., 1981).

Community Empowerment

This intervention is aimed at increasing the capacity and equity of elderly individuals. Capacity is defined as a group's ability to utilize power to solve problems affecting them and ability to gain access to institutions and organizations that service them. Equity is based upon whether groups define their investment as equal to their return and whether they see themselves as getting their fair share of resources (Naparstek, Biegel, & Spiro, 1982).

The Neighborhood and Family Services Project of the University of Southern California, Washington Public Affairs Center (Biegel & Sherman, 1979), developed a model that builds on the unique strengths and resources of communities and utilizes these strengths to enhance service delivery to neighborhood residents. In doing so, the model creates linkages between community and professional helping networks. Community residents increase their capacities to develop programs to meet needs that they have identified. Professionals act in an advisory capacity to community groups instead of in the usual manner.

The overriding objective of this effort is to strengthen networks, lay and professional, and to remove impediments to partnerships between community helpers and leaders and agency professionals. Development of specific intervention programs serves as both means and ends. The end is achieved because intervention programs— whether they are self-help groups, hotlines, or referral directories— address a specific need that has been identified by the community organization in collaboration with the professional advisory committee. The means, namely, the planning and developmental process, achieves the end of enhancing the capacity of lay people, first to work together and then to work in concert with professionals as full partners.

In New York City, the Citizens Committee for New York City, Inc., sponsors a new program called MAP (Mutual Aid Project). The goal is to help older people in neighborhoods provide services for themselves. Staff organizers are available to local groups and furnish advice, technical support, and organizational assistance. The residents themselves decide what projects are needed; the staff functions only in a supportive role to help the residents develop projects they have identified. MAP has published a handbook of projects organized by member groups. Examples include self-protection projects, projects for the homebound, consumer education projects, urban gardening, and cooperative and exchange projects. Another example is the Mutual Help Model developed by Phylis Ehrlich, which utilizes networking methods to organize neighborhood groups to help themselves with problems regarding aging services (Worts & Melton, 1982).

Dangers, Obstacles and Limits of Social Network Interventions

The previous section attests to a growing number of exciting, innovative strategies for strengthening and/or creating informal support systems for the at-risk elderly. Lest this process seem too easy or too promising, a few words are in order concerning the limitations of social networks and the dangers, obstacles, and limitations of social network interventions.

Social networks can do harm as well as good. Some networks may be judgmental or require conformity. Other networks may be ineffective in dealing with "difficult" individuals. Networks can enforce notions of pride and privacy, leading individuals to avoid seeking professional help when such care is warranted.

In 1978, the President's Commission on Mental Health issued its Final Report. Its first recommendation called for recognition, understanding, and utilization of informal support systems to address the mental health needs of the nation's population. The Commission cautioned that informal support systems should not be seen as a rationale to cut needed professional services. Despite this caveat, the worst fears of many of those involved in social network interventions have come true. Needed professional services are indeed being cut to reduce the federal and state deficits, and families, friends, neighbors, and other informal service providers are being asked to pick up the burden. There is a very real danger that such actions could seriously overload and weaken informal support systems. Another danger is that professionals might not fully understand the difficulty and time required to develop social network interventions. They may attempt "cookbook" replications of successful projects without regard to the process involved or the skills and training needed by staff. Such interventions may have the unintended effect of weakening intead of strengthening informal support systems. Finally, there is the danger of romanticizing informal support systems and failing to realize that such systems are not always positive and can sometimes do harm as well as good.

There are also a number of obstacles that may prevent full utilization of social network interventions. Professionals may not be knowledgeable about the role and functions of informal support systems or may believe that only those with professional education and training should offer help to people in need. Informal helpers may in turn be intimidated by professionals and may be uncomfortable interacting with them. Professionals may not have the necessary skills for assessing and intervening with informal support systems. Depending on the intervention, specialized skills may be needed in counseling and therapy, consultation, group work, or community organization. While not all staff need all of these skills, a particular intervention may require additional training and expertise by agency staff. This may be especially burdensome because of current cutbacks of public and private dollars for training. This suggests another obstacle, namely, that some interventions may take a considerable amount of "front end" time to develop, and the agency wishing to undertake the intervention may not have the funds or the time with which to do so. In fact, as the public dollar becomes tighter, many agencies are being forced to deliver only treatment or clinical services. Social network interventions of a preventive nature, like many of those we have discussed above, may not be supported. Other obstacles include administrative, fiscal, and legal procedures of funding bodies and service agencies that may militate against social network interventions. Most aging network agencies are reimbursed on a unit-of-service basis for agreed-upon services. If we expect these agencies to utilize informal networks, then reimbursement formulas must reflect this new role.

Finally, there are a number of limitations of social network interventions. As we have seen, evaluations of specific interventions are fairly primitive. Some interventions have not been evaluated at all; others have been evaluated either through client self-reports or anecdotally through program reports. Only a few interventions have utilized before-and-after measures, and then only rarely with a control or comparison group. There is need for more thorough and scientific program evaluations, not only to ascertain the relative success of the intervention, but specifically to assess which components seem to be successful for which participants and whether particular intervention strategies are more successful than others. A key question in future evaluations is the relationship between professional and informal services: Are some needs more appropriately met by professionals and others by the informal network? What is the proper balance of informal and professional services? How can we maximize efficient uses of both types of support systems?

References

American Foundation for the Blind. (1982). Self-help groups for older persons with sensory loss. New York: The U.S.E. Program.

Antonucci, T., & Bornstein, J. (1978). Changes in informal support networks. Research Report, NIMH Grant #MH-14618.

Baum, M., & Baum, R. (1980). *Growing old: A societal perspective.* Englewood Cliffs, NJ: Prentice-Hall.

Biegel, D. (1982). *Help seeking and receiving in urban ethnic neighborhoods.* Ph.D. thesis, University of Maryland.

Biegel, D. E., & Sherman, W. R. (1979). Neighborhood capacity building and the ethnic aged. In D. Gelfand & A. Kutzik (Eds.), *Ethnicity and aging.* New York: Springer Publishing Company.

Biegel, D., & Naparstek, A. (1982). The neighborhood and family services project: An empowerment model linking clergy, agency professionals and community residents. In A. M. Jeger & R. S. Slotnik (Eds.), *Community mental health and behavioral-ecology.* New York: Plenum.

Brice, G. C., & Nowak, C. A. (1981). *Education as a family mental health intervention.* Presented at the 35th Annual Scientific Meeting of the Gerontological Society of America, Boston, MA.

Brody, E. M. (1982). Older people, their families and social welfare. In *The social welfare forum, 1981.* New York: Columbia University Press.

Butler, R. N. (1981). Overview on aging: Some biomedical, social and behavioral perspectives. In S. B. Kiesler, J. N. Morgan, & V. C. Dopenheimer (Eds.), *Aging: Social change.* New York: Academic Press.

Cantor, M. H. (1975). Life space and the support system of the inner city elderly of New York. *The Gerontologist, 15*(1), 23–27.

Cantor, M. H. (1979). The informal support system of New York's inner city elderly. In D. Gelfand & A. Kutzik (Eds.), *Ethnicity and aging.* New York: Springer Publishing Company.

Caplan, G., & Killilea, M. (1976). *Support systems and mutual help.* New York: Grune & Stratton.

Cassel, J. (1976). The contribution of the social environment to host resistance. *American Journal of Epidemiology, 102*(2), 107–123.

Cohen, C. I., & Sokolovsky, J. (1981). Social networks and the elderly: Clinical techniques. *International Journal of Family Therapy, 3*(4), 281–294.

Collins, A., & Pancoast, D. (1976). *Natural helping networks.* Washington, DC: National Association of Social Workers.

Crawford, L., Smith, P., & Taylor, L. (1978). *It makes good sense: A handbook for working with natural helpers.* Portland, OR: Technical Report, Portland State University, School of Social Work.

Crowe, A. H., et al. (1981). *The elder program: An educational model in network building among the elderly.* A paper presented at the 34th Annual Meeting of the Gerontological Society, Toronto, Canada.

Dean, A., & Lin, N. (1977). The stress-buffering role of social support: Problems and prospects for systematic investigation. *Journal of Nervous and Mental Disease, 165*(6), 403–417.

Department of Human Services. (1983). Report on home based care. Report to the Joint Committee on Appropriations and Financial Affairs, by the DHS, State of Maine.

Eaton, W. (1978). Life events, social supports and psychiatric symptoms: A reanalysis of the New Haven data. *Journal of Health and Social Behavior, 19,* 230–234.

Fischer, C. S., Jackson, R. M., Stueve, C. A., Gerson, D., Jones, L. M., & Baldesare, M. (1977). *Networks and places: Social relations in the urban setting.* New York: The Free Press.

Frankfather, D. L., Smith, M. J., & Caro, F. G. (1981). *Family care of the elderly.* Lexington, MA: Lexington Books.

Froland, C., et al. (1979). *Professional partnerships with informal helpers: Emerging forms.* Paper presented at the Annual Meeting of the American Psychological Association.

Froland, C., Pancoast, D. L., Chapman, N. J., & Kimboko, P. J. (1981). *Helping networks and human services.* Beverly Hills, CA: Sage Publications.

Garrison, J. E., & Howe, J. (1976). Community intervention with the elderly: A social networks approach. *Journal of the American Geriatrics Society, 24,* 329–333.

Gelfand, D., & Gelfand, J. (1982). Senior centers and support networks. In D. Biegel & A. Naparstek (Eds.), *Community support systems and mental health: Practice, policy and research.* New York: Springer Publishing Company.

Gore, S. (1978). The effects of social support in moderating the health consequences of unemployment. *Journal of Health and Social Behavior, 19,* 157–165.

Guttmann, D., et al. (1979). *Informal and formal support systems and their effects on the lives of elderly in selected ethnic groups.* Technical Report, The Catholic University of America, Washington, DC. Final Report, ADA Grant #90-A-1007.

Guttmann, D. (1982). Neighborhood as a support system for Euro-American elderly. In D. Biegel & A. Naparstek (Eds.), *Community support systems and mental health: Practice, policy and research.* New York: Springer Publishing Company.

Hooyman, N. (1983). Social support networks in services to the elderly. In J. K. Whittaker & J. Garbarino (Eds.), *Social support networks: Informal helping in the human services.* Hawthorne, NY: Aldine.

Kahn, R. L., & Antonucci, T. C. (1981). Convoys of social support: A life course approach. In S. B. Kiesler, J. N. Morgan, & V. C. Dopenheimer (Eds.), *Aging: Social change.* New York: Academic Press.

Kaplan, B. H., & Fleisher, D. (1981). *Are neighbors a viable support system for the frail elderly?* A paper presented at the 34th Annual Meeting of the Gerontological Society, Toronto, Canada.

Kulka, R. A., & Tamir, L. (1978). *Patterns of help-seeking and formal support.* Technical Report. Research Report, NIMH Grant MH-14618.

Litwak, E. (1979). *Support networks and the disabled: The transition from the community to institutional setting.* Paper presented at the meeting of the Gerontological Society, Washington, DC.

Lopata, H. Z. (1973). *Widowhood in an American city.* Cambridge, MA: Schenkman.

Lowenthal, M. F., & Haven, C. (1968). Interaction and adaptation: Intimacy as a critical variable. In B. Neugarten (Ed.), *Middle age and aging.* Chicago: University of Chicago Press.

Maguire, L., & Biegel, D. (1982). The use of social networks in social welfare. In *Social Welfare Forum, 1981.* New York: Columbia University Press.

Maguire, L. (1983). *Understanding networks: Intervention strategies with indi-*

viduals, self-help groups, organizations and communities. Beverly Hills, CA: Sage Publications.

Naparstek, A., Biegel, D., & Spiro, H. (1982). *Neighborhood networks for humane mental health care*. New York: Plenum Press.

Nowak, C. A., & Brice, G. C. (1983). *A review of familial support systems in later life: Implications for mental health and social service providers*. Unpublished paper. Buffalo, NY: Center for the Study of Aging, State University of New York at Buffalo.

Office of Aging Studies. (1979). *Training to enhance informal support systems of the elderly*. Final report to DHEW from the School of Social Welfare, Louisiana State University.

Palmore, E. (1974). *Normal aging II*. Durham, NC: Duke University Press.

Pancoast, D. L., & Chapman, N. J. (1982). Roles for informal helpers in the delivery of human services. In D. Biegel & A. Naparstek (Eds.), *Community support systems and mental health: Practice policy and research*. New York: Springer Publishing Company.

President's Commission on Mental Health. (1978). *Report of the task panel on community support systems*. Washington, DC: U.S. Government Printing Office.

Rose, A. M., & Peterson, W. A. (Eds.), (1965). *Older people and their social world*. Philadelphia: F. A. Davis.

Shanas, E., et al. (1968). *Old people in three industrial societies*. New York: Atherton Press.

Shanas, E. (1979). The family as a social support system in old age. *The Gerontologist, 9*(2), 169–174.

Silverman, P. R. (1970). The widow as a caregiver in a program of preventive intervention with other widows. *Mental Hygiene, 54*, 540–547.

Slater, P. (1970). *The pursuit of loneliness: American culture at the breaking point*. Boston: Beacon Press.

Smith, S. A. (1975). *Natural systems and the elderly: An unrecognized resource*. Unpublished monograph, Portland, OR.

Smyer, M. A. (1983). Supporting the supporters: Working with families of impaired elderly. *Journal of Community Psychology, 12*(4), 323–333.

Snyder, J. (Fall 1971). The use of gatekeepers in crisis management. *Bulletin of Suicidology, 8*.

Spiegel, D. (1982). Self-help and mutual support groups: A synthesis of the recent literature. In D. Biegel & A. Naparstek (Eds.), *Community support systems and mental health*. New York: Springer Publishing Company.

Sussman, M. B. (1976). The family life of old people. In R. H. Binstock & E. Shanas (Eds.), *Handbook of aging and the social sciences*. New York: Van Nostrand.

Townsend, P. (1975). *The family life of old people*. London: Routeledge and Kegan Paul.

Trimble, D. (1980). A guide to network therapies. *Connections, Bulletin of the INSNA, 3*(2), 9–21.

U.S. General Accounting Office. (1977). *Report to the Congress: The well-being of older people in Cleveland, Ohio*. Washington, DC: U.S. Government Printing Office. Doc No. HRD-77-70.

Worts, F., & Melton, K. (1982). *A guide to the utilization and support of informal resources to serve the aging*. Technical Report, North Philadelphia Initiative for Long Term Care. Prepared for the Pennsylvania Department of Aging.

Zimmer, A. H., & Mellor, M. J. (1981). *Caregivers make the difference: Group services for those caring for older persons in the community*. Unpublished paper of the Natural Supports Program, Community Service Society of New York.

Index

Index

Activity theory, xii, 161-162
  description of, 23-24, 26, 27
  vs. disengagement theory, 26
Adams, B. N., 47, 97, 128, 138
Adult children, xii, 41-59, 78-79, 81-82, 108
  antecedents of relations between
    elderly parents and, 54-56
  attitudes toward filial
    responsibility, 51-54
  consequences of relationships
    with, for physical and social
    well-being of elderly parents,
    56-58
  major findings on relations with
    elderly parents, 43
  proximity of elderly parents to,
    41-43
  quantity and quality of contact
    with elderly parents, 43-47
  reciprocity, concept of, 48, 55
  research priorities, 58-59
  types of assistance provided by,
    to elderly parents, 48-50
  types of assistance provided to,
    by elderly parents, 50-51
  visiting patterns with parents, 44
  see also Kin, extended
Affectional support
  from friends and neighbors, 144-145
  in marriage, 75-76
Allan, G., 97
Andersen, R. J., 185
Antonovsky, A., 208, 211
Antonucci, T. C., 6

Area Agencies on Aging, 180
Arling, G., 192
Asian Americans, 201, 203, 204, 214;
  see also Ethnic minorities
Atchley, R. C., 184
Attachment theory in sibling
  relations, 100, 103

Babchuck, N., 140, 141, 161, 162,
  163, 164, 165-166, 167, 172
Baum, M., 113, 212-213
Beckman, L. J., 225
Bell, D., 204
Bell, W. G., 239
Bernard, J., 72
Biegel, D. E., 191
Bild, B. R., 95
Blacks, 201, 202, 213, 214
  family interaction among, 46, 114-115
  women, 219
  see also Ethnic minorities
Booth, A., 166, 173
Britton, J. H., 54
Brody, E., 236, 237
Brody, S., 112
Brothers, see Siblings
Butler, R. N., 186

Cantor, M. H., 80, 111, 113, 127,
  128, 130, 131, 136, 137, 140, 148,
  205, 211, 213, 224
Caregivers Assistance and Resource
  for the Elderly's Relatives Series
  (CARERS), 259

Carp, F., 171
Case management as intervention,
    261–262
Cassel, J. C., 8–9
"Central figures," concept of, 5–6
Chicanos, 210–211; see also Ethnic
    minorities; Hispanics
Children, see Adult children
Cicirelli, V. G., 93–94, 95, 96–97, 98,
    101, 103, 104
Citizens Committee for New York
    City, 267
Clark, M., 31, 32, 34, 53
Clemente, F., 166
Clergy, Agency and Community
    Case Study/Brown Bag
    Luncheons, 263
Clinical treatment as intervention,
    257–258
Cohen, C. I., 257–258
Cohler, B. J., 244
Collins, A. H., 5, 15, 262
Comer, J. P., 213
Community empowerment as
    intervention, 266–267
Confidants, friends and neighbors
    as, 139–142
"Convoy," concept of, 6
Coward, R. T., 11–12, 16, 191
Cuber, J. F., 75
Cuellar, E., 210
Cumming, E., 103–104, 161
Cutler, S. J., 162, 163, 164–165, 166,
    167, 172

Demography of the elderly, 7, 252
    household composition, 41–43
    marital status, 67, 68–71
    siblings, 93–94
    women, 219
Disengagement, 24–26, 27, 30–31
Disengagement theory, xii, 161
    vs. activity theory, 26
    description of, 24–26, 27, 30–31
    and exchange theory, 27
Disentitlement, marital status and,
    83–84

Divorce statistics, 69, 70
Divorced women, support system
    of, 225–226
Dono, J. E., 127, 130, 145, 147
Dowd, J. J., 26–29, 30, 33
Downing, J., 185
Dumazedier, J., 173
Durkheim, E., 168
Dyad model in gerontologic
    research, 85, 87 (fig.)

Economic status
    and marital status, 74
    and voluntary association
        participation, 166–167
Eggan, F., 205–206
Eggert, G. M., 56, 58
Ehrlich, I., 187
Ehrlich, P., 267
Elderly
    children of, see Adult children
    extended family of, see Kin,
        extended
    siblings of, see Siblings
    spouses of, see Married couples
Estes, C. L., 179, 182
Ethnicity, conceptual definition of,
    200–202
Ethnic minorities, social networks
    of, xiii, 199–216
    conceptual definition of minority,
        200–202
    dependence on social networks
        for survival, 203–205
    extended kin system among, 46,
        114–115
    misnomer of "ethnic minority,"
        202–203
    research needs on social networks,
        214–216
    social networks as resistance
        resources to stress, 207–209
    social networks as social worlds,
        209–211
    traditional kinship approach in
        study of social networks, 205–
        207

Exchange theory, xii
    description of, 27–32
Extended family, *see* Kin, extended

The Family After Forty Project, 259
Family caretaker enhancement as
    intervention, 258–261
Family Support Project, 260
Fengler, A., 81, 171
Filial responsibility, attitudes
    toward, 51–54; *see also* Adult
    children
Financial aid in parent-child
    relations, 48, 50, 110
Florida Dept. of Health and
    Rehabilitative Services, 262
Food Stamps, 181, 184, 190
Formal networks
    definition of, 178
    health services for the elderly,
        181–182
    nature and scope of, 179–184
    relationship to informal, xiii,
        11–14, 118, 193
    role of, 10–11
    social services, 182–184
    support of informal care
        networks, 187–191
    utilization of, 184–187
    see also Voluntary associations
Frail elderly, social support for the,
    xiii, 234–245
    care responsibilities, debate over,
        236–237
    definitions, 235
    future research issues, 243–245
    impact of in-home service cuts (in
        Washington State), 241–243
    institutionalization, 78–79
    policy reforms, directions for,
        240–241
    responsibility for, 238–240
    spousal caregiving, 77–82
    variables shifting the sources and
        forms of caregiving, 237–238
Frankfather, D. L., 260
Friends, xiii, 33, 109, 123–153

    as components of informal
        support system, 126–131
    as confidants, 139–142
    future research on, 149–151
    homogeneity in selection of, 137–
        139
    literature on, 123–124
    neighborhood, 136–137
    vs. neighbors, 131–132
    in old age, 131–142
    social policy, social research, and
        informal support systems, 125–
        126
    as support givers, 142–147

Gadow, S., 235
Garrison, J. E., 257
Gelfand, D. E., 201
Gender differences
    in friendship behavior, 134–135
    roles, 220–221
    in voluntary association
        participation, 165–166
Geographic mobility and parent-
    child relationship, 54
Geographic proximity
    and parent-child relationship, 42,
        45
    and sibling relationship, 94–95
Gibson, G., 43, 44
Gibson, M. J., 189
Glazer, N., 14
Gordon, C. W., 160, 161
Gottlieb, B. H., 5, 10
Gouldner, A. W., 220
Gourash, N., 5
Graney, M. J., 169, 170
Greeley, A. M., 201

Hanson, S. L., 51, 52
Hareven, T., 58, 59
Health status
    and friendship relations, 134
    and marriage status, 71–72
    and voluntary association
        participation, 167–168
    see also Frail elderly

Hempel, C., 22
Hess, B. B., 48, 54–55, 135, 136
Hierarchical-compensatory model of
     informal support systems, 131,
     148
Hill, R., 50
Hispanics, 201, 202, 203, 204, 207,
     214; see also Ethnic minorities
Hochschild, A. R., 172
Holmes-Rahe Stress Scale, 223
Homeostatic flexibility, 208
Hooyman, N., 264
Household composition, see Adult
     children; Married couples
Hoyt, D. R., 223
Hunter, K. I., 171
Husbands, see Married couples

Illness
     and dependence on adult
          children, 49–50
     and friends and neighbors, 145
     see also Frail elderly
Informal networks vs. informal
     support networks, 33
Informal support networks, 32–33
     changes in, 6–8
     by children, see Adult children
     definition of, 4–5
     by family, see Kin, extended
     by friends, see Friends
     vs. informal networks, 33
     limitations, 253–254
     nature of, 4–6
     by neighbors, see Neighbors
     network theory and, 251–269
     overlapping among, 130–131
     relationship to formal, xiii, 11–14,
          178–193
     by siblings, see Siblings
     and social policy, 125–126
     by spouses, see Married couples
     strengths, 253
     substitution or interchange among,
          130
In-home services for frail elderly,
     240–243

Institutionalization, 238
     and kin relations, 111–112
     and marital status, 79 (tab.)
     and parent-child relations, 55–57
Interactment theory, see Activity
     theory
Isolation and marital status, 84
Italian Americans, 213; see also
     Ethnic minorities

Jews, 202, 204, 213, 215; see also
     Ethnic minorities
Johnson, C. L., 227

Kahn, R. L., 6
Kalish, R. A., 204
Kaplan, B. H., 111–112
Kart, G. S., 181
Kerckhoff, A. C., 52
Kieffer, C. M., 227
Killilea, M., 9
Kin, extended, xii, 108–118
     contact patterns, 44–46
     extended family, 115–116
     family helpers, 108–110
     minority groups, 114–115
     social networks, 117–118
     types of help, 110–114
Kinship approach to study of social
     networks, 205–207
Kivett, V. R., 50
Knoke, D., 161, 162, 163
Kohen, J. A., 140, 141

Laurie, W. F., 57
Laverty, R., 97
Lee, G. R., 46, 181, 182, 184
Lemon, B. W., 23, 172
Levin, J., 186
Levine, J., 59
Life satisfaction, see Well-being
Little, V. C., 112
Litwak, E., 110, 116, 127, 148, 206,
     238, 239
Longevity and married status, 71
Longino, C. F., Jr., 170, 174, 222,
     224, 227

Lopata, H. Z., 33, 47, 49, 111, 209–210, 224, 225
Lowenthal, M. F., 24, 141, 214
Lowy, L., 180, 182

Maddox, G. L., 236
Maguire, L., 255
Mahoney, K., 113
Maine Department of Human Resources, 260–261
Marital satisfaction, 72–73
Marital status differences among elderly, 69–71
Married couples, xiii, 67–88, 221–223
    affectional supports, 75–76
    ages of partners, 68–69
    caregiver characteristics, 80–81
    caregiving, 76–80, 108
    caregiving context, 81–82
    demographics, 68–71
    dependency needs, 80
    disentitlement, 83–84
    dyadic model in research, 85, 87 (fig.)
    health and marriage, 71–72
    isolation among, 84
    longevity and marriage, 71
    longitudinal designs in research, 85–87
    marital satisfaction, 72–73
    material supports, 74
    penalties of marriage, 83–84
    processual models in research, 85, 86 (fig.)
    research needs, 84–87
    well-being and marriage, 72
McKinlay, J., 185, 186
Meals-on-Wheels, 181, 184
Medicaid, 76, 83, 180, 181, 190, 240
Medicare, 76, 180, 181–182, 190, 240
Men, elderly
    friendship behavior among, 134–135
    marital status, 69–70
    see also Gender differences
Mentally impaired, see Frail elderly
Mindel, C. H., 80

Minorities, see Ethnic minorities
Moen, E., 185–186
Morbidity and marital status, 71–72; see also Illness
Moroney, R. M., 239
Mortality rates and marital status, 71
Multigenerational households, 54, 55
"Multiplexity," role, 131, 148
Mutual aid as intervention, 265–266
Mutual Aid Program (MAP), 267
Mutual Help Model, 267

National culture society, 209
Native Americans, 201, 204, 212, 214–215; see also Ethnic minorities
Neighborhood helping as intervention, 262–264
Neighbors, xiii, 123–153
    as components of informal support system, 126–131
    as confidants, 139–142
    vs. friends, 131–132
    future research, 149–151
    literature on, 123–124
    in old age, 131–142
    role of, in friendships, 136–137
    social policy, social research, and informal support systems, 125–126
    as support givers, 142–147
Nelson, G. M., 239
Network Analysis Profile, 257
Network theory and research, application to field of aging, xiii, 251–269
    dangers, obstacles, and limits of interventions, 267–269
    social network interventions, 255–267
    social support and elderly, research on, 251–254

Old age, stereotypes of, 29
Older Americans Act of 1965, 10, 179, 180
    1973 amendments to, 180, 181

Older Americans Act of 1965
    (*continued*)
  social services under, 182–183
Older Women's League Education
    Fund, 219
Olsen, M. E., 173

Pancoast, D. L., 264
Parron, E., 223, 228
Parsons, T., 205
Patterson, R. D., 187
Peers, *see* Friends; Neighbors
Pennsylvania Dept. of Aging,
    261
Pennsylvania State Univ.,
    Gerontology Center, 259
Philblad, C., 132
Physically impaired, *see* Frail
    elderly
Pilisak, M., 6, 7
Pinker, R. A., 189
Polish Americans, 209, 210, 213; *see
    also* Ethnic minorities
Political society, 209
Poverty
  and ethnicity, *see* Ethnic
    minorities
  and marital status, 74
Powers, E. A., 186, 228
President's Commission on Mental
    Health (1978), 202, 212, 268
Primary group-based services,
    definition of, xi
Processual models in gerontologic
    research, 85, 86 (fig.)
Professional-social network
    relationships, building, 14–15
Project LINC, 266
Public policy on the elderly, 10–11
  and friends and neighbors, 151–
    153
  and informal support systems,
    125–126
  see also Ethnic minorities; Frail
    elderly

Racial minorities, *see* Blacks; Ethnic
    minorities

Reciprocity, 109, 220
  and extended family, 116
  and friends and neighbors, 151–
    152
  and parent-child relations, 48, 55
Religious minorities, *see* Ethnic
    minorities
Research needs
  adult children, 58–59
  ethnic minorities, 214–216
  female elderly, 229–231
  frail elderly, 243–245
  friends and neighbors in support
    system, 149–151
  married couples, 84–87
  siblings, 104–105
  social networks, 214–216
  voluntary associations, 172–175
Resistance resources, 208
Resource theory, 28–29, 30
Robinson, B., 112
Role "multiplexity," 131, 148
Rosenberg, G. S., 94, 95
Rosow, I., 6–7, 228
Ross, H. G., 99–100

Salamon, S., 30
Schoor, A., 240
Schulman, N., 55, 136, 144
Self-help groups, 265–266
Service exchange, 265–266
Sexual relations and marital status,
    76
Sexual roles, 220–221
Shanas, E., 41, 42, 44, 49, 51, 57,
    58, 95, 108, 112–113, 143, 191,
    228
"Shared responsibility," concept of,
    235, 236
Siblings, xii, 93–105, 113–114, 117
  antecedents of helping patterns,
    102–103
  attachment theory, 100, 103
  changes in relationship with age,
    98–100
  consequences of relationship to
    well-being of elderly, 103–104
  prevalence of, 93–95

quantity and quality of contact
  with elderly, 95–100
research priorities, 104–105
rivalries, 97–98
substitution theory, 100, 103
type of help provided, 101–102
vicinity of, 94–95
Silverstone, B., 102
Sisters, *see* Siblings
Smith, K. F., 55
Smyer, M. A., 259–260
Social class and kin interaction, 45
Social exchange
  processes: implications for
    network involvement among
    the elderly, 32–34
  and social network, 27–32
Social exchange theory, *see*
    Exchange theory
Social mobility and parent-child
    relations, 45, 54
Social networks
  aid, types of, provided, 5
  building professional-social
    network relationships, 14–15
  conceptual definition of, 200
  dependence on, for survival, 203–
    205
  and ethnic minority elderly, 211–
    214
  formal, 10–11; *see also* Formal
    networks
  informal, 4–8; *see also* Informal
    support networks
  informal and formal, relationship
    between, xiii, 11–14, 178–193
  kinship approach in study of, 205–
    207
  research needs, 214–216
  as resistance resources to stress,
    207–209
  role of, in care for the elderly, xii,
    3–16
  and social exchange, 27–32
  as social worlds, 209–211
  theoretical perspectives, xii, 21–34;
    see also Theoretical perspec-
    tives on social networks

and well-being, 8–10
Social networks interventions
  case management, 261–262
  clinical treatment, 257–258
  community empowerment, 266–
    267
  danger, obstacles, and limits of,
    267–269
  family caretaker enhancement,
    258–261
  framework for examining, 255,
    256 (tab.)
  mutual aid/self-help, 265–266
  neighborhood helping, 262–
    264
  volunteer linking, 264
Social Security system, 179–180
Soldo, B. J., 179
Spouses, *see* Married couples
Status generalization, 29
Stereotypes of old age, 29
Streib, G. F., 51, 235
Stress, social networks as resistance
    resources to, 207–209
Substitution theory in sibling
    relations, 100, 103
Supplemental Security Income
    (SSI), 184, 239–240
Sussman, M. B., 48, 50, 51, 110, 114,
    115, 117, 118, 206, 207, 260

Task-specific model of informal
    support relationships, 131
Theoretical perspectives on social
    networks, xii, 21–34
  exchange processes: implications
    for networks involvement
    among the elderly, 32–34
  major approaches to social
    gerontology, 23–27
  social network and social
    exchange, 27–32
Theory, defining concept of, 21–
    22
Tocqueville, A. de, 159, 168
Tolsdorf, C. C., 24, 33
Townsend, P., 48
Trela, J. E., 167

Tribal society, 209
"Triple jeopardy," 252
Troll, L. E., 41, 42, 43, 44, 54, 97,
    225, 227

Unger, D. G., 5, 13
University of Louisville Gerontology
    Center, The Elder Program, 266
University of Southern California,
    Neighborhood and Family
    Services Project, 267

Verbrugge, L., 72
Voluntary associations, xiii, 159–175
    age and health status, involvement
        by, 167–168
    age-homogenous groups and
        volunteerism, 171
    benefits to the elderly from
        involvement in, 168–171, 174–
        175
    defining and classifying, 160–161
    extent of elderly involvement in,
        161–165, 172–173
    facilitators and inhibitors of
        elderly involvement in, 165–168,
        173–174
    future research, 172–175
    gender, involvement by, 165–166
    membership vs. participation in,
        164–165
    race, involvement by, 166
    socioeconomic status,
        participation by, 166–167
Volunteer linking as intervention,
    264

Walker, K. N., 4
Waller, W., 28
Ward, R. A., 169, 170, 171, 181
Ward, R. L., 226–227
Warren, D. I., 5, 13, 14

Washington State in-home services
    for the frail elderly, 241–243
Well-being
    and marriage status, 72
    and parent-child relations, 57
    and sibling relations, 103–104
    and social support, 8–10
    and voluntary association
        participation, 169–170
Western Gerontological Society,
    219
What Are Friends For?, 265
White House Conference on Aging
    (1981), 200, 202, 214, 216
Whitfield, S., 190
Widowers, 69–70, 71
Widows, 69–70, 71
    support systems for, 224–225
Wirth, L., 201
Wives, see Married couples
Women
    changing role of, 7–8
    confidants of, 141
    contacts with adult children, 45
    current research priorities on, 229–
        231
    demographics, 219
    divorced, social supports for, 225–
        226
    friendship behavior among, 134–
        135
    marital status of, 69–70
    married, social supports for, 221–
        223; see also Married couples
    never-married, social support for,
        226–227
    principle of family substitution,
        227–228
    spouseless, support system for,
        223–227
    support systems for, xiii, 219–231
    widowed, 69–70, 71, 224–225
Work Exchange, Inc., 265